THE
WRITER'S
LEGAL GUIDE

THE WRITER'S LEGAL GUIDE

Tad Crawford

HAWTHORN BOOKS, INC.
Publishers/NEW YORK

Grateful acknowledgment is made to the following for permission to reprint copyrighted materials:

Poets and Writers, Inc., for the article "Vanity Press: Stigma or Sesame?" by Nelson Richardson, © 1976 by Poets and Writers, Inc.

Society of Authors' Representatives, Inc., for their model book contract, © 1974 by the Society of Authors' Representatives, Inc.

The Nation for the article "A Publishing Alternative" by Tad Crawford, © 1975 by The Nation Associates, Inc.

Writer's Digest for an article on taxation and writers by Tad Crawford, © 1975 by *Writer's Digest*.

THE WRITER'S LEGAL GUIDE

Library of Congress Catalog Card Number: 76–56516
ISBN: 0–8015–8937–1
1 2 3 4 5 6 7 8 9 10

For the people I have been fortunate to know—and the many others like them—who give generously of themselves to assist and encourage writers.

Contents

Acknowledgments

Special thanks to the following people whose expertise and constructive criticism assisted in the development of *The Writer's Legal Guide:* Arthur F. Abelman, Esq.; Alan Berlin, Esq.; Jeffrey Cooper, Esq.; Prof. Jack Crawford, Jr.; Darcie Denkert, Esq.; Donald C. Farber, Esq.; Eileen Farley; James L. Garrity, Esq.; Paul Jacobs, Esq.; Prof. John Kernochan; Elsie Mills; Jean V. Naggar; Prof. Joseph M. Perillo; Nelson Richardson; Carolyn Trager; and Carl Zanger, Esq.

THE
WRITER'S
LEGAL GUIDE

1
Copyright

The Constitution of the United States provides that "the Congress shall have the power . . . To promote the Progress of Science and useful Arts, by securing for limited Times to Authors and Inventors the exclusive Right to their respective Writings and Discoveries . . ." Historically, laws protecting literary property had evolved under English common law and statutes. Congress responded to its constitutional prerogative by enacting and periodically revising copyright laws which, if properly utilized, can protect nearly every kind of original writing. It is not expected, however, that the writer who uses this handbook will become a legal expert with respect to copyright or the other legal areas which are discussed. The handbook is not intended to serve as a substitute for consultation with an attorney who can carefully evaluate each writer's unique legal problems. But, at the least, greater familiarity with relevant legal principles and likely areas of difficulty will enable the writer to know when the assistance of an attorney, accountant, agent, or other professional adviser will be valuable in order to gain both aesthetic and financial protection. For the writer who may find legal assistance difficult to afford, consideration should be given to use of one of the groups of volunteer lawyers for the arts which are discussed in an appendix on p. 227. Membership in writers' organizations, such as those listed in some of the reference sources in the selected bibliography, can also increase the writer's awareness of legal and business risks and potentials.

The value of copyright protection can be shown by comparing two instances of literary piracy, one involving the early plays of Eugene O'Neill and the other involving the early short stories of J. D. Salinger. Eugene O'Neill, during 1913, 1914, and 1915, copyrighted a number of his plays by registering them with the Copyright Office. He did not value these works highly, nor did he wish to see them published. However, in the 1940s he failed to renew his copyrights for additional twenty-eight-year terms after the original twenty-eight-year terms had expired. The result of this omission was that the plays went into the public domain, available to all who might wish to copy, perform, or publish them. New Fathoms Press, Ltd. published them as the *Lost Plays of Eugene O'Neill* and advertised this collection of "lost" work as a historic literary event. O'Neill not only had to suffer this unauthorized and unwished for publication, but also received no income from the exploitation of the *Lost Plays of Eugene O'Neill.*

J. D. Salinger similarly wished to let his early short stories, which had appeared between 1940 and 1948 in such magazines as *The Saturday Evening Post, Colliers,* and *Esquire,* remain in obscurity. However, in 1974 a pirated collection of these stories appeared under the title *The Complete Uncollected Short Stories of J. D. Salinger, Vols. 1 and 2.* In San Francisco, Chicago, New York, and elsewhere, different men using the alias John Greenberg sold between twenty-five thousand and thirty thousand copies of the book. Salinger, perturbed by this invasion of his privacy, broke a twenty-year public silence to denounce the pirated collection. But Salinger's situation differed from O'Neill's, because Salinger had valid copyrights on these short stories. He sued the bookstores that had sold the book, obtained an injunction to prevent them from making further sales, and demanded damages of two hundred and fifty thousand dollars. Beyond this, however, federal prosecutors also commenced an investigation, because a violation of the copyright laws can sometimes be punished by criminal penalties. *The Complete Uncollected Short Stories of J. D. Salinger, Vols. 1 and 2* slipped back into the obscurity which the writer had wished for his early stories, his objections to unauthorized publication sustained because of the protection provided by the copyright laws.[1]

This chapter will explain how the writer obtains and benefits from copyright protection available under the common law and the Copyright Act of 1909, both of which will remain in force through January 1, 1978. The next chapter will examine the Copyright Revision Act of 1976, finally enacted into law after fifteen years of debate. The Copyright Revision Act of 1976 will apply to all copyright matters arising after its effective date of January 1, 1978, and is best understood by seeing its relationship to the common law and the Copyright Act of 1909. The rest of this chapter, therefore, concentrates on the common law and the Copyright Act of 1909.

The writer will find it helpful, in reading the copyright chapters, to have an up-to-date Copyright Information Kit, which can be obtained free upon request from the Copyright Office, Library of Congress, Washington, D.C. 20559. The Copyright Information Kit contains copyright application forms and circulars explaining numerous aspects of obtaining copyrights and the role of the Copyright Office.

What Is Copyrightable

Only original work can benefit from copyright protection. Originality doesn't require brilliance or an artistic breakthrough. The writer must merely create work which has some minimal artistic qualities. And, of course, the work cannot be copied from the copyrighted work of another person. If two writers, by an unlikely chance, happened independently to create identical works, both works would be copyrightable. But if one writer copied from the other, the copied work would be an infringement and noncopyrightable. Or, as Judge Learned Hand wrote, "Borrowed the work must indeed not be, for a plagiarist is not himself pro tanto an 'author'; but if by some magic a man who had never known it were to compose anew Keats's 'Ode on a Grecian Urn,' he would be an 'author,' and, if he copyrighted it, others might not copy that poem, though they might of course copy Keats's."[2] Two writers who used the same subject, such as the same historical event or well-known person, could, of course, each copyright the resulting work.[3]

Derivative works, which are distinguishable variations that

have been substantially copied from earlier works, can be copyrighted in appropriate circumstances. A writer who owns a copyright can add new elements to the previously copyrighted work and copyright the new elements. Also, if a work is in the public domain (which means the work is not protected by copyright and may be freely copied by anyone) the writer can create a copyrightable work by adding original elements to such a work copied from the public domain. For example, a writer could create a copyrightable work by copying Keats's "Ode on a Grecian Urn" and adding new artistic elements. But if the writer copyrighted the new poem, the writer would only be able to prevent copying of the new elements, not "Ode on a Grecian Urn," which would remain in the public domain.[4] Such derivative works as compilations, abridgments, adaptations, dramatizations, and translations all require original effort and are copyrightable in their own right. But if the derivative work is based on copyrighted material, the consent of the copyright owner must be obtained for the derivative work to be copyrightable.[5]

An idea is not copyrightable, but the creative expression of the idea that forms an independent work is copyrightable. For example, the idea to use a particular subject is not copyrightable. It is the writer's special realization of the subject which is copyrightable. Thus, common plots and stock characters can be fleshed out to create copyrightable works. However, the disclosure of an idea can be protected by a contract (preferably written, with a clear description of the benefit received by each party to it) requiring payment if any use is made of the idea. Protection of ideas is discussed at greater length on pp. 80–82. The importance of sequels, spinoffs, and the like has raised the issue of whether a character can be copyrightable apart from the story containing the character. It appears that a unique character can have some protection per se, but methods of protecting characters other than copyright will be considered in later chapters.[6] Titles, names, and short phrases are not generally copyrightable because they lack a sufficient amount of creative expression. Works which are obscene, an ambiguous term at best, will also not be copyrightable.

The Register of Copyrights can refuse to register a work on the ground that it is not copyrightable, but this exercise of the Register's discretion can be reviewed by the courts.[7]

Common Law Copyright

Common law copyright comes into existence upon the creation of the work (without any action on the part of the writer) and lasts until the work is published or registered for statutory copyright protection. Publication can be simply defined as making a work available to the general public, but the concept is explained more fully later in the chapter. If a work is published with copyright notice, a statutory copyright is obtained as explained in the next section. If a work is published without copyright notice, the common law copyright is lost to the public domain. Thus, common law copyright protects works that are being submitted to potential markets prior to publication.

If a work were never to be published or registered, common law copyright would last indefinitely. For example, Mark Twain wrote a story in 1876 titled "A Murder, A Mystery and A Marriage." The story was submitted to the *Atlantic Monthly* with Twain's proposal that a number of well-known contemporary writers—including Bret Harte and William Dean Howells, the editor of the *Atlantic Monthly*—write their own final chapters to the story. This idea did not come to fruition and the story was never published. Nor was a manuscript of the story found in Twain's estate upon his death in 1910. But in 1945 the manuscript was purchased at an auction by a person who then sought to publish the story. A copyright, of course, is separate from the physical manuscript and may or may not pass with the manuscript. The New York Court of Appeals concluded that Twain had shown no intent to transfer his common law copyright, which still belonged to his estate. Accordingly, an injunction was issued to prevent the publication of the story by the owner of the physical manuscript.[8] The possibly infinite duration of common law copyright was also illustrated in a case involving notes written in 1803, 1804, and 1805 by Captain William Clark during the Lewis and Clark expedition. While the issues in the case revolved around ownership of the common law copyright, the copyright itself had lasted more than one hundred and fifty years.[9]

Common law copyright also protects the writers of letters.[10] The general rule is that the writer of the letter owns the copyright in the contents of the letter while the recipient of the letter owns the physical letter. This would not be true, however, if the writer showed an intent to transfer the copyright to the recipient or place the copyright in the public domain, or if the vindication of the character or rights of individuals necessitated publication of the letter.

However, the protection afforded by common law copyright could not prevent A. E. Hotchner from using conversations he had had with Ernest Hemingway in Hotchner's book, *Papa Hemingway*. The objections made to such use on behalf of Hemingway's estate were ineffective, because the court concluded that Hemingway was willing to have Hotchner publish the conversations and gave an implied consent. On the other hand, the court did believe that common law copyright might protect certain unique kinds of spoken dialogue with respect to which the speaker indicated an intention to mark the speech off from ordinary conversation and control its publication. The decision also pointed out, "The public delivery of an address or a lecture or the performance of a play is not deemed a 'publication,' and accordingly, it does not deprive the author of his common-law copyright in its contents."[11]

A frequent misconception is the belief that common law copyright must be obtained by sending a registered, self-addressed envelope containing a manuscript through the mail. Because this is inexpensive, it is sometimes referred to as the "poor man's copyright." But common law copyright exists from the moment the work is created, so sending a copy of the work through the mails is irrelevant as far as obtaining copyright protection is concerned.

Such a mailing is not irrelevant, however, for the writer who seeks to establish the date on which a work came into existence. The best method to establish such a date would be registration of the work with the Copyright Office, but most works by writers can't be registered until after publication (as explained in detail later in the chapter). Also, certain materials which could be pirated, such as ideas and titles, are uncopyrightable. The Authors League of America has, therefore, created a registration bureau for the ideas or synopses of its members. And The Writers Guild has a similar service available to all writers for any kind of manuscript. A local writers' organization could easily provide such a registration mechanism for its members or writers in its locality. Since the purpose of this kind of registration is proof of who created something first, use of a third party (perhaps a local notary public) is a wise step. Of course the writer's own records as to date of a work's creation or a self-addressed, sealed envelope containing a manuscript would also have some value as proof in an infringement action, but can be subjected to doubt if the other party charges that tampering or fraud has occurred.[12] The Copyright Revision Act of 1976 will eliminate much of the need for private registration, since the Copyright Office will register all classes of work, whether published or unpublished. Uncopyrightable material, however, still could not be registered.

Statutory Copyright

Statutory copyright is obtained by either registering an unpublished work (but only certain classes of work can be registered while unpublished) or by publishing a work with the statutory copyright notice correctly placed in the work. Both methods of gaining statutory copyright protection are explained later in this chapter. For the writer, the statutory copyright protection of greatest interest exists in classes "A" for books, "B" for periodicals, "C" for lectures or similar material for oral delivery, "D" for a dramatic or dramatico-musical composition, and "E" for musical compositions.

Exclusive Rights

The exclusive rights of the copyright owner include the following:

(a) to print, reprint, publish, copy, and vend the copyrighted work;

(b) to translate the copyrighted work into other languages or dialects, or make any other version thereof, if it be a literary work; to dramatize it if it be a nondramatic work; to convert it into a novel or other nondramatic work if it be a drama . . .

(c) to deliver, authorize the delivery of, read, or present the copyrighted work in public for profit if it be a lecture, sermon, address or similar production, or other nondramatic literary work; to make or procure the making of any transcription or record thereof by or from which, in whole or in part, it may in any manner or by any method be exhibited, delivered, presented, produced, or reproduced; and to play or perform it in public for profit, and to exhibit, represent, produce, or reproduce it in any manner or by any method whatsoever . . .

(d) to perform or represent the copyrighted work publicly if it be a drama or, if it be a dramatic work and not reproduced in copies for sale, to vend any manuscript or any record whatsoever thereof; to make or to procure the making of any transcription or record thereof by or from which, in whole or in part, it may in any manner or by any method be exhibited, performed, represented, produced, or reproduced; and to exhibit, perform, represent, produce, or reproduce it in any manner or by any method whatsoever . . .

(e) to perform the copyrighted work publicly for profit if it be a musical composition; and for the purpose of public performance for profit, and for the purposes set forth in subsection (a) hereof, to make any arrangement or setting of it or of the melody of it in any system of notation or any form of record in which the thought of an author may be recorded and from which it may be read or reproduced . . .[13]

A person who uses any of these exclusive rights without permission of the copyright owner will usually be an infringer. Infringement is discussed later in the chapter.

Who Is Protected

Common law copyright protects all writers' works regardless of citizenship or domicile.[14]

Statutory copyright protection is limited, however, to citizens of the United States and foreign nationals residing permanently in the United States. Other foreign writers must avail themselves of the provisions of international copyright conventions and presidential proclamations to gain statutory copyright protection in the United States.[15]

Duration of Copyright

The common law copyright lasts until a publication occurs— regardless of what length of time may pass. The statutory copyright lasts for an initial twenty-eight-year term (which runs from the earlier of either registration or publication) and a twenty-eight-year renewal term.[16] The writer should maintain careful records showing when copyrights obtained prior to 1978 must be renewed (the renewal application must be filed during the final year of the initial twenty-eight-year term). Also, statutory copyrights that would have expired at the end of the renewal term on or after September, 19, 1962, have been extended, due to the deliberations over copyright revision, and their term is specified under the Copyright Revision Act of 1976 as discussed on pp. 30–31.

Publication

The term *publication* has been used to indicate an event that ends common law copyright. After this, work is either protected by statutory copyright or is in the public domain and freely available to all users. Publication generally occurs when copies of the work are offered for sale, sold, or publicly distributed by the copyright owner or the owner's authority. As pointed out earlier, a performance of a play or reading of a lecture will not destroy the common law copyright. Delivery of a manuscript to a publisher and printing of copies are not publications, but delivery of the copies to retail dealers for sale is a publication even prior to sales taking place.[17]

A common law copyright is not terminated, however, by a limited publication. The judicial definition has been "that a limited publication which communicates the contents of a manuscript to a definitely selected group and for a limited purpose, and without the right to diffusion, reproduction, distribution, or sale, is considered a 'limited publication,' which does not result in loss of the author's common-law right to his manuscript; but that the circulation must be restricted both as to persons and purpose, or it can not be called a private or limited publication."[18] Thus, the circulation of an unpublished manuscript to a literary circle for criticism, to a group of editors for possible publication, or to agents in seeking representation would be a limited publication that would not end the common law copyright. Registration for statutory copyright does end common law protection, but an invalid attempt at registration leaves the common law copyright in effect.[19]

Publication is also important because statutory copyright can be gained simply by publication with the statutory copyright notice correctly placed in the work. And a publication which would not be extensive enough to cause a loss of common law copyright if correct copyright notice were not present might still be sufficient to gain statutory protection if correct copyright notice were present. The rationale behind this distinction is the desire of the courts to avoid the piracy of literary property.[20]

Published Works

The categories of work which must be published to gain statutory copyright protection are class "A" for books and class "B" for periodicals. The regulations define class "A" more extensively as including "such published works as fiction and nonfiction, poems, compilations, composite works, directories, catalogs, annual publications, information in tabular form, and similar text matter (with or without illustrations) as books, either bound or in loose-leaf form, pamphlets, leaflets, cards, single pages or the like." Periodicals in class "B" are defined as including "such works as newspapers, magazines, reviews, bulletins, and serial publications, published at intervals of less than a year." Contributions to periodicals are also copyrighted in class "B."[21]

Upon publication the copyright notice "shall consist either of the word 'Copyright,' the abbreviation 'Copr.,' or the symbol ©, accompanied by the name of the copyright proprietor, and if the work be a printed literary, musical, or dramatic work, the notice shall include also the year in which the copyright was secured by publication."[22]

If Alice Writer owned the copyright in a book first published in 1977, valid copyright notice could be Copyright Alice Writer 1977, Copr. Alice Writer 1977, or © Alice Writer 1977. If the writer is generally known by another name, such as a pseudonym, trade name, or nickname, this name may validly be used in the notice.[23] Appropriate copyright notice to gain protection in foreign countries is discussed on pp. 18–19.

The copyright law states that the notice must be placed as follows: "in the case of a book or other printed publication, upon its title page or the page immediately following, or if a periodical either upon the title page or upon the first page of text of each separate number or upon the title heading, or if a musical work either upon its title page or the first page of music . . ."[24] The courts are strict in following these requirements regarding the placement of notice. The title page, which need not be the first page in a book, has been defined as the first page to be devoted in part or whole to the title or a general classification of the contents.[25] The page immediately following the title page is the reverse side of the ordinary title page.[26] Copyright notice placed on other pages, such as the final page, will be invalid.[27]

Circular 42a, *Copyright for Contributions to Periodicals*, advises that notice for a contribution should sometimes appear on the title page of the contribution itself. This is because copyright notice must be in the name of the copyright owner. Also, the copyright law provides that the exclusive rights encompassed by copyright are indivisible.[28] This doctrine of indivisibility requires the transfer of the entire bundle of rights with the assignment of a copyright. If less than all the rights are to be assigned, the arrangement will be merely a license and not an assignment of copyright ownership. But notice in the licensee's name may be invalid, since the licensee only has a right to use the copyrighted material but is not the copyright owner. Therefore, if a writer transfers all rights in a work protected by common law copyright to a collective work such as a magazine or anthology, the copyright notice of the collective work will protect the copyright in the contribution. Of course the owner of the copyright in the collective work will own the copyright in the contribution. But if the writer wishes to keep ownership of the copyright and only gives a license, such as first North American rights, to the collective work, the notice of the collective work will not be in the name of the copyright owner and will not protect the writer's copyright in the contribution. The writer should, therefore, insist on a separate copyright notice in the writer's name if the writer retains the copyright and grants only a license. Another approach to this problem is to have the writer transfer all rights to the collective work with the written understanding that the copyright will be transferred back to the writer after publication. In this way the magazine owns the copyright at the time of publication, and notice in the magazine's name protects the writer.

The courts have strained to avoid having writers lose copyrights because of the doctrine of indivisibility. For example, in a leading case the court held that a writer's contributions, previously unpublished and without copyright notice, were protected by the copyright notice of *The Saturday Evening Post* despite the fact that the writer had licensed only serialization rights instead of assigning the entire copyright. However, the court also stated that "placing a special notice in the author's own name on each installment appearing in the magazine would be a more careful practice than we find here. . . ."[29] And if a writer assigns a copyright to the publisher of a book, then the publisher's name should appear in the copyright notice as the copyright owner.

The writer should advise the publisher of all dates upon which any material in a work may have been previously published or registered in order to be certain the year in the copyright notice is correct. The year in the notice must be the year of first publication (or registration as discussed under unpublished works).[30] For example, a work first published in 1963 would have notice in the form © Alice Writer 1963. If that same work were republished in 1973 with only trivial or insubstantial changes, the correct notice would remain © Alice Writer 1963 because 1963 would still be the year of first publication. But if the work were published in 1973 with substantial revisions or new material, the 1973 version would be considered a derivative work first published in 1973.[31]

The correct notice would be © Alice Writer 1973. All derivative works, such as film versions, compilations, adaptations, and translations are copyrightable in their own right. The correct notice for a derivative work need, therefore, only contain the year in which the derivative work itself is first published. The underlying material—for example, the novel upon which a derivative film is based—is protected by the copyright in the derivative work, although the term of copyright on the underlying work is measured from the year in its copyright notice. If a novel copyrighted in 1967 is made into a film which is copyrighted in 1977, the novel's copyright term will still run from 1967. If any doubt exists as to whether changes in a work are trivial or substantial, it would be best to include both the earlier and later date.

The year in the copyright notice may be in arabic numbers (1977), spelled out (One Thousand Nine Hundred Seventy-Seven), or in roman numerals (MCMLXXVII).[32]

Because statutory copyright for published works is obtained by publication with copyright notice, defective notice can cause copyright protection to be lost. If, for example, a year later than the year of first publication is placed in the notice, copyright protection is lost. There are, however, exceptions. For example, the use in the notice of a year prior to that of first publication will merely reduce the copyright term, but not invalidate the copyright.[33] Also, if an attempt at compliance is made and copyright notice is omitted by accident or mistake from a relatively small number of copies, the copyright will continue to be valid, although an innocent infringer will not be liable for the infringement.[34]

Upon copyright renewal, the form of notice should include the year of publication and the year of renewal, with the year of renewal indicated as such.[35]

Unpublished Works

There are, as mentioned earlier, two types of statutory copyright protection, one for unpublished work and the other for published work. The types of work that can be protected under the statute when unpublished are those registerable in class "C" (lectures or similar productions prepared for oral delivery), class "D" (dramatic or dramatico-musical compositions), and class "E" (musical compositions).

The regulations of the copyright office specify with respect to class "C" that "this class includes the scripts of unpublished works prepared in the first instance for oral delivery, such as lectures, sermons, addresses, monologs, panel discussions, and variety programs prepared for radio or television." In class "D" are included "published or unpublished works dramatic in character such as the acting version of plays for the stage, motion pictures, radio, television and the like, operas, operettas, musical comedies and similar productions, and pantomimes." And class "E" includes "published or unpublished musical compositions in the form of visible notation (other than dramatico-musical compositions), with or without words, as well as new versions of musical compositions, such as adaptations or arrangements, and editing when such editing is the writing of an author. The words of a song, when unaccompanied by music, are not registerable in Class 'E.' "[36]

If an unpublished work is registered with the copyright office, no notice need be placed on the work to secure protection. If the same work is subsequently published, the appropriate copyright notice on the published work will bear the year of the unpublished work's registration. If a derivative work based on the registered work is subsequently published, the year in the derivative work's notice would be that of the derivative work's publication.

Registration

The registration of unpublished works is necessary to gain statutory copyright protection, but such protection can be gained for published works merely by publication with the appropriate copyright notice. Failure to register does not invalidate copyright protection for a work published with copyright notice, but registration must be complied with prior to commencing any action based on a copyright infringement or renewing copyright protection.[37] Also, the issuance of the certificate of registration by the Copyright Office is *prima facie* evidence of the validity of the facts set forth in the certificate.[38]

Registration for unpublished works in classes "C," "D," and "E" can be obtained by sending one complete copy of the work with an appropriate application form and a fee of $6 to the Register of Copyrights, Library of Congress, Washington, D.C., 20559. Registration for published works is accomplished in classes "A," "B," C," "D," and "E" by deposit of two complete copies of the best edition of the work as it was published with copyright notice, by filing of an application form for the appropriate class, and by payment of a fee of $6 to the Register of Copyrights. An innocent error in classifying a work upon registration will not invalidate the copyright.[39]

Circular 30, *Postage-Free Mailing Privilege*, explains how the copies and applications can be mailed without charge to the Copyright Office. However, the registration fee must be sent in a separate envelope with regular postage.

Manufacturing Requirement

The purpose of the manufacturing requirement is to protect book manufacturers in the United States from foreign competition. It requires that all books and periodicals in the English language (or of United States origin in any language) be printed from type set or plates made in the United States. If lithography or photoengraving is used, the whole process must be accomplished in the United States (and separate lithographs or photoengravings, such as fine art prints, are covered). Finally, books or periodicals subject to the manufacturing requirement must be bound in the United States.[40]

There are, however, several exceptions to the manufacturing requirement. It does not apply to works in raised characters for the blind, to books or periodicals of foreign origin and in a foreign language, to books or periodicals protected under the Universal Copyright Convention (as long as the writer is not a United States citizen or domiciliary), to illustrations of a scientific work or work of art located abroad, or to books or periodicals covered by *ad interim* copyright. *Ad interim* copyright generally applies to books or periodicals in the English language that are manufactured and first published outside of the United States. This would normally violate the manufacturing requirement, but instead *ad interim* copyright lasting five years can be obtained by deposit of a complete copy of the work, an appropriate application form, and the registration fee with the Copyright Office within six months of the foreign publication.[41] After *ad interim* copyright has been obtained, up to fifteen hundred copies of the work can be legally imported into the United States. If a publication satisfying the manufacturing requirements takes place in the United States within the five years, the statutory copyright is extended to the full term.[42] Upon such publication in the United States, the year in the copyright notice should be the year of first publication abroad.

International Protection

If the writer's work is to be published abroad, care should be taken to benefit from the international copyright protection available under bilateral and multilateral arrangements. Up-to-date information on the copyright relationship of the United States to each foreign country is contained in Circular 38a, *International Copyright Relations of the United States.*

The Universal Copyright Convention, joined by nearly seventy nations, including the United States, requires the symbol ©, the name of the copyright proprietor, and the year of first publication.[43] A work which has been registered when unpublished should have the date of first publication in the notice to comply with the convention, as well as the date of registration to comply with the requirements of the United States copyright law. The convention provides that both unpublished and published works by a citizen of a nation that is a signatory to the convention, as well as any works first published in a signatory nation, shall be protected in a signatory nation to the extent that nation would protect the work of its own citizens.

The Buenos Aires Convention, which includes as signatories a number of Latin-American nations as well as the United States, provides that a copyright obtained in one signatory nation shall gain protection for the work in all signatory nations. No further formalities are necessary, except that the work indicate that property rights have been reserved by use of a phrase such as "Derechos Reservados" or "All Rights Reserved."

The United States is not a signatory to the Berne Convention, but the passage of the Copyright Revision Act of 1976 makes it far more likely the United States will join the more than sixty member nations. The Berne Convention gives writers whose works are either unpublished or first published in a signatory nation the same protection that nation would accord its own citizens. Since a writer can gain protection by first publishing in a nation that is a signatory to the convention, many United States publishers follow the practice of simultaneously publishing a work in the United States and a nation such as Canada, which is a party to the convention. No formalities are necessary under the convention, and this simultaneous publication gains "back door" protection for United States writers. The convention also provides for the writer's moral rights: "Independently of the author's economic rights, and even after the transfer of the said rights, the author shall have the right to claim authorship of the work and to object to any distortion, mutilation, or other modification of, or derogatory action in relation to, the said work, which would be prejudicial to his honor or reputation."[44] The convention provides for each member nation to protect legislatively these rights, so the extent of moral rights would depend on United States law in the event the United States joined the convention.[45]

Works for Hire

The rule is established that in the absence of other contractual arrangements an employer will own the copyright in work created by an employee writer in the course of employment.[46] Less clear, however, has been the ownership of copyright in a commissioned work. The general rule appears to be that in the absence of an agreement under which the writer is to own the copyright, the party commissioning the work will own the copyright.[47] Of course, whether selling a finished work or doing an assignment on commission, the writer should always insist on a written contract specifying what publication rights are being conveyed in the work.

Transfer of Copyright

An agreement to transfer a common law copyright can be oral. However, assignment of a statutory copyright must be written.[48] Moreover, the assignment of a statutory copyright should be recorded in writing with the Register of Copyrights within three months after execution if within the United States, or within six months after execution if outside the United States. The failure to file will render the assignment "void as against any subsequent purchases or mortgages for valuable consideration, without notice, whose assignment has been duly recorded."[49] If any doubt exists as to whether a transaction is an assignment of the entire copyright, recordation of the relevant contract should be made with the copyright office to be completely safe.

Statutory copyright is subject to certain automatic reversionary interests with respect to the renewal term that benefit a deceased writer's surviving spouse and children (including illegitimate children) or estate, or, in the absence of a will, the writer's next of kin.[50] The automatic reversionary interests mean that a writer's assignment of rights in a renewal term is only binding if the writer survives to renew. If the writer does not survive to renew, the spouse, children, or executor are free to assign the renewal to whomever they please. The rationale of this is the inability of the writer to be certain at the time of assigning a copyright that a fair agreement has been reached, since only future exploitation will reveal the copyright's true value.

One form for assigning a copyright is shown here.

ASSIGNMENT OF COPYRIGHT

Assignment, made this _____ day of _____, 19_____, by
_____ (the "Writer"), residing at
_____, to _____ (the
"Purchaser"), residing at _____.
    WHEREAS, the Writer has created an original work titled _____
_____, and described as _____
_____ and is the sole proprietor of the
copyright   in   such   work,   and

WHEREAS, the Purchaser wishes to acquire the entire interest of the Writer in said work.

NOW, THEREFORE, in consideration of $_____, the receipt of which is hereby acknowledged, the Writer hereby assigns and transfers to the Purchaser, his heirs, executors, administrators, and assigns, all of the Writer's right, title, and interest in the said work and the copyright thereof throughout the world, including any statutory copyright together with the right to secure renewals and extension of such statutory copyright throughout the world, for the full term of said copyright or statutory copyright and any renewal or extension thereof which is or may be granted throughout the world.

IN WITNESS WHEREOF, the Writer has executed this instrument as of the day and year set forth above.

_____

Writer

(It would be advisable for the Writer to sign before a Notary Public.)

Fair Use and Permissions

The *fair use* of a limited part of a copyrighted work or works may be allowed without the permission of the copyright owner for purposes of review, critical commentary, news articles, and similar restricted uses which do not compete with the work. Whether such a use is a fair use or a copyright infringement, however, depends upon the circumstances of the particular use. For example, a writer quoted disconnected lines of a popular 1931 song in a story for *Collier's National Weekly* which involved characters listening to a radio. Although the song was copyrighted, the court found that the writer had made a fair use of the quoted lines because of the "extent and relative value of the extracts; the purpose and whether the quoted portions might be used as a substitute for the original work; the effect upon the distribution and objects of the original work."[51] Parody, which of necessity is similar to the work being parodied, often faces a fine dividing line between being a fair use or being a copyright infringement.

It is wise to obtain permission to use a copyrighted work if any doubt exists as to whether an intended use will indeed be a fair use. For a small fee, the Reference Division of the Copyright Office will search its own records to determine who is the copyright owner of a given work, as explained in Circular 22, *How to Investigate the Copyright Status of a Work.* A sample permission form appears on p. 23, but the writer must be certain in each case that the permission form actually covers the specific use which will be made of the material. A permission for one use will not extend to other unspecified uses.

The writer offered a permission form like this one should consider whether it is fair. For example, shouldn't a fee be paid for the material which the editor wishes to use? Especially for anthologies, the editor should agree to keep roughly 50 percent of the royalties and divide the other 50 percent pro rata among the writers whose works are used. The writer can seek an advance against such royalties. If only a flat fee is being paid, the payment should be made when permission is granted, not when publication occurs. In the flat fee arrangement, the permission should limit the use of the material to a single edition for a given period of time, so that additional payments will have to be made for additional uses. The form of the copyright notice, the credit for authorship, and the credit for permission to republish the material will all have to be specified. The writer will probably want artistic control in the form of a guarantee that the material will not be altered in any way. A way to enforce this would be to have the writer see a copy of the galleys. In any case, provision should be made for the writer to receive free copies of each edition in which his or her work appears. The exact demands of the writer giving a permission will vary based upon the intended use, but consideration should be given to the general principles discussed in chapter 7, "Marketing Literary Property."

PERMISSION FORM

Dear Sir/Madam:

I am preparing a book titled _____ to be published
by _____. May I have your permission to include the following material from

_____
by_____
page _____, line _____ through page _____, line_____
total number of words _____ beginning, " _____
_____," and ending, " _____"

in my book and in future revisions and editions thereof, including nonexclusive world rights in all languages. These rights will in no way restrict
republication of your material in any other form by you or others authorized
by you. Should you not control these rights in their entirety, would you let me
know whom else I must write.

Unless you indicate otherwise, I will use the following credit line [indicate
credit line] and copyright notice [indicate copyright notice].

I would greatly appreciate your consent to this request. For your convenience
a release form is provided below and a copy of this letter is enclosed for your
files.

Sincerely yours,

Alice Writer

. . . .

I (We) grant permission for the use requested above.

_____

_____

Date _____

Infringement

The plaintiff in an infringement suit must prove that the plaintiff owned the copyright and that the work was copied by the infringer.[52] Copying is often inferred from a defendant's access to a work and the substantial similarity of the work alleged to be infringing. The standard for judging substantial similarity is whether an ordinary person in seeing both works would consider one to be pirated from the other. Infringement of common law copyright is remedied under state law by damages which, generally, are based on the market value of the work or, as a possible alternative measure, the profits of the defendant. If malice can be shown in the infringement of a common law copyright, punitive damages can be awarded.

The statutory damages are specified as "such damages as the copyright proprietor may have suffered due to the infringement, as well as all the profits which the infringer shall have made from such infringement."[53] There is uncertainty as to whether the damages and profits are to be awarded in the alternative or added together. There is also provision for *in-lieu* damages, generally between $250 and $5,000 per infringement in the court's discretion, which may be awarded in cases in which the damages and profits standard would be difficult to meet.[54] Other sanctions against infringers include injunctions, impounding and destruction of infringing copies and plates, criminal penalties, mandatory court costs, and a discretionary award of reasonable attorney's fees.[55]

Writers and Copyright

Copyright is a valuable protection for writers determined to exert maximum control over their creations. It is a right easily and inexpensively obtained, but of long duration and significant effect. The writer who wishes to benefit from copyright protection prior to January 1, 1978, must be familiar with the common law and Copyright Act of 1909 discussed in this chapter. After January 1, 1978, the writer will gain copyright protection under the Copyright Revision Act of 1976, which is described and explained in the next chapter.

2
Copyright
Revision Act of
1976

Sixty-five years of technological evolution in the media required changes in the copyright laws. After fifteen years of deliberation, copyright revision was at last achieved in the Copyright Revision Act of 1976 (referred to as "the act"), the effective date of which is January 1, 1978. A new Copyright Information Kit should be obtained from the Copyright Office after the effective date of the act in order for the writer to have the most current copyright information.

Copyright Revision: An Overview

The revised copyright law will take effect on January 1, 1978. Probably the most important concept of the revised copyright law is the creation of statutory copyright protection as soon as an original work of authorship is fixed in tangible form. This means that common law protection is greatly limited and applies only to unpublished works not fixed in tangible form. The term of copyright is changed to the writer's life plus fifty years, which will lengthen the term in almost every case. The manufacturing requirement is greatly reduced and will be ended completely as of July 1, 1982. In terms of international protection, the change in the term of protection and the elimination of the manufacturing requirement make it far more likely that the United States will become a signatory of the Berne Copyright Convention, which would increase the safeguards for United States writers whose work is of interest in foreign markets. Another provision, which bears on the possibility of joining the Berne Copyright Convention, is the act's refusal to give effect to the seizure or expropriation of a copyright by any government. For example, if a foreign government were to seize the copyright of a foreign writer, the United States would not recognize that seizure and would still offer the protection of the United States copyright law to the writer. This provision, directed against the coercion of writers, gives an added stature to the act.[1]

Publication is a less important concept under the act than it previously was. Publication with copyright notice is no longer necessary to gain statutory copyright protection, since such protection will exist as soon as a work is fixed in tangible form. Copyright protection can be lost if publication takes place without proper copyright notice, but defective notice can be cured in many cases. Particularly for contributions to collective works, such as magazines and anthologies, the notice of the owner of copyright for the entire collective work will now definitely protect the copyrights in the individual contributions. The act also specifies what rights the copyright owner of the collective work will have to use the individual contributions, assuming no express transfer of rights is made by the writer.

Registration is permissive and specifically not a requirement for copyright protection, but valuable remedies may be lost if registration is not obtained as soon as possible. Registration is permitted for all classes of work, regardless of whether publication has occurred. The registration fee is increased from $6 to $10, but in some cases works that were published separately can be registered on one application. The concept of works for hire is clearly defined and limited in scope in a manner beneficial to writers. Transfers of copyright must be evidenced by a writing signed by the copyright owner, a significant change for the works which might previously have been protected by common law copyright instead of statutory copyright. Also, provision is made for the termination of copyright transfers and licenses after the passage of thirty-five to forty years, a significant gain for writers. Copying for fair use or library and archival reproduction is carefully delineated and restricted, as are performances or displays of works in various educational and nonprofit situations.

This chapter explains in greater detail the provisions of the act.

What is Copyrightable

The act continues the requirement of originality, stating, "Copyright protection subsists . . . in original works of authorship fixed in any tangible medium of expression, now known or later developed . . ."[2] The definition of "works of authorship" includes literary works, musical works (with accompanying words), and dramatic works (with accompanying music). To show that the manner of fixation in tangible form can take place in many different ways, the act further defines literary works as "works, other than audiovisual works, expressed in words, numbers or other verbal or numerical symbols or indicia, regardless of the nature of the material objects, such as books, periodicals, manuscripts, phonorecords, film, tapes, disks, or cards, in which they are embodied."[3]

A derivative work, which is drawn from a preexisting work or works, is also copyrightable. Derivative works would include translations, dramatizations, fictionalizations, film versions, abridgments, condensations, and any other forms in which a work could be "recast, transformed, or adapted." It is specified that a "work consisting of editorial revisions, annotations, elaborations, or other modifications which, as a whole, represent an original work of authorship, is a 'derivative work'."[4]

Another form of copyrightable work is the compilation, which is a gathering and arranging of preexisting materials or data in a manner which results in an original work of authorship. Compilations include collective works, such as magazines, which are copyrightable as a whole despite the fact that the individual contributions are also copyrightable.

Derivative works and compilations represent the avenues by which use of preexisting works or data can result in new copyrightable works. However, copyright protection will not be extended to any part of a derivative work or compilation which is an infringement of a copyright in the preexisting material.[5] On the other hand, the fact that part of a work is uncopyrightable as an infringement does not render the rest of the work uncopyrightable. If a translation is an infringement of a novel, the translation is not copyrightable at all because the entire work is an infringement. But if a poetry anthology contains one poem which has been infringed, the balance of the anthology would still be copyrightable.

Copyrights in derivative works or compilations do not give the person creating the derivative work or compilation any exclusive rights in the preexisting material. Also, the copyright in the derivative work or compilation is independent of the copyright in the preexisting works and does not affect "the scope, duration, ownership, or subsistence of, any copyright protection in the preexisting material."[6]

Works written by employees of the United States government in the course of their employment are not copyrightable.[7] These works benefit the public domain and are freely available to all who wish to reproduce them (but, in this case, only in the United States). However, a free-lance writer who prepares a work for the government under a grant or contract may be allowed to copyright the work. This will ultimately depend on the specific legislation, agency regulations, or contracts which govern the writer's relationship with the government.

Common Law Copyright

The act eliminates common law and state copyright protection for any works covered under the act, which are those works "fixed in a tangible medium."[8] Thus, a writer's works that are not fixed in a tangible medium, such as an extemporaneous speech or an improvised and unwritten dramatic sketch, might be protected under common law or state statutes. Also, the act does not affect types of legal actions unrelated to copyright, such as invasion of privacy or defamation, nor does it affect copyright suits based on matters arising before the effective date of the act.

Statutory copyright under the act protects all works fixed in tangible form, whether published or unpublished.

Exclusive Rights

The act grants the copyright owner, with respect to the copyrighted work, the exclusive rights to make or authorize the reproduction of copies, the preparation of derivative works, the distribution of copies (by sale, other ownership transfer, rental, lease, or lending), and the public performance or public display of the work.[9] However, the lawful owner of a copy of a work (a copy is defined to include an original manuscript) may sell that particular copy, so nothing would prevent a library or a person who had purchased a book from reselling it.[10] And the lawful owner of a copy can display the copy without the permission of the copyright owner, as long as the people who see the display are present at the location of the physical copy. Certain other exceptions (such as fair use) limit the copyright owner's exclusive rights and are discussed in greater detail later in the chapter. Subject to these exceptions, any use of a copyrighted work without the copyright owner's permission is an infringement.

Who Is Protected

The act protects unpublished works, "without regard to the nationality or domicile of the author." "Published works will be protected if any one of the following conditions is met: (1) One or more of the authors is a national or domiciliary of the United States, a stateless person, or a national or domiciliary of a nation which participates in a copyright treaty to which the United States is a party. (2) The work is first published in the United States or a nation which is a party to the Universal Copyright Convention. (3) The work comes within the scope of a presidential proclamation extending protection to nationals and domiciliaries of a foreign nation and works first published in that nation if reciprocal protection has been determined to exist for United States nationals and domiciliaries and works first published here. (4) The work is first published by the Organization of American States, the United Nations, or any of the specialized agencies of the United Nations.[12]

Duration of Copyright

The act ends common law copyright with its possibility of perpetual protection, except for such common law protection as may exist for works not fixed in tangible form. Federal copyright protection will no longer be two twenty-eight-year terms, but the life of the writer plus fifty years.[13]

In the case of a work created jointly, the term shall be the life of the last surviving writer plus fifty years.[14] For works created anonymously, under a pseudonym, or as a work for hire, the term shall be either seventy-five years from first publication of the work or one hundred years from the work's creation, whichever period is shorter.[15] If the name of the writer who has created a work anonymously or used a pseudonym is recorded in the Copyright Office, the term shall run for the life of the writer plus fifty years. Because the date of a writer's death is important for determining the copyright term, the Copyright Office will maintain records as to the date of death of writers who have copyrighted work.[16] However, a presumption will exist that the copyright term has elapsed if seventy-five years from publication or one hundred years from creation of a work have passed and the Copyright Office records do not disclose any information indicating the copyright term might still be in effect.[17]

Rules are given to determine the terms of copyrights in existence on the effective date of the act.

Works which are protected by common law copyright on January 1, 1978, the effective date of the act, will be protected as if they had been created on that date.[18] A writer who created a work in 1977, but never published the work or filed for copyright, would automatically have the work protected under the act as of January 1, 1978. The term of protection would be the writer's life plus fifty years. In no case, however, would the copyright expire before December 31, 2002. Also, if the work were published on or before December 31, 2002, the term would automatically extend at least until December 31, 2027.

Works registered for statutory protection prior to January 1, 1978, shall have a term of twenty-eight years, but can be renewed for another term of forty-seven years.[19] Works already in their copyright renewal term (that is, the second twenty-eight-year term) on January 1, 1978, shall be extended to create a term of seventy-five years from the date copyright originally was obtained.[20] For example, F. Scott Fitzgerald's *The Great Gatsby*, originally copyrighted in 1925 and renewed in 1953, will have a seventy-five-year term which will expire in the year 2000. Also, copyrights that would have had their renewal term expire after 1962, except for the special extensions of their renewal terms during consideration of copyright revision, will have a term of seventy-five years from the date copyright was originally obtained.

The act provides that all copyright terms shall run to the end of the year in which they would expire. This will greatly simplify determining the duration of a copyright. For example, the copyright on *The Great Gatsby* will expire on December 31, 2000.

Publication

Because the act creates copyright protection as soon as a work is fixed in tangible form, the concept of publication has diminished importance. But publication without notice (subject to the provisions discussed later regarding defective notice) can cause the copyright on the work to enter the public domain. Publication is defined as "the distribution of copies . . . of a work to the public by sale or other transfer of ownership, or by rental, lease, or lending. The offering to distribute copies . . . to a group of persons for purposes of further distribution, public performance, or public display, constitutes publication."[21] The definition of copies is interesting as well as important. Copies are the material objects in which a work is fixed and "from which the work can be perceived, reproduced, or otherwise communicated, either directly or with the aid of a machine or device."[22] Copies include the original object in which the work was first fixed, such as a manuscript.

The definition of publication specifically states that "a public performance or display of a work does not of itself constitute a publication."[23] For example, the performance of a play, reading aloud of a short story, or showing of a film would not be publication. If any doubt exists as to whether a publication may occur, copyright notice should be placed on the copies of the work.

Registration

The act will permit the registration for copyright protection of all unpublished as well as published works.[24] An unpublished work that has been registered can be registered again when published, even if the published work is substantially the same as the unpublished work.[25]

Registration is not required as a condition for having copyright in either unpublished or published works. However, it is definitely advantageous to register both unpublished and published works as soon as possible. Otherwise certain remedies will not be available to a writer if an infringement occurs (as discussed under infringement later in the chapter). The issuance of a certificate of registration, either before or five years after first publication, is "*prima facie* evidence of the validity of the copyright and of the facts stated in the certificate."[26] The court in its discretion will determine the weight to be given a certificate issued more than five years after first publication. Also, registration is required to commence a suit for infringement.[27] If, however, the Copyright Office has refused to register a work (and the application was correctly made) the applicant can institute an action for infringement. Notice of the action must be given to the Register of Copyrights, who may intervene on the issue of whether the denial of registration was correct.

The deposit requirements for registration are one complete copy of the work for an unpublished work and two complete copies of the best edition for a published work.[28] If the registration is for a contribution to a collective work, only one complete copy of the best edition of the collective work need be deposited.[29] To avoid undue hardship, the regulations to be established by the Register of Copyrights may allow "the deposit of identifying material instead of copies or phonorecords, the deposit of only one copy . . . where two would normally be required, or a single registration for a group of related works."[30] More specifically, however, the act requires that the regulations permit a single registration for a group of works by the same individual writer, all first published as contributions to periodicals or newspapers within a twelve-month period, if (1) each of the works had separate copyright notice, and the writer's name or abbreviated name or alternative designation was the same in each notice; and (2) the deposit consists of the entire periodical or complete section of the newspaper in which the contribution first appeared; and (3) the application identifies the works separately, indicating for each the date of first publication and the name of the periodical or newspaper.[31] These liberalized registration requirements will be of great assistance to writers who regularly contribute to periodicals. Similar provisions will ease the renewal of some copyrights which were in their first twenty-eight-year term on January 1, 1978.[32] An individual writer may use a single renewal registration for a group of works first contributed to periodicals, including newspapers, if (1) the renewal applicant is the same for each work; (2) the works were all copyrighted on first publication, either by separate notice in the writer's name or a general copyright notice for the entire periodical; (3) the renewal application and fee are received not more than twenty-eight or less than twenty-seven years after the December 31st of the calendar year in which all the works were first published; and (4) the application identifies the works separately, stating the date of first publication and the name of the periodical or newspaper.

The act raises the copyright application fee from $6 to $10.[33] The renewal fee is raised from $4 to $6.

Copyright Notice

The act requires that copyright notice be placed on "all publicly distributed copies from which the work can be visually perceived, either directly or with the aid of a machine or device."[34] The notice consists of ©, Copyright, or Copr., the year of first publication of the work, and the name of the copyright owner[11] or an abbreviation by which the name can be recognized, or a generally known alternative designation of the owner."[35] The position of notice must be such "as to give reasonable notice of the claim of copyright."[36] The register will prescribe nonexhaustive regulations as to what constitutes reasonable notice prior to the act's effective date. It is specified that a derivative work or compilation need only include the year of first publication of that work, not the years of publication of the underlying works contained therein. Also, a pseudonym, nickname, or trade name can all appropriately be used in the notice.

The act provides that the omission of copyright notice—or the omission of a name or date or the use of a date more than one year later than the actual date of publication—will not invalidate a copyright if (1) notice has been omitted from a relatively small number of copies; (2) registration has been previously made or is made within five years of the publication without notice and a reasonable effort is made to add notice to all copies; or (3) the omission of notice violates a written requirement by the copyright owner that such notice appear on all copies.[37] If a year earlier than the actual publication date appears in the notice, the copyright is still valid and the copyright term is computed from the earlier date.[38]

The notice problems, which existed under the prior law with respect to contributions to collective works, are resolved by the act. A collective work is defined as "a work, such as a periodical issue, anthology, or encyclopedia, in which a number of contributions, constituting separate and independent works in themselves, are assembled into a collective whole."[39] The act protects the copyrights of contributors to collective works by specifying that the copyright in each contribution to a collective work is separate from the copyright in the entire collective work, and that the copyright in the contribution vests initially in the writer.[40]

The act further serves writers by providing that there is no loss of the copyrights of contributors (except for advertisers) to collective works, "where the person named in a single notice applicable to a collective work as a whole is not the owner of copyright in a separate contribution that does not bear its own notice."[41] The fact that a writer does not have separate copyright notice on a contribution will not, therefore, create a risk of the copyright going into the public domain. More generally, the act protects any copyright owner when, in the course of a publication authorized by the owner, an incorrect name appears in the notice. In such a case the owner's (or contributor's) copyright will remain valid, the person named in the notice will have to account for receipts, and infringers will be highly restricted as to defenses.[42]

The act also aids writers by determining what use can be made of a contributed work by the owner of the copyright in the collective work: "In the absence of an express transfer of the copyright or of any rights under it, the owner of copyright in the collective work is presumed to have acquired only the privilege of reproducing and distributing the contribution as part of that particular collective work, any revision of that collective work, and any later collective work in the same series."[43] This means, for example, that a magazine wishing to acquire complete ownership of a submission will need a written agreement in which the writer expressly transfers such ownership to the magazine. The owner of the copyright in a collective work could reprint an article from one issue of a magazine in a later issue of the same magazine or could reprint an article from a 1980 edition of an encyclopedia in a 1990 revision of the encyclopedia. But the owner of the copyright in the collective work could not revise the contribution or use it in a different magazine or in a new anthology. The writer will be free to submit the contribution elsewhere for additional publication and remuneration unless a written transfer has been made which would prevent such additional publication. The writer should make a practice of obtaining explicit, written agreements—even by letter—as to what rights in a work are being transferred. If this isn't done, however, the writer should, if possible, have copyright notice appear on the contribution in the writer's name, since this may limit the publisher of the collective work to just a one-time use, instead of also conveying the right to use the contribution in future revisions of that work and in works in the same series.[44]

Manufacturing Requirement

The act completely eliminates the manufacturing requirement as of July 1, 1982.[45] Prior to that date the act greatly reduces the manufacturing requirement, which is applicable only to, "copies of a work consisting preponderantly of nondramatic material that is in the English language and is protected under this title . . ." Thus, the manufacturing requirement does not extend to dramatic works, foreign language or multilingual works, public domain material, or other works consisting preponderantly of work not subject to the manufacturing requirement. Preponderance is determined by importance. That is, if the material which would not be subject to the manufacturing requirement is more important than the material which would be, the work consists preponderantly of the work not subject to the manufacturing requirement. A preface, captions, and brief descriptions of pictorial material, for example, would be a situation where the material subject to the manufacturing requirement (that is, the literary material) would be less important than the material not subject to the manufacturing requirement (that is, the pictorial material). On the other hand, if the pictorial material were merely illustrating a textual narrative, regardless of the relative amounts of space taken by each, the literary material would be of greater importance and the manufacturing requirement would apply. In such case, however, the literary material would have to be, "manufactured in the United States or Canada"—such manufacture in Canada being another relaxation of the manufacturing clause—but the illustrations would not have to be.

Works by foreign writers, or by American and foreign writers, or by American nationals domiciled abroad for one year, are exempt from the manufacturing requirement except in the case of works for hire for United States employers. Other exemptions allow (1) the importation of 2,000 copies of a work if the copyright owner obtains an import statement from the Copyright Office; (2) importation under the authority of or for the use of the federal, state, or local governments (but not for use in schools); (3) importation by a person of one copy of a book for use, but not for sale; (4) importation by a person of copies forming part of personal baggage, as long as the person is coming from outside the United States and is bringing the copies for use and not for sale; (5) importation by a scholarly, educational, or religious organization for library use; and (6) importation in a situation in which an individual American writer has transferred the rights of first publication to a foreign publisher, and no edition has been published in the United States.

The act clearly states that compliance with the manufacturing requirement is not a condition to gaining copyright protection. Thus, even when copies are imported in violation of the manufacturing requirement, the rights of the copyright owner will not be lost. However, if the copyright owner seeks to bring an action for infringement of the exclusive rights to reproduce and distribute copies of the work, the infringer will have a complete defense with respect to the nondramatic literary material in the work (and other parts of the work if owned by the same person owning the copyright in the nondramatic literary material) if the infringer proves: (1) the copyright owner has violated the manufacturing requirement; (2) the infringing copies do not violate the manufacturing requirement; and (3) the infringement began prior to the registration of an edition of the work complying with the manufacturing requirement. Therefore, a violation of the manufacturing requirement can be remedied and infringement prevented simply by registering an edition which complies with the manufacturing requirement.

International Protection

The requirements for international copyright protection will remain the same regardless of the passage of the act, although passage does make it far more likely the United States will become a signatory to the Berne Copyright Convention. This is due to the act following certain of the Berne standards, such as adopting the copyright term of the writer's life plus fifty years and providing for the elimination of the manufacturing requirement. Joining the Berne Convention would give United States writers even greater international protection than existed previously.

Works for Hire

The act details copyright ownership of works for hire.[46] In the case of an employee working regularly for an employer, the employer will own the copyright in work created by the employee pursuant to the employment.[47] Of course, the employer and employee could make a valid written agreement under which the employee would own the copyright. On the other hand, a purchaser would not own the copyright in "a work specially ordered or commissioned for use as a contribution to a collective work, as a part of a motion picture or other audiovisual work, as a translation, as a supplementary work, as a compilation, as an instructional text, or as an atlas, (unless) the parties expressly agree in a written instrument that the work shall be considered a work for hire."[48] The failure to expressly agree in writing that a work is for hire will leave the writer the owner of the copyright in all the cases listed. Also, since the definition of work for hire is restrictive, the writer will remain the copyright owner for all classes of work which are not listed unless there is a written transfer of the writer's copyright to another party.[49] In the delineation of works for hire, supplementary works are defined to include works, "by another author for the purpose of introducing, concluding, illustrating, explaining, revising, commenting upon, or assisting in the other work."[50] Examples of supplementary works would be forewords, afterwords, charts, editorial notes, and indexes.

Transfer of Copyright

The act specifically provides that copyright is divisible from its physical embodiment, such as a manuscript, and can be separately transferred.[51]

The act also emphatically rejects the doctrine of indivisibility by providing that any of the exclusive rights in a copyright can be transferred individually. A transfer of copyright ownership is defined as a transfer "of a copyright or of any of the exclusive rights comprised in a copyright, whether or not it is limited in time or place of effect, but not including a nonexclusive license."[52] For example, the writer might transfer the right to make copies to one person and the right to make derivative works to another person. The exclusive rights can also be subdivided. So, for example, rights to make different kinds of derivative works could be transferred to different persons. Any such transfer of a copyright or an exclusive right in a copyright must be evidenced by a writing signed by the owner of the rights being conveyed or signed by the owner's authorized agent. The signing need not be done before a notary, but notarization will be *prima facie* evidence that the transfer was signed by the owner or agent.[53] The time for recording transfers is shortened to within one month of the execution if within the United States or within two months of the execution if outside the United States. Failure to so record a transfer can cause a later conflicting transfer to prevail over an earlier transfer.[54]

Due to the greater length of the new terms, transfers and licenses which were granted by the writer can be terminated during a five-year period beginning at the end of thirty-five years after the execution of the grant or, if the grant includes the right of publication, during a five-year period beginning at the end of thirty-five years from the date of publication or forty years from the date of execution, whichever term ends earlier.[55] This right of termination does not apply to works for hire or grants made by will. Also, transfers and licenses granted by the writer, certain family members, or the writer's executors, in works registered for copyright protection prior to January 1, 1978, can be terminated during a five-year period that begins on January 1, 1978, or the end of fifty-six years after the copyright was obtained, whichever is later. Again, this termination right does not apply to works for hire or grants made by will. The right of termination is exercised by the writer or other person who made the grant or by the writer's surviving family in an order prescribed by the act. Termination is made on two to ten years' advance notice to the grantee of the copyright or the grantee's successors. The notice is recorded in the Copyright Office. A grant may be terminated despite an agreement not to terminate the grant, including an agreement to will a copyright or to make a future grant of a copyright.

A copyright can be transferred by will or, if the writer dies without a will, can be transferred by the laws of intestacy.[56]

Fair Use

The act provides statutory recognition of fair use by stating that copying "for purposes such as criticism, comment, news reporting, teaching (including multiple copies for classroom use), scholarship, or research, is not an infringement of copyright."[57] To determine whether a use is a fair use depends on four enumerated factors: "(1) the purpose and character of the use, including whether such use is of a commercial nature or is for nonprofit educational purposes; (2) the nature of the copyrighted work; (3) the amount and substantiality of the portion used . . . and (4) the effect of the use upon the potential market for or value of the copy-righted work."[58] If a writer wishes to use another's copyrighted work and is uncertain whether the use will be a fair use, written permission should be obtained from the owner of the copyright. A release form for such a permission appears on p. 23.

Reproduction by Libraries and Archives

The act specifically permits libraries or archives to reproduce no more than one copy of a work in the following cases: (1) When the work is unpublished, it may be duplicated in facsimile form for purposes of preservation and security or for deposit in another library or archive. (2) When the work is published, it may be re-produced in facsimile form to replace a damaged or missing copy which cannot be purchased commercially at a reasonable price. (3) One contribution to a collective work or a small part of any other copyrighted work may be duplicated on the request of a user of a library or archive, as long as the use will be for private study or research and the user will own the duplicate. (4) An out-of-print work can be duplicated if it is not obtainable at a reasonable price commercially, but the duplicate must be for private study or research and must become the property of the user who requests the duplication. The act explicitly distinguishes between "the iso-lated and unrelated reproduction or distribution of a single copy . . . of the same material on separate occasions . . . ," which is allowed, and concerted or systematic attempts to repro-duce and distribute multiple copies, which is forbidden. Also, to qualify to make copies at all under this exemption, the libraries or archives must gain no direct or indirect commercial advantage, must be open to the public or at least open to nonaffiliated re-searchers in a specialized field, and, lastly, must include a notice of copyright on all copies which are made.[59]

Exemption of Certain Performances and Displays

The copyright owner's exclusive rights include those over the public performance or public display of the work. Because of this, the act provides an exemption for certain performances and displays, which can be undertaken without the permission of the copyright owner. It should be noted, however, that a performance or display does not include copying a work.[60] A work is "displayed" when it is shown, either directly or by mechanical means. A film is displayed when its images are shown nonsequentially. A work is "performed" when, either directly or by mechanical means, it is recited, danced, acted, or, in the case of a film, shown in any sequence.

Thus, the act states that no infringement occurs when a work is displayed "by instructors or pupils in the course of face-to-face teaching activities of a nonprofit educational institution."[61] Similarly, certain transmissions by nonprofit educational institutions or governmental bodies for instruction are, in the case of performing a nondramatic literary work or displaying any work, permitted under the act without permission of the copyright owner.[62] The performance of a nondramatic literary work or display of any work in the course of services at a religious assembly or place of worship is similarly exempt.[63]

Next the act provides a more general exemption for performance of nondramatic literary works, as long as (1) no transmission is taking place; (2) no direct or indirect commercial advantage accrues from the performance; and (3) no performer, promoter, or other organizer is paid a fee.[64] After these conditions are met, to be exempt there must either be no admission charge, or all proceeds, after deducting the reasonable costs of production, must be used for educational, religious, or charitable purposes. If an admission fee is charged, the copyright owner is given the right to prevent the performance. Otherwise, the copyright owner might be placed in the position of having proceeds from performances of work used to support causes which the copyright owner personally opposed.

Lastly, permission of the copyright owner need not be obtained for certain performances and transmissions of nondramatic literary works or dramatic literary works published ten years prior to the performance, when the performance is for the benefit of deaf, blind, or otherwise handicapped persons.[65]

Infringement

The owner of a copyright or any of the exclusive rights in a copyright may recover damages for "the actual damages suffered by him or her as a result of the infringement, and any profits of the infringer that are attributable to the infringement and are not taken into account in computing the actual damages."[66] The act provides for injunctions, impounding and disposition of infringing articles, higher *in-lieu* damages, criminal penalties, discretionary court costs, and reasonable attorney's fees.[67] However, *in-lieu* damages and attorney's fees will not be available if an infringement prior to the date of registration is of an unpublished work or of a published work which was not registered within three months of first publication.[68] Suits for infringement must be brought within three years after the accrual of the claim.[69]

The act provides special rules regarding defenses for certain infringements, such as the defenses discussed earlier which are available to an infringer of copies imported in violation of the manufacturing requirement. Special rules also apply to infringers using works published with defective notice. If notice is entirely omitted, or if the name or date is omitted from the notice, or, lastly, if the year in the notice is more than one year later than the year in which publication actually occurred, an infringer who commences the infringement in reliance on a copy with such incorrect notice will not be liable for any infringements committed prior to receiving notice that the work is, in fact, registered.[70] If the only error in the copyright notice is an incorrect name (for example, when a contributor to a magazine retains the copyright but does not have a separate notice on the contribution) the infringer's defense is severely restricted. To avoid liability for the infringement, the infringer must prove that, having been misled by the notice, the infringement was undertaken in good faith based on a permission granted by the person named in the notice.[71] In addition, even this defense will not be allowed if, before the infringement started, copyright registration was made in the name of the owner of the copyright, or a document executed by the person named in the notice was recorded in the Copyright Office and indicated the true owner of the copyright. Also, where an infringer can rely on this defense, the person who was named in the copyright notice and granted permission to use the work will have to account to the copyright owner for all monies paid for the permission.

Copyright

Copyright is a crucial right for writers, not only for financial reasons but for purposes of artistic control as well. The act offers more extensive protections to the writer than were previously available from statutory copyright. To benefit, the writer must gain a familiarity with the fundamentals of the revised copyright law. Once the writer has mastered a working knowledge of the act, the noncopyright protections discussed in the next chapter can be viewed from a better perspective.

3
Rights of the Writer

"The Defendant, a publisher, advertised for sale certain poems, which he represented by the advertisement to be the work of Lord Byron, on whose behalf a Bill was filed (His Lordship being himself abroad), for an Injunction to restrain the publication under the title described in the advertisement. . . .

"Notice having been given pursuant to this Order the application was now renewed before the Lord Chancellor, who approved of the course which had been taken by the Vice-Chancellor, and, upon the Defendant declining to swear as to his belief that the poem in question was actually the work of Lord Byron, granted the motion."[1]

This success of Lord Byron's friends in restraining the publication of falsely attributed poems occurred in 1816. Cases regularly arise in which writers are aggrieved by conduct that cannot be prevented or remedied under the copyright laws. Yet other doctrines and statutory rights may prevent false attribution, a failure to give authorship credit, an unauthorized use of a title or a character, or alterations made in the course of using a work. Each situation must be resolved with respect to its own facts, but this chapter will serve to alert the writer to general legal principles that provide protections beyond the scope of copyright.

Moral Rights

Moral rights as such are not recognized in the United States, but they provide a good starting point to discuss what rights a writer does have in the United States. Moral rights are not economic. They are not based upon the ownership of property. Instead they derive from the belief that the creative person should have certain powers over his or her work, regardless of who the owner of the property rights may happen to be. Thus, the moral rights provided by the Berne Copyright Convention state that "the author shall have the right to claim authorship of the work and to object to any distortion, mutilation or other modification of, or other derogatory action in relation to said work, which would be prejudicial to his honor or reputation."[2]

France provides an example of a well-established system of moral rights, codified in 1957.[3] The moral rights are perpetual and inalienable. They last forever and cannot be transferred by the writer. The right of disclosure gives the writer the sole power to determine when a work is completed and ready to be communicated to the public. Once the work has been disclosed, the writer has a right to reconsider or retract the work. This affords an opportunity to withdraw work that the writer no longer considers valid or worthy of being before the public. An important limitation on this right, however, is the obligation of the writer to pay in advance for any losses which such a withdrawal will cause the party owning the right of economic exploitation. The right of paternity guarantees that the writer's name and authorship will be acknowledged with respect to any of the writer's works. An agreement under which a writer is required to use a pseudonym will not be valid since the right of paternity would be violated. Also, the writer may prevent the use of his or her name in association with a work created by someone else. Finally, the right of integrity provides that there shall be no alterations or distortions of a work without obtaining consent. The writer has the right to reshape the work—including rearranging, adapting, or translating it—and to prevent others from doing so. The power to enforce the rights of paternity and integrity can be transmitted to heirs or third parties under the writer's will, while the right of disclosure is enforced by the writer's executors, descendants, spouse, other heirs, general legatees, and finally the courts.

There is an ongoing disagreement as to whether doctrines available to protect writers in the United States amount to the equivalent of moral rights in countries such as France.[4] The better view is that moral rights offer greater protections than the doctrines explained in the balance of this chapter. But the importance of these doctrines should not be discounted, since often the writer will gain protections much like those afforded by moral rights.

Unfair Competition

"The essence of an unfair competition claim is that the defendant assembled a product which bears so striking a resemblance to the plaintiff's product that the public will be confused as to the identity of the products. . . . The test is whether persons exercising 'reasonable intelligence and discrimination' would be taken in by the similarity."[5] The application of unfair competition can be even broader than this definition indicates. In proper factual situations, it can prevent the writer being presented as the creator of works which he or she did not create; prevent the writer being presented as the creator of distorted versions of the writer's own works; prevent another person from claiming to have created works in fact created by the writer; protect titles which, although not usually copyrightable, may become so well recognized that use of the title again (such as *Gone with The Wind*) would create confusion of the new work with the original work; and generally prevent competitors from confusing the public to benefit unfairly from the reputation for quality of the writer's work.

Gilbert Patten, using the pen name of Burt L. Standish, wrote more than one thousand stories about an idealistic young man named Frank Merriwell (whose name appeared in each title). In 1934, nearly forty years after the first Frank Merriwell story was published, a motion picture company decided to produce and distribute a dozen three-reel featurettes titled "Frank Merriwell, Flash (The Talking Horse), and Captain (King of Dogs)." These films were about the Canadian Mounted Police and had nothing to do with the Frank Merriwell character created by Burt L. Standish, except that the name Frank Merriwell appeared in the title and designated a leading character. The court forbade such a use, stating "The plaintiff's copyrights do not cover the titles to the stories. . . . But a name which has become descriptive, and is closely identified in the public mind with the work of a particular author, may not, during the life of the copyright, be used so as to

mislead. . . . Nor may such a name be used even after the expiration of the copyright, unless adequate explanation is given to
guard against mistake. . . . In the present case, the name 'Frank
Merriwell' has become associated in the public mind solely and exclusively with the plaintiff's authorship; it is a name which is
highly descriptive of his work; and ordinary principles of unfair
competition are peculiarly applicable."[6] Similarly, although the
phrase "fifth column" was a common usage, Ernest Hemingway's
play *The Fifth Column* acquired a sufficient secondary meaning
associated with or suggesting his play to the public that the title
Fifth Column Squad could not be used for someone else's film.[7]
Unfair competition does not merely prevent other literary uses,
but also commercial uses. For example, the producers of the television series "Sesame Street" were successful in preventing
"Sesame Street" from being used for commercial services or goods
(although the defendant children's schools were allowed to continue a limited use as long as a disclaimer showed the absence of
any affiliation with the "Sesame Street" television series).[8] Of
course, the likelihood of the public being deceived can change as
time passes and a title or name is forgotten.[9] And if a title or name
is so little known that the public never associates it with a particular work, the doctrine of unfair competition would not be applicable. For instance, the authors of an unpublicized and unproduced
play titled *Virgin Queen* about Queen Elizabeth could not prevent
the use of the title *The Virgin Queen* for an independently con-
ceived film based on her life.[10]

A case involving the distortion of work arose when Norman
Granz, a well-known promoter and producer of jazz concerts,
sold the right to make "How High the Moon" and "Lady Be Good"
into records for marketing under the credit line "Presented by
Norman Granz." The music was rerecorded from a 78 rpm master
to a $33\frac{1}{3}$ rpm master, after which 10-inch $33\frac{1}{3}$ rpm records were
sold. The $33\frac{1}{3}$ rpm master and records deleted at least eight
minutes of the original musical performance. The court stated,
"Disregarding for the moment the terms of the contract, we think
that the purchaser of the master discs could lawfully use them to
produce the abbreviated record and could lawfully sell the same
provided he did not describe it as a recording of music presented
by the plaintiff. If he did so describe it, he would commit the tort

of unfair competition."[11] One of the judges, in a concurring opinion, wrote, "Under the authorities, the defendant's conduct here, as my colleagues say, may also be considered a kind of 'unfair competition' or 'passing off.' The irreparable harm, justifying an injunction, becomes apparent when one thinks what would be the result if the collected speeches of Stalin were published under the name of Senator Robert Taft, or the poems of Ella Wheeler Wilcox as those of T. S. Eliot."[12] The theory primarily relied upon by the court, however, was that the required credit line, "Presented by Norman Granz," created a contractual obligation that the music in fact be as Norman Granz had presented it.

This leads to an important qualification of unfair competition: It does not by itself entitle a writer to authorship credit. There is no question that in the United States a contract is valid even if a writer agrees either to work under a pseudonym or not to receive authorship credit. If a work is published without using the writer's name, it would be difficult to contend that alterations or distortions were misrepresenting the writer's work to the public. So the writer, to use unfair competition in cases involving distortion, must be receiving authorship credit.

But if a contract is silent as to whether the writer will receive authorship credit, is there still an implied obligation to give such credit? An artist named Vargas entered into an agreement with *Esquire* to create "Vargas girls," but the contract had no provision for authorship credit for the artist. *Esquire* chose to publish the work under the name "Esquire girls" and Vargas had no right to be credited as the artist upon publication. Despite his argument that the phrase "Vargas girls" implied he would receive credit, the court decided that he would be entitled to such credit only if the contract expressly so stated.[13] The writer in the United States who does not contractually reserve authorship credit is taking a risk, although the customary trade practices in the relevant medium might conceivably be shown to require such credit in the absence of any specific contractual provision.[14] The writer should ideally reserve authorship credit, especially since such credit can be a precondition to obtaining relief in an unfair competition case involving altered or distorted work.

It should also be pointed out that unfair competition—or the closely similar doctrines relating to trademarks and trade names—cannot enlarge the copyright protections available to a writer. Samuel Clemens used the pen name Mark Twain in publishing a number of literary sketches which appeared prior to 1880. He did not copyright these sketches, so they became part of the public domain. A publisher then brought them out in a book using the name of Mark Twain as author. Clemens objected to use of the name Mark Twain on the theory that his pen name had become a trademark which no one could use without his permission (the same argument would seem to apply whether or not the name was a pen name). The court found in favor of the publisher, stating, "Trade-marks are the means by which the manufacturers of vendible merchandise designate or state to the public the quality of such goods, and the fact that they are the manufacturers of them . . . An author cannot, by the adoption of a *nom de plume*, be allowed to defeat the well-settled rules of the common law in force in this country, that the 'publication of a literary work without copyright is a dedication to the public, after which any one may publish it.' No pseudonym, however ingenious, novel, or quaint, can give an author any more rights than he would have under his own name."[15]

Protection Against Defamation

Defamation is an attack on the reputation of another person. Both libel and slander are forms of defamation, libel being expressed by print, writing, pictures, or signs, and slander being expressed by spoken words.[16] For a writer to bring an action for defamation, the defamatory material must have reached the public. Also, the defamatory material must be false, since the truth of the alleged defamatory material will be a defense to a law suit based on defamation (except in a minority of states that require, in addition to truthfulness, that the publication be made without malice or for justifiable ends).

In 1913 Antonio d'Altomonte, an Italian of noble birth and a leading authority on criminology and African life and politics, was represented to be the author of a sensational article about cannibals which appeared in the *New York Herald*. The article, accompanied by a one-half page illustration and a biography of the alleged author, recounted in the first person the remarkable exploits of D'Altomonte in "Stopping a Congo Cannibal Feast." The article went on to state that a young American rescued by D'Altomonte was named John Harris Walton and he still lived in San Paolo di Loando. The court concluded that the false attribution of this article was libelous to someone of D'Altomonte's reputation, because "if false and a forgery, it is calculated to destroy his influence as a writer and a lecturer . . ."[17]

It is probably more common for a false attribution to involve material at least partially written by the person claimed to be the author. For example, a lawyer named Joseph Clevenger wrote and edited *Clevenger's Annual Practice of New York* from 1923 to 1956. In 1956 he terminated his editorship and revoked the publisher's right to use his name as editor of any subsequent editions. Despite this, the 1959 edition stated that it was "Annually Revised" without any indication that the revisions were done by the publisher's staff. Clevenger argued that numerous mistakes in the text would be associated by the public with his name in the title, causing irreparable damage to his reputation as a competent lawyer and legal commentator. The court concluded that a jury might reasonably find that the wording and arrangement of the title page were libelous, so Clevenger's complaint could not be dismissed.[18] But Clevenger presumably would have had no grounds for a libel action if there had been a correct indication that other persons had revised the book or that the book was only derived from Clevenger's.[19]

The writer may sometimes have to meet a higher standard in showing libel than would an ordinary private citizen. For instance, an important distinction is made between defamation and criticism. A writer who places work before the public invites criticism of the work. The criticism, no matter how hostile or fantastic or extravagant, is not by itself defamatory. However, if untrue statements are made disparaging the work, or if the writer is attacked personally in a way unconnected with the work, the critic may well have crossed the border into the area of defamation.[20] William Buckley and Gore Vidal, both writers and well-known personalities, engaged in acrimonious television debates during the 1968 presidential campaign. These and later exchanges in magazines led to Buckley's filing a libel suit. Vidal counterclaimed for libel on the basis of Buckley's calling *Myra Breckinridge* porno-graphy, describing Vidal as "nothing more than a literary pro-ducer of perverted Hollywood-minded prose," and writing to *Esquire* to warn that an article Vidal had submitted there might be libelous to Buckley. The court stated that the relevant issue was not whether *Myra Breckinridge* was pornographic (and Vidal therefore a pornographer) but whether Buckley's comments were reasonable or fair and within the extensive latitude allowed to critics. After briefly discussing the contents of *Myra Breckinridge*, the court concluded that Buckley had expressed his honest opin-ions, which were within the protection of the rule allowing fair comment. The letter to *Esquire* was found to be a reasonable exer-cise of the privilege to protect one's own reputation from threats of defamation.[21]

Closely related to the fair comment rule is the concept that the writer may be a public figure. Pat Montandon, who had written *How to Be a Party Girl* and was to publicize the book on televi-sion, was found to be a public figure under the following defini-tion: " 'Public figures' are those persons who, though not public officials, are 'involved in issues in which the public has a justified and important interest.' Such figures are, of course, numerous and include artists, athletes, business people, dilettantes, anyone who is famous or infamous because of who he is or what he has done."[22] In order to recover for libel, a public figure must show by clear and convincing evidence that the defamation was done with malice—that is, with the knowledge that the statement was false or with a reckless disregard as to whether the statement was true or false. Montandon, through a bizarre series of events, was pre-sented in *TV Guide* as planning to speak on the topic of "From Party Girl to Call Girl." The obvious implication was that Mon-tandon had experience as a call girl, which was utterly without foundation. The court found in her favor on the libel claim, since the jury could reasonably have found that the call girl reference had been published with reckless disregard for its truth or falsity.

The limitations of defamation actions are shown in a case in-volving four well-known pro-Soviet Russian composers who sought to prevent the use of their music and names in connection with a film allegedly having an anti-Soviet theme. This espionage film, eighty-seven minutes long, used as incidental background music forty-five minutes of public domain compositions by Dmitri Shostakovich, Aram Khachaturian, Serge Prokofieff, and Nicolai Miakovsky. A credit line indicated that the music was from the selected works of these composers. The libel charge was based on the idea that the public would believe the composers had consented to the use of the music and, therefore, had acted in a disloyal and unpatriotic manner. The court stated that work in the public domain can be freely copied by all, so no implication of consent can be found either from the use of the music or the credit line. The composers' reputations would not be damaged and distribution of the film was allowed.[23] But when suit was brought in France, the court found the film violated the composers' moral rights.[24] In another transatlantic case, a New York court decided that suit for a bad French translation would have to be brought against the French publisher in France—not against the United States publisher who sold the translation rights. The court did speculate that, since no contractual right had been given to distort or alter the work, "sufficient has been shown to establish such substantial alteration as would warrant the granting of some relief to an author who was entitled to and interested in the preservation and integrity of his work, if the parties responsible for the alteration of his work were before the court."[25]

The protection against defamation is personal and protects only the writer while he or she is alive, not assignees or heirs. Defamation and the next topic, invasion of privacy, are discussed again on pp. 57–63 and pp. 63–68.

Right to Privacy

The right to privacy is the right to be free from unwanted and unnecessary publicity or interference which could injure the personal feelings of the writer or present the writer in a false light before the public. This right is recognized in varying forms by almost every state. New York's Civil Rights Law Section 50, for example, prohibits using "for advertising purposes, or for the purposes of trade, the name, portrait or picture of any living person without having first obtained the written consent of such person . . ." Under Section 51, however, this right is specifically not applicable to use of "the name, portrait or picture of any author, composer or artist in connection with his literary, musical or artistic productions which he has sold or disposed of with such name, portrait or picture used in connection therewith."

A professor's privacy was invaded when his name was used in the unauthorized publication of his course lecture notes. The use of his name implied the professor's consent when, in fact, he reasonably believed the publication might jeopardize his professional standing.[26] It may be that false attribution is an invasion of privacy, although the cases are not all in agreement on this.[27] At least one decision indicates that no invasion of privacy occurs if a work in the public domain is published using the writer's real name, even though the book originally appeared under a pen name.[28] And the courts have also determined that the right of privacy does not protect pen names, only real names.[29]

The right to privacy diminishes when the writer gains stature as a public figure, particularly with respect to those areas of the writer's life in which the public has a legitimate interest. Ayn Rand's review of *Chaos Below Heaven* by Eugene Vale was accurately quoted on the book's jacket without her permission. The court viewed the use of her name not as a blatant commercial exploitation of her personality, but rather as a comment by a public figure on a matter of current interest. Her suit based on an invasion of privacy was denied.[30]

The right to privacy is personal and only the living writer may assert it, not assignees or heirs.

Right to Publicity

The right to publicity is a relatively new right independent of the right of privacy. The right to publicity states that a person with a public reputation has a right to benefit from the commercial value associated with that person's name or picture. Sports figures, for example, have the right to financial benefits from use of their names and pictures on baseball cards or in a baseball game.[31] But the right to publicity will be of little value to the writer who is not well known.

The right to publicity does not prevent advertising uses of a famous person's name and picture if such uses are incidental to a legitimate news article. Joe Namath was the subject of many newsworthy articles on football in *Sports Illustrated*. However, when *Sports Illustrated* used photographs from the articles to illustrate advertising, Namath contended that his right to publicity had been violated. The court concluded that the use of the name and photographs of Namath were only uses incidental to establishing the quality and news content of *Sports Illustrated*. To allow damages might well violate the First Amendment guarantees of freedom of speech and press, so Namath lost the case.[32]

The right to publicity, unlike the protections against defamation and invasion of privacy, can be assigned or enforced by heirs.[33]

Protection Against Misappropriation

A misappropriation is a wrongful taking or use of someone else's property. Some cases involving literary property do not fit easily under copyright infringement or unfair competition, but can be decided under the designation of misappropriation.[34] Such a case revolved about Amos Burke, a fictional detective created by Pulitzer Prize-winning playwright Frank D. Gilroy. Burke developed out of a television program, "Who Killed Julie Greer," and became the main character in the ABC series "Burke's Law," which ran from 1963 through 1966. Gilroy assigned only his television rights in the character to ABC, retaining the publishing rights for himself since he planned to write a series of detective novels using Burke as the protagonist. However, the defendants— ABC, Four Star Television, Barbety Television Enterprises, Simon & Schuster, and Dell Publishing Company—cooperated in publishing two paperback novels and three comic books using the character of Burke. In 1965 Gilroy brought suit in New York State Supreme Court based upon this misappropriation of his literary property.

Seven years later a verdict was handed down in Gilroy's favor. The court agreed that the defendants had misappropriated the character of Burke and awarded Gilroy $15,000 in damages, the amount of the profits realized by the defendants from their publications. Gilroy appealed, arguing that the value of his property had been far greater than $15,000. It was contended that a writer of his ability could have made far more than that by writing a series of detective novels, but that the books published by the defendants had been of inferior quality and ruined the market for sequels dealing with Burke. Moreover, it was argued that expert testimony should have been permitted to establish reasonable damages based on the profit potential of the Burke character if used in a series of books written by Gilroy.

The Appellate Division agreed with these contentions, stating, "The proper measure of damages flowing from defendants' wrongful appropriation of plaintiff's literary property is the reasonable value thereof and 'Opinion evidence of the value of the property' is admissible."[35] The case was remanded to the Supreme Court for a new trial on the issue of damages. At the new trial expert testimony was given by Marc Jaffe, senior vice president of Bantam Books, and Henry Morrison, a literary agent. The jury, after listening to their appraisals of what a series of Amos Burke books would have earned, returned a verdict of $745,000 in favor of Gilroy. The addition of interest and costs increased the total award to $1,185,737.

The defendants appealed to the Appellate Division, arguing that the damages were speculative and not based on any reasonable certainty of what would have been earned. The Appellate Division concluded, "We think that what the defendant misappropriated had value. To some extent, at least, plaintiff's difficulty in demonstrating the amount of value is due to what we have determined to be defendant's fault . . . We think, however, that the present verdict cannot stand for the reason that it rests on evidence that is wholly speculative, essentially an estimate of royalties without any 'stable foundation for a reasonable estimate of royalties.' . . . On the whole, we think the interest of substantial justice will best be achieved by reducing plaintiff's recovery to the principal amount of $100,000 together with appropriate interest thereon."[36] The principal with interest amounted to nearly $200,000. The Appellate Division's reasoning that the damages were speculative rested on the fact that Gilroy had never written a mystery novel, so the expert testimony had gone too far in assuming the sales and prices of a series of mystery novels to be written at the rate of two per year over a period of fifteen years. Yet the $100,000 award was far in excess of the $15,000 originally given Gilroy. In suitable cases, therefore, expert testimony will be admissible to establish the reasonable earning potential of literary property which has been misappropriated.

Writers in the United States

The enlightened approach often found abroad which explicitly creates moral rights for writers has yet to be adopted in the United States. The different doctrines which protect the writer here focus far more closely on economic rights, while leaving risks that the writer may not receive proper authorship credit or will have no recourse to prevent alterations or distortions of work. Carefully drawn contracts, the creation and terms of which are discussed later in the book, are the writer's best avenue to obtain protections similar to moral rights. Such contracts can resolve troublesome issues long before costly litigation arises, although resort to the courts may still be necessary when wrongful use is made of a writer's name or literary creations.

4
Content of
Written Works

The First Amendment of the United States Constitution provides that "Congress shall make no law . . . abridging the freedom of speech, or of the press . . ." This guarantee is not unlimited, however, and the writer must be aware that the content of a written work can sometimes give rise to civil or criminal liability. For example, copyright, the doctrine of unfair competition, the rights to privacy and publicity, and protection from defamation safeguard not only the writer but the writer's competitors as well. Significantly, other private citizens also have rights protecting them from invasion of privacy or defamation, which the writer will have to consider when creating work. In addition, the public at large through governmental agencies may seek to suppress works that are considered obscene or that might deny a fair trial to a criminal defendant because of excessive publicity.[1] And school boards will sometimes act as censors of textbooks or library books thought undesirable for a student readership.

Defamation

Defamation is an attack upon a person's reputation by print, writing, pictures, signs, or spoken words. Whether the defamation is a libel or a slander depends on the medium in which the defamation occurs. Printed materials and films give rise to actions for libel, while spoken words give rise to actions for slander. Whether television and radio broadcasts give rise to libel or slander is gradually being resolved by statutes enacted in the various states, the importance of the issue being that a libel suit is often easier for the plaintiff than one based on slander (in which damages to reputation sometimes have to be proven, instead of simply assumed from the nature of the defamatory statement).[2] Generally, everyone who participates in publishing defamatory material will be liable to the defamed person.[3] While the truth of an alleged defamation is generally a defense to such an action as mentioned on p. 49, the burden of proving truthfulness is on the person who asserts truth as a defense.[4]

Injury to reputation is the essence of defamation. One decision states: "Reputation is said in a general way to be injured by words which tend to expose one to public hatred, shame, obloquy, contumely, odium, contempt, ridicule, aversion, ostracism, degradation or disgrace, or to induce an evil opinion of one in the minds of right-thinking persons, and to deprive one of their confidence and friendly intercourse in society."[5] Statements found defamatory upon their face include allegations that a person "has attempted suicide, that he refused to pay his just debts, that he is immoral or unchaste, or 'queer,' or has made improper advances to women, or is having 'wife trouble,' and is about to be divorced; that he is a coward, a drunkard, a hypocrite, a liar, a scoundrel, a crook, a scandal-monger, an anarchist, a skunk, a bastard, a eunuch, or a 'rotten egg'; that he is 'unfair' to labor, or that he has done a thing which is oppressive or dishonorable, or heartless, because all of these things obviously tend to affect the esteem in which he is held by his neighbors."[6] The injury to reputation need only occur in the eyes of any substantial and respectable group in society, rather than society-at-large.[7] And a statement which is defamatory at one time and place might not be defamatory in a different context.

The words used must be interpreted as they were reasonably understood in view of all the circumstances, including the entire statement which was made. The court decides whether the words could reasonably be understood as defamatory, after which the jury decides whether the words in fact were understood in that sense. Humor, ridicule, sarcasm, questions, and insinuations can all be defamatory if they are reasonably understood to disgrace someone. A distinction is made between statements of fact and those of opinion. Opinion, such as abusive name-calling done in anger, may very well be considered not to contain any specific charge which could be considered defamatory. But just because a statement is made in the form of an opinion will not give protection against defamatory assertions of fact necessarily included in the opinion.[8] A person who repeats a defamatory statement is liable for defamation, even if the person gives the original source, indicates that he or she does not believe the statement to be true, uses the customary newspaper phrase "it is alleged," or states the story is based on rumors.[9]

A defamatory statement need not refer to a person by name in order to be actionable. The problems this can cause with fictional works based on real events or the writer's own experiences are substantial.[10] For example, MGM made a film depicting Rasputin as the cause of the destruction of imperial Russia. In the course of the film, a character named Princess Natasha is either seduced or raped by Rasputin. Many other facts included in the film indicated that Princess Natasha in real life was Princess Irina Alexandrova. The court sustained as reasonable the jury's finding in favor of the Princess and awarding her £25,000. One justice, in weighing the defendant's arguments, rejected "the contention that no reasonable jury could come to the conclusion that to say of a woman that she had been ravished by a man of very bad character when as a matter of fact she never saw the man at all and was never near him is not defamatory of the woman. I really have no language to express my opinion of that argument."[11] Thomas Wolfe, whose fiction was highly autobiographical, had publication of one book held up because of the threat of a libel suit by a former mistress and, in another case, was actually sued by a former landlady and had to settle out of court despite his desire to fight the suit.[12]

Fictional works will often use a disclaimer, such as, "All circumstances in this novel are imaginary, and none of the characters exist in real life." The problem is that such a disclaimer means little if, in fact, the characters are drawn from real life. An authoritative source states: "The fact that the author or producer states that his work is exclusively one of fiction and in no sense applicable to living persons is immaterial except as to punitive damages, if readers actually and reasonably understand otherwise. Such a statement, however, is a factor to be considered by the jury in determining whether readers did so understand it, or, if so, whether the understanding was reasonable."[13] Punitive damages are extra damages beyond what is necessary to compensate a plaintiff for injuries suffered. They are awarded because the acts complained of by the plaintiff are reckless or malicious. A carefully drafted disclaimer, relevant to the particular content of the book, can thus have value.

A different approach to the problem of libel in fiction is to alter the fictional characters that may be the basis for libel suits. This can work very well, since changing a work's locale, plot, and all facts of characters' lives—including appearance and mannerisms—can insure that no real persons will suffer a libel. The problem, of course, is whether the fictional work retains its integrity after the alterations. Some writers will be able to work out a compromise between what they want to say and what they dare to say, and others won't.

A lawyer's advice is a necessity if a piece is to be reworked due to fear of a libel suit. Similarly, a lawyer should be consulted if a release is to be sought from the person who might otherwise bring the libel suit. A release form would indicate that the person knows he or she will be the model for a character which may have additional fictional characteristics or experiences. The person—in return for a consideration such as a payment of money—agrees not to make a claim or sue for libel, invasion of privacy, or any other reason based on the content of the work or the advertising and promotion for the work.[14] A problem, however, arises if the person is approached but refuses to sign the release. If the publisher or producer proceeds, the person defamed can argue for punitive damages on the basis that prior knowledge of the defamatory content is shown by the request for the release.

A different problem with fiction can arise when characters and names are completely imaginary, but happen to correspond closely with a real person. An English newspaper published a fictional article of humor about the double life of a Mr. Artemus Jones, a blameless churchwarden who lived at Peckham with his wife except when he was secretly across the Channel at Dieppe "betraying a most unholy delight in the society of female butterflies." A real Mr. Artemus Jones sued for libel. This Mr. Jones was an unmarried lawyer who lived in North Wales. He complained only of the use of his name. The jury gave Mr. Jones a substantial award for damages. The defendant's appeals were to no avail, and the headnote to the final decision states, "In an action for libel, if the language used is, in the opinion of the jury, defamatory and people reading it may reasonably think that it refers to the plaintiff, damages are recoverable, even although the writer or publisher may not have intended to refer to any particular individual."[15]

The requirement of reasonableness, however, saves fiction writers from facing an impossible task in the choice of names. James T. Farrell wrote a novel titled *Bernard Clare* after the name of the main character. The novel, while clearly fictional, draws in part on Farrell's own experiences as a young man journeying from Chicago to New York in order to become a writer. The character's name derived from County Clare in Ireland and was intended to connote an Irish background. A newspaperman named Bernard Clare claimed that he had been libeled by the novel. This real Bernard Clare had worked in Minnesota, Michigan, and Wisconsin, and had nothing in common with Farrell's fictional character except sharing the same name. The court granted Farrell's motion for summary judgment, stating, "It would be an astonishing doctrine if every writer of fiction were required to make a search among all the records available in this Nation which might tabulate the names and activities of millions of people in order to determine whether perchance one of the characters in the contemplated book designated as a novel may have the same name and occupation as a real person . . . It is inconceivable that any sensible person could assume or believe from reading this book of fiction that it purported to refer to the life or career of the Bernard Clare who was a newspaper writer in Minneapolis."[16]

Defamatory statements directed at a large group will not be considered to defame an individual member of the group. To avoid unchecked group defamation in attacks on various minority groups, some states have enacted criminal statutes to punish such defamation. An individual can sue for defamation when the group defamed is small. "All of A's sons are murderers" is a defamation for which each son can sue individually. But the statement that "Some of A's sons are murderers" would be a much more difficult statement upon which to bring suit because not all of the sons are defamed and the ones defamed are not identified.[17]

The First Amendment provides important limitations on the extent to which actions for defamation can successfully be pursued. The right of a public figure, in particular, to sue for libel is limited to false statements made with actual malice or reckless disregard of the truth.[18] The term "public figure" is itself subject to definition. For example, a woman successfully sued a magazine for unfavorably misreporting the grounds of her divorce decree. Although the woman was often mentioned in society columns and actually gave news conferences because of the widespread reporting of her divorce proceedings, the Supreme Court reasoned she was not a public figure because she had no major role in society's affairs and had not voluntarily joined in a public controversy with an intention to influence the outcome.[19] Similarly, when a magazine accused a prominent lawyer of having framed a policeman as part of a Communist conspiracy to discredit the police, the attorney was determined not to be a public figure. The Supreme Court stated, "The communications media are entitled to act on the assumption that public officials and public figures have voluntarily exposed themselves to increased risk of injury from defamatory falsehoods concerning them. No such assumption is justified with respect to a private individual."[20]

The Supreme Court determined that the states should have discretion to determine the standard of liability for defamation where a private individual is involved in a matter of public interest, so long as the states require some negligence or fault on the part of the person accused of the defamation. Thus, where a matter of public interest is involved, a public figure will have to show actual malice or reckless disregard for the truth to recover for defamation while a private individual will only have to show negligence (assuming negligence has been selected as the relevant state standard). Where a private person is defamed on a matter not of public interest, there is no requirement even to show an intent to defame. Recovery in such a case is allowed on the basis of the defamation alone and malice or reckless disregard for the truth is only relevant in fixing punitive damages.[21]

Damages for defamation can be lessened by a retraction of the defamatory statement. The retraction must be a complete and un-equivocal attempt to repair the injury to reputation which has taken place. The retraction should be given the same prominence and publicity as the defamation, and come as soon after the de-famation as possible. Such a retraction can be used to show that the plaintiff's reputation was not so badly damaged or that there was an absence of the malice necessary for punitive damages. In many states statutes limit the amount of damages which can be re-covered if a retraction is made or if no retraction is requested by the injured person.[22]

Defamation is also discussed on pp. 49–52. It is mentioned there that only the living person who has been defamed may bring the suit for defamation, not assignees or heirs. Statutes in a num-ber of states do make defamation of the dead into a crime, but these statutes have been held not to give surviving relatives a right to sue.[23]

Invasion of Privacy

The right of privacy is now recognized in varying forms by nearly every jurisdiction. This right has been said to protect four quite different types of interests: (1) the appropriation of a per-son's name or likeness for business or commercial uses; (2) the dis-closure to the public of embarrassing private facts; (3) the placing of a false image of a person before the public; and (4) intrusion into a person's seclusion or private life, such as by invading some-one's home or eavesdropping by the use of wire taps.[24]

Protection against appropriation is exemplified by New York Civil Rights Law Section 51, which provides: "Any person whose name, portrait or picture is used within this state for advertising purposes or for the purposes of trade without . . . written con-sent . . . may maintain an equitable action in the supreme court of this state against the person, firm or corporation so using his name, portrait or picture, to prevent and restrain the use thereof; and may also sue and recover damages for any injuries sustained by reason of such use and if the defendant shall have knowingly used such person's name, portrait or picture in such manner as is forbidden or declared to be unlawful . . . the jury, in its discretion, may award exemplary damages." Exemplary damages are the same as punitive damages. Appropriation involves the use of a name or picture which identifies someone. A picture of a person's hand or foot without further identification would not be an appropriation. The mere fact that by coincidence a name in a novel is the same as a person's name in real life is not an appropriation. Nor is there an appropriation if an incidental mention of a person's name occurs in a book or motion picture. And, as discussed with respect to Joe Namath on p. 54, magazines and newspapers can use articles and accompanying photographs for advertising the newsworthy qualities of the publication. When Betty Friedan, a feminist leader and well-known writer, did a series of pieces for *New York Magazine* titled "The Year We Entered Modern Times," part of the series described her life twenty-five years before, including an illustrative photograph of her with her son and former husband. The court held the former husband's right to privacy had not been violated because Betty Friedan had become a public figure and the course of her life twenty-five years before was of public interest. Moreover, television commercials for *New York Magazine* based on the article were not an invasion of privacy either, since "it has long been held that, under New York law, an advertisement, the purpose of which is to advertise the article, 'shares the privilege enjoyed by the article' if 'the article itself was unobjectionable.' "[25]

The public disclosure of embarrassing private facts is an aspect of the right of privacy which has been made largely ineffectual by the doctrine permitting the publication of newsworthy information. A leading case involved William James Sidis, a child prodigy who at the age of eleven lectured on four-dimensional bodies to distinguished mathematicians and at the age of sixteen graduated from Harvard College. But after his graduation he suffered a nervous breakdown, felt revulsion for his feats as a child, and sought obscurity. Nearly a quarter of a century after his youthful fame, a writer for the *New Yorker* sought him out for a brief biographical sketch that the magazine published in 1937. The article was admittedly factual, but appeared against Sidis's will. It discussed not only his early renown, but the failed efforts to prevent discovery of his identity, his choice of a clerk's position in which his mathe-

matical skill would not have to be used, and his curious interests—collecting streetcar transfers and studying the lore of the
Okamakammessett Indians. The writer accurately portrayed
Sidis's peculiar manner of speech and laughter as well as his
shabby and untidy living quarters. Despite all the time that had
passed, the court affirmed the dismissal of Sidis's suit for invasion
of privacy because he "was once a public figure. As a child prodigy, he excited both admiration and curiosity. Of him great deeds
were expected. . . . Since then Sidis has cloaked himself in obscurity, but his subsequent history, containing as it did the answer to
the question of whether he had fulfilled his early promise, was still
a matter of public concern."[26] But the court did not make the doctrine of newsworthiness so unlimited as to prevent an invasion of
privacy suit for an unusual or shocking public disclosure of private facts. The court continued, "Revelations may be so intimate
and so unwarranted in view of the victim's position as to outrage
the community's notions of decency."[27]

A recent case which followed this rule with respect to newsworthiness involved the well-known body surfer Mike Virgil. He
gave an interview to a writer for *Sports Illustrated* in which he
frankly told of his "putting out cigarettes in his mouth and diving
off stairs to impress women, hurting himself in order to collect
unemployment so as to have time for bodysurfing at the Wedge
during summer, fighting in gang fights as a youngster, and eating
insects . . ."[28] Virgil revoked his consent to the publication when
he realized the article would include these juvenile transgressions
as well as his prowess as a body surfer. But the revocation did not
help him, since the court concluded that "the personal facts concerning Mike Virgil were included as a legitimate journalistic attempt to explain Virgil's extremely daring and dangerous style of
body surfing at the Wedge. There is no possibility that a juror
could conclude that the personal facts were included for any inhe-
rent morbid, sensational, or curiosity appeal they might have."[29]
The court stated that the final test of newsworthiness or legitimate
public interest depends upon the values of the community.

One revelation which did violate a person's right to privacy involved a man who had been convicted of hijacking a truck eleven
years before, but who had since reformed and hidden his criminal
past from his friends and his daughter. *Reader's Digest* ran an arti-

cle about hijacking which mentioned the man by name and related the hijacking incident without stating when it had occurred. The court concluded that "identification of the *actor* in reports of long past crimes usually serves little independent public purpose. . . . Unless the individual has reattracted the public eye to himself in some independent fashion, the only public 'interest' that would usually be served is that of curiosity."[30] The facts of the crime could be reported since past crimes remained newsworthy, but use of the name of the rehabilitated individual did not serve the public interest and constituted an invasion of his privacy. Of course, this rule only prevents the use of names in special circumstances. It would not apply if the criminal reattracted public attention—for example, by committing more crimes or running for public office—or if the crime itself had great notoriety like that surrounding the Saint Valentine's Day Massacre.

The placing of a person in a false light before the public is a form of invasion of privacy which is quite similar to an action for libel (except that a false light invasion could be laudatory instead of defamatory). It was probably this aspect of the right of privacy which enabled Lord Byron to prevent publication of poems falsely attributed to him. The false light cases frequently involve a personality or event of public interest which is presented to the public in a fictionalized form. If true, the account would be protected by the First Amendment as newsworthy. But if transformed into a version which is substantially fictional, its newsworthiness is lost along with the protection of the First Amendment.

The United States Supreme Court considered this issue in a case in which *Life Magazine* ran a fictionalized account of a true incident. The article truly stated that three escaped convicts had imprisoned a suburban Philadelphia family for nineteen hours, but it added fictional acts of violence and verbal sexual abuse. The family, which had since moved and sought obscurity, sued for invasion of privacy. The court stated, "We hold that the constitutional protections for speech and press preclude the application of the New York statute to redress false reports of matters of public interest in the absence of proof that the defendant published the report with knowledge of its falsity or in reckless disregard of the truth."[31] The case was sent back to the lower courts for a determination as to whether *Life Magazine* had published with knowledge of the falsity or in reckless disregard of the truth.

Another false light invasion of privacy case involved the well-known baseball pitcher Warren Spahn. The New York courts found that a biography of Spahn for a juvenile audience contained gross errors of fact, invented dialogue, and a manipulated chronology of events. The facts had been altered to fit a dramatic portrayal appealing to the readership but remote from Spahn's actual life. The writer never interviewed Spahn or anyone who knew Spahn, but instead worked from uncorroborated newspaper and magazine clippings. Although Spahn admittedly was a public figure, the court concluded that he had shown the biography to be published with knowledge of the falsifications or a reckless disregard for the truth. He was awarded $10,000 in damages and the publisher was enjoined from printing or distributing *The Warren Spahn Story*.[32]

An obvious corollary of the Spahn decision is that an essentially truthful biography of a public figure will not be grounds for an invasion of privacy suit. Random House published a biography titled *Howard Hughes* by John Keats. Hughes, a well-known public figure, sought to prevent publication on an invasion of privacy theory. The court noted that Hughes had not even proven that *Howard Hughes* contained false statements, so the issue of whether there had been knowledge of falsity or a reckless disregard for the truth could not be reached. Random House was able to proceed with publication of the biography.[33]

The final category of invasion of privacy involves intrusions into another person's seclusion or private life. The intrusion may be physical, such as a trespass into someone's home, but often relates to unauthorized electronic surveillance. There need be no publication in order to recover damages based on intrusion, since the intrusion itself is the invasion of privacy. In a much publicized case, former employees of Senator Thomas Dodd (aided by some current staff members) entered his office, removed and photocopied documents, and returned the original documents to their place in the files. Copies of these documents were turned over to the syndicated columnists Jack Anderson and Drew Pearson, who published articles based on the information. Anderson and Pearson had no involvement in the plans to get the documents, but in fact knew of the intrusion into Dodd's office prior to publishing the articles. The court reasoned that "in analyzing a claimed breach of privacy, injuries from intrusion and injuries from publication should be kept clearly separate. Where there is intrusion, the intruder should generally be liable whatever the content of what he learns. . . . On the other hand, where the claim is that private information concerning plaintiff has been published, the question of whether that information is genuinely private or is of public interest should not turn on the manner in which it has been obtained."[34] Pearson and Anderson could not be liable for injuries caused by the intrusion for they had no part in the intrusion. And, since Dodd was a public figure, they could not be liable for publishing truthful articles pertaining to his qualifications as a United States senator. The summary judgment granted against Dodd was affirmed.

An invasion of privacy did take place, however, when *Life Magazine* equipped two employees with hidden radio transmitters and cameras and had them pose as patients in order to gain entry to the private home of a quack doctor. The court observed, "The First Amendment has never been construed to accord newsmen immunity from torts or crimes committed during the course of newsgathering."[35] It also permitted the amount of the damages for intrusion to be increased because of the subsequent publication of an article based on information obtained by the hidden devices.

The complexity of the doctrines relating to invasion of privacy makes resort to a lawyer necessary if difficulties are anticipated. The lawyer may determine that a release from any claims for invasion of privacy should be sought from people who might bring suit.[36] Privacy is also discussed on pp. 52–53.

Obscenity

The First Amendment protection of expression does not extend to obscene works. Historically, the censors in England sought to prevent sedition against the Crown or blasphemy against the Church.[37] The suppression of sexually impure expression gained impetus with the Victorian era, and in this century has all but replaced the original concerns of the censors. Just a few examples of books challenged for obscenity in the United States include Giovanni Boccaccio's *Decameron*, John Cleland's *Memoirs of a Woman of Pleasure*, Gustave Flaubert's *November*, Henry Miller's *Tropic of Cancer*, James Joyce's *Ulysses*, D. H.

Lawrence's *Lady Chatterley's Lover*, Eugene O'Neill's *Strange Interlude*, and Edmund Wilson's *Memoirs of Hecate County*. The crucial issue becomes the definition of what is obscene. Courts have contributed so little to a clear definition of what validly comes within the scope of the obscene, that it is perhaps of equal interest to hear what writers have had to say on the subject.

Henry Miller's writing found audiences in France and Japan long before the original English-language versions of his books were permitted publication in his native Brooklyn, New York. In his essay "Defense of the Freedom to Read," which sought to prevent the suppression of his book *Sexus* in Norway, he wrote, "But it is not something evil, not something poisonous, which this book *Sexus* offers the Norwegian reader. It is a dose of life which I administered to myself first, and which I not only survived but thrived on. Certainly I would not recommend it to infants, but then neither would I offer a child a bottle of *aqua vite*. I can only say one thing for it unblushingly—compared to the atom bomb, it is full of life-giving qualities." D. H. Lawrence criticized society's guidelines for obscenity in his essay, "Pornography and Obscenity," in which he said, "There's nothing wrong with sexual feelings in themselves, so long as they are straightforward and not sneaking or sly. The right sort of sex stimulus is invaluable to human daily life. Without it the world grows grey. . . . But even I would censor genuine pornography, rigorously. It would not be very difficult. In the first place, genuine pornography is almost always underworld, it doesn't come into the open. In the second, you can recognize it by the insult it offers, invariably, to sex, and to the human spirit." Lawrence noted as well that concepts of obscenity change with different societies and epochs. But our contemporary legal definition of obscenity excludes both violence and insult to the human spirit. Instead there is a categorization of meaningless terms, such as prurient, lascivious, lewd, and vile, which connote no more than the word obscene itself.

But what is the latest definition of obscenity handed down by the United States Supreme Court? In 1973 a new standard was adopted, providing that the guidelines for obscenity are "(a) whether 'the average person, applying contemporary community standards' would find that the work, taken as a whole, appeals to the prurient interest. . . ; (b) whether the work depicts or describes, in a patently offensive way, sexual conduct specifically defined by the applicable state law; and (c) whether the work, taken as a whole, lacks serious literary, artistic, political, or scientific value."[38] This standard made findings of obscenity more likely, since the prior test had held all expressive material protected under the First Amendment unless "utterly without redeeming social value."[39] Moreover, reliance upon an average person who applies contemporary community standards allows each community to write its own definition of obscenity.[40] It would appear that there must soon be a clarification of what is intended by the phrase "contemporary community standards." It has, however, been ruled that the new standards do not apply retroactively—that is, to conduct prior to June 21, 1973.[41]

In the final analysis, it is impossible for the writer or his or her distributors to know when and where a work containing sexual motifs may be found obscene. At the least, no violation of the obscenity laws will occur while the work is kept in the privacy of the study. But obscenity laws, if applicable, can cover such uses of work as possession for sale or exhibition, sale, distribution, exhibition, mailing, and importation through customs. If minors have access to the work, an even higher standard than that applicable to obscene works may be applied by the states without violating the First Amendment.[42] Procedural safeguards, however, are provided by the First Amendment.[43] Law enforcement agencies cannot simply seize works, but must give notice so that a hearing can be held. Each side can be represented at this hearing and the judge must consider all relevant evidence bearing on the obscenity question. Only after observance of these procedural requirements can the censors, if victorious, have their way.

Obscenity is a complex legal area. The writer who fears that an obscenity issue may arise should consult a lawyer, especially since most contracts require a warranty against obscenity (as discussed on pp. 76–77 and pp. 114–115).

Censorship by School Boards

The control of school boards over such matters as curriculum, textbooks, and library books can have a significant effect on the access of students to books and the ideas contained in books. While state statutes usually give school boards the authority to dictate these decisions free from outside interference, several cases have been fought over attempts to place First Amendment limitations upon these decisions, particularly with respect to the removal of books from school libraries.

In a 1972 case the Community School Board No. 25 in Queens, New York, removed Piri Thomas's *Down These Mean Streets* from all junior high school libraries in the district. The vote on the board was five to three in favor of removal of a work described by the Second Circuit Court of Appeals as ugly, violent, replete with obscenities, containing normal and perverse sex, and depicting the use of heroin. The court, noting that no one had argued against the right of the board to initially decide which books would be purchased by the library, stated, "It would seem clear to us that books which become obsolete or irrelevant or where improperly selected initially, for whatever reason, can be removed by the same authority which was empowered to make the selection in the first place."[44]

In a 1976 case the Board of Education in Strongsville, Ohio, refused to approve Joseph Heller's *Catch 22* and Kurt Vonnegut's *God Bless You, Mr. Rosewater* as either textbooks or library books, despite favorable faculty recommendations. The board also ordered *Catch 22* and Vonnegut's *Cat's Cradle* removed from the high school library. The Sixth Circuit Court of Appeals decided that there had been no constitutional or procedural violation in the board's decisions not to use *Catch 22* and *God Bless You, Mr. Rosewater* as textbooks. However, the court did feel that the removal of library books curtailed freedom of speech and thought, particularly since the board members apparently found the books personally distasteful. The court stated, "Neither the State of Ohio nor the Strongsville School Board was under any federal constitutional compulsion to provide a library for the Strongsville High School or to choose any particular books. Once having created such a privilege for the benefit of its students, however, neither body could place conditions on the use of the library which were related solely to the social or political tastes of school board members."[45]

These conflicting decisions, and the volatile nature of the issue of censorship by school boards, make future litigation in this area a certainty.[46]

5
Contracts:
An Introduction

A contract is an agreement creating legally enforceable obligations between two or more parties.[1] The writer's relationships with publishers, producers, and agents are all contractual. A contract provides the legal framework within which the rights and obligations of the writer and other party can be specified. While verbal contracts can sometimes be valid, the better approach is to use written contracts (as discussed more extensively later in the chapter). This chapter develops a background of the law relating to contracts so that subsequent chapters dealing with such matters as agency contracts and marketing literary property can be more helpful.

Offer and Acceptance

An offer invites entry into a contract. It is a promise which can be accepted by a return promise or, less usual, by performance based on the terms of the offer. If a publisher says to a writer, "I am willing to pay you $250 for first North American serial rights in your story, 'The Doves of Peace,' " an offer has been made. The publisher has promised to purchase in definite terms which can be accepted by the writer's return promise to sell the story. If the publisher says, "This story would be a gem in my upcoming anthology," or "This story should sell for a fortune," or, "I'm going to keep this story for a few weeks," no offers have been made. If the publisher says, "You write this story and we'll agree later about the price," or, "You write this story and I'll pay you as I see fit," no offers have been made because a material term—the price—has been omitted. However, if the publisher says, "Write this article and I will pay you $250 if satisfied," a valid offer has been made. The writer should beware of such an offer, because the courts generally rule that a satisfaction clause means that a dissatisfied employer may reject the work, even though a reasonable person would have been satisfied.[2] In other words, the writer is working on speculation, an arrangement which should be avoided if possible.

The person making an offer can usually revoke it at any time prior to acceptance. Another way in which an offer can be terminated is by limiting the time for acceptance—for example, "I will purchase your story for $250 if you will sell it to me within the next ten days." This offer would terminate at the end of ten days. If no such time limit is set, the assumption is made that the offer ends after a reasonable amount of time has passed. An offer is also terminated by a counter offer. For example, if the publisher offers $250 for a story and the writer demands $500, the original offer of $250 is no longer effective.

Acceptance is usually accomplished by agreeing to the offer. If the publisher offers to pay $250 to have a story written, the writer can accept by stating, "I agree to write this story for $250." The end result of the process of offer and acceptance is a meeting of the minds, a mutual understanding between the parties to the contract. If a final contract is ambiguous, a court may try to determine the parties' intentions by examining customs in the profession, prior dealings between the parties, and the conduct of the parties with respect to the particular contract.[3] Once performance has been completed under a contract which is ambiguous, the court will try to rectify the ambiguities by a standard of reasonableness. If a writer does an article which a magazine publishes, the writer should be paid a reasonable compensation even if no price had been agreed upon.[4]

Consideration

Every contract, to be valid, must be based on consideration, which is the giving of value by each party to the other. The consideration each party to a contract receives is what induces entry into the contract. Where the publisher promises to pay $250 for a story which the writer promises to write, each party has received value from the other in the form of a promise. The consideration must be bargained for at the time of entering into the contract. If a publisher says, "Your story is so good that I'm going to pay you an extra $250 even though I don't have to," the publisher is not obliged to pay. The writer has already written the story and been paid in full, so the promise to pay an additional $250 is not supported by consideration.

The one situation where consideration is not required occurs when a person relies on a promise in such a way that the promise must be enforced to avoid injustice. If a patron makes a promise and should reasonably know that the writer will rely upon it, such as offering $250 as a gift for the writer to buy a typewriter, the patron cannot refuse to pay the money after the writer has in fact relied on the promise and purchased the typewriter.

Competency of the Parties

The law will not enforce a contract if the parties are not competent. The rationale is that there can be no meeting of the minds or mutual understanding in such a situation. A contract entered into by an insane person is not enforceable. Similarly, contracts entered into by minors will, depending on the law of the specific state, be either unenforceable or enforceable only at the choice of the minor. The age of reaching majority has traditionally been twenty-one, but many states such as New York and California have now lowered the age of majority to eighteen.[5]

Legality of Purpose

A contract for a purpose that is illegal or against public policy is not binding. For example, the novelist Anita Roddy-Eden sued comedian Milton Berle for breach of a contract under which Berle would take credit as sole author of a book in fact written by Roddy-Eden. It was hoped the public would buy more copies of the book because of Berle's name. But after Roddy-Eden finished a satisfactory book, Berle refused to go ahead with the contract. The court held that Roddy-Eden could not recover damages because the goal of the contract was to perpetrate a fraud upon the public. The court distinguished this from the common practice of using a pseudonym: "In such a case, regardless of the pen name employed by the writer, he is, in truth, the real author and is not exploiting the ability, talent and authorship of another, palming it off under the false pretense that it is his own."[6]

Written and Oral Contracts

While not all contracts need be written to be enforced, it is certainly wise to insist on having them in writing. The terms of a contract may come into dispute several years after the creation of the contract. At that time reliance on memory to provide the terms of the contract can leave much to be desired, especially if no witnesses were present and the parties disagree as to what was said.

A written contract need not even be a formal document. An exchange of letters can create a binding contract. Often a letter agreement is signed by one party, and the other party completes the contract by also signing at the bottom of the letter beneath the words CONSENTED AND AGREED TO. A check can create or be evidence of a contract—for example, a check from a magazine to a writer stating "This check for $250 is accepted as payment in full for world rights in perpetuity to the story 'Doves of Peace'."[7] If such a check conflicts with a prior written or oral agreement, it should be returned to the magazine so that any terms on the check accurately reflect the prior understanding. Both parties may not have signed an agreement, but a memorandum signed by the party against whom enforcement is sought can be found to constitute a valid contract. Even where the parties merely show, from their conduct, an intention to agree, a contract—called an "implied contract"—can come into existence. But when part of a contract is in writing, the writer should not rely on an oral agreement to the effect that compliance with all the written provisions will not be insisted upon. Courts are reluctant to allow oral evidence to vary the terms of a written contract, except in cases where the written contract is procured by fraud or under mistake or is too indefinite to be understood without the additional oral statements.

The copyright revision act requires that any transfer of a copyright or an exclusive right in a copyright must be evidenced by a writing.[8] While this would cover most of a writer's transactions, it does not apply to nonexclusive licenses.[9] It also would not apply to literary property which might not be copyrightable—for example, an idea. However, the Uniform Commercial Code might still apply (in every state except Louisiana), requiring written evidence—indicating price and subject matter and signed by the party against whom enforcement is sought—of a contract for the sale of intangible personal property if the amount being paid exceeds five thousand dollars.[10]

The writer may often contract to render services, such as writing an article on commission. An oral contract for such services is usually enforceable if the services can be performed within one year.[11] If the services will take longer than one year to perform, there must be a writing evidencing the contract and containing all essential terms of the contract. The ownership of the copyright of works for hire is discussed on p. 19 and pp. 37–38.

Warranties

Caveat emptor—let the buyer beware—expressed the traditional attitude of the courts toward the purchasers of property. Warranties, however, are express or implied facts or promises upon which the purchaser can rely. Warranties can be created orally, even if the contract must be written. They can be created during negotiations, at the time of making the contract, or, in some transactions not usually relevant to writers, after entry into the contract.[12] An express warranty is created when the writer asserts facts or promises relating to the character or ownership of the work which the purchaser relies upon in making the purchase.[13] The writer will often be required to give a publisher an express warranty to the effect that the work does not infringe any copyright, violate any property rights, or contain any scandalous, libelous, or unlawful matter. If this warranty proves untrue, the writer must pay the publisher for any losses which result. However, sales talk or opinions by the writer as to the value or merit of the work will not create warranties. If, for example, the writer speculates that the work will earn a fortune over the next few years, the publisher cannot rely upon such an opinion and no warranty is created. An implied warranty comes into existence by operation of law (rather than express representations of the parties) based on the circumstances of the transaction or the relationship of the parties.[14] In some sales, for example, there is an implied warranty that the seller has title or the right to convey title in the goods being sold, but it has been held that no warranty of marketable title will be implied in the sale of literary property.[15]

Assignments of Contracts

Sometimes one party to a contract can substitute another person to take over the burdens or rewards of the contract. This is not true, however, for contracts which are based upon the special skills of one party to the contract. Where such personal ability is crucial to the contract—for example, in a contract for the writing of a story—the writer may not delegate the contractual duties for performance by another writer.[16] But even though the writer is unable to delegate the performance of duties, assignment to another person of the writer's right to receive money due or to become due under the contract will be permissible.[17] A well-drafted contract will state the intention of the parties as to the assignment of rights or delegation of duties under the contract.

Nonperformance Excused

There are a variety of situations where the writer's failure to perform contractual obligations will be excused. The most obvious case is that the death of the writer is not a breach of contract which would permit a recovery from the writer's estate. Similarly, because the writer's work is personal, disabling physical or mental illness will excuse performance by the writer (although a provision might be made specifically extending the writer's time for performance in the event of ill health).

Grounds other than the personal nature of the writer's work

will also permit the writer to refuse to perform. If the other party waives the writer's performance or if both parties have agreed to rescind the contract, no performance will be necessary. If the writer is prevented by the other party from performing, performance will be excused and the writer will have an action for breach of contract.[18] Similarly, no performance is required where performance would be impossible, as in the case of the interviewer who cannot conduct an interview because of the subject's death. Also, performance is excused if it would be illegal due to a law passed after entering into the contract.

Remedies for Breach of Contract

A party who refuses to perform a contract can be liable to pay damages. There must, however, be some detriment or loss caused by a breach of contract before the recovery of damages will be allowed. The damages will generally be the amount of the reasonably foreseeable losses (including out-of-pocket costs and lost profits) caused by the breach.[19] Also, the injured party must usually take steps to minimize damages. Contracts will frequently set damages in advance to avoid the necessity of extensive proofs to establish proper damages at trial. The courts will enforce such provisions for damages, known as "liquidated damages," as long as damages would be difficult to establish and the amount specified is not unreasonable or a penalty.

The writer may wonder what happens when performance under a contract is either nearly completed or is completed but varies slightly from what was agreed upon. Unless the contract specifies that strict compliance is necessary to be paid for performing the contract, the writer should be able to recover the contract price less the costs necessary to pay for the defects in performance. For example, where an artist created stained glass windows in substantial compliance with the designs except that less light came through the windows than the parties had apparently intended, the court stated, "Where an artist is directed to produce a work of art in accordance with an approved design, the details of which are left to the artist, and the artist executes his commission in a substantial and satisfactory way, the mere fact that, when completed, it lacks some element of utility desired by the buyer and not specifically contracted for, constitutes no breach of the artist's contract."[20] A similar rule should apply to a writer who, for example, does an article or book from an agreed upon outline.[21]

The question, however, of what constitutes substantial performance is an area where litigation is likely. The reason for this is another rule: that part performance under a contract will not allow recovery based on the price specified in the contract for full performance. Moreover, such part performance will not, in most states, even be paid for on the basis of reasonable value unless the part performance is of substantial benefit to the other party who accepts and retains the benefits of such performance. This rule would not apply, of course, if one party prevented the other from performing. Also, where one part of a contract can be separated from another part, such as a number of payments for a number of different articles, recovery will usually be permitted for the partial contract price specified for each partial performance.[22]

In some situations damages may not be adequate to compensate for the loss caused by a breach of contract. If a famous writer is hired to do a story, the writer's refusal to honor the contract might be difficult to value in money damages. But since involuntary servitude is prohibited, the creation of the story cannot be forced upon the writer.[23] On the other hand, if a story with unique value is already in existence, a publisher might be able to require specific performance of a contract to sell the copyright. This would mean that a court would order the owner to transfer to the publisher the specific copyright for which the publisher had contracted.[24] Specific performance can only be used, however, where the payment of money would not be a sufficient remedy.

Statutes of Limitation

A statute of limitation sets forth the time within which an injured party must bring suit to have the injury remedied. After the limitation period has passed, no lawsuit can be maintained. The limitation period runs from the time of the breach. The limitation period for actions based on contracts varies from state to state—for example, six years in New York and four years in California (except that the period is reduced to two years in California if the contract is not written).[25] The limitation period in many states is longer for written contracts than for contracts which are oral, partly in writing, or implied.[26] The writer contemplating legal action is well advised to seek redress promptly so that no question will arise regarding statutes of limitation.

Bailments

A bailment is a situation where one person gives his or her lawfully owned property to be held by another person. For example, a writer might leave a manuscript with unique photographic transparencies at the office of an agent, a publisher, or a printer. In all of these relationships, where both parties benefit from the bailment, the person who takes the writer's property must exercise reasonable care in safeguarding it.[27] If that person is negligent and the work is damaged or lost, the writer will recover damages. Even if the work has no easily ascertainable market value, damages would still be awarded based on the intrinsic value of the work.

However, the reasonable standard of care required in a bailment can be changed by contract. The writer might, for example, be asked to sign a contract under which the writer would assume all risks of injury to the work. The writer should seek just the opposite—that is, to have the other party agree to act as an insurer of the work. This would mean that the other party would be liable if the work were damaged for any reason, even though reasonable care might have been exercised in safeguarding it. Of course, these considerations will hardly be significant if the manuscript is one of many copies and contains no valuable art work or transparencies.

Protection of Ideas

Ideas are denied copyright protection but can still be protected by contract.[28] The idea may be a format, a theme, a situation, and so on. The problem comes upon submission of the idea, since the writer must feel assured of reimbursement if the idea is used. At the outset, it should be noted that many purchasers of literary property have release forms which must be signed by persons submitting ideas (and, often, unsolicited manuscripts) before any consideration will be given the submission. Such release forms bar any claims by the writer based upon a subsequent use of similar material by the potential purchaser. In addition, if the writer should be able to sue and recover despite the release form, the maximum reasonable value of the material is stipulated (for example, two hundred dollars) and the total recovery possible is limited to such an amount. These provisions are accompanied by a recital from the writer, such as "I recognize that there is always a likelihood that this material may be identical with, like, or competitive to material which has or may come to you from other sources. Identity or similarity of material in the past has given rise to claims and disputes between various parties and has caused misunderstandings. You have advised me that you will refuse to examine or consider material unless you obtain for yourself complete protection from me against the possibility of any such claims." The writer can expect to be bound by such provisions, so caution should be exercised before signing a release form in order to submit an idea or manuscript.

The writer will be best served by an express contract providing for payment in the event the purchaser does use the idea. This is likely to be difficult to obtain, but the writer who simply volunteers an idea is basically at the mercy of the other party. The express contract should specify the consideration and other details of the transaction. If a standard price is paid for such material, it should be stated. Otherwise, a reasonable standard of value should be required as compensation. The submission agreement need not be complex, although it must suit the individual circumstances. For example, the writer might use a brief letter:

Dear Sir/Madam,

   I understand it is your practice to entertain or receive program materials, ideas, or suggestions for [specify the market]. I have developed such an [indicate what will be submitted] for submission and would like to disclose this to you. I understand that if you use it you will pay me a reasonable compensation based on current industry standards. Please advise me if I should send this to you.

Sincerely yours,

Alice Writer

It is not uncommon, however, for the writer to disclose ideas without having thought to obtain an express contract. Recovery may still be possible under a variety of doctrines which will only be mentioned here: implied contract (where the parties indicate by their conduct that a contract exists), confidential relationships (applicable to some cases in which the party with less bargaining power trusts in the other party's good faith and discloses the idea), and quasi contract (in which the law implies an obligation that the party receiving the idea pay for the benefits conferred).[29] Especially for a confidential relationship or quasi contract, however, the courts may require that the idea be concrete, elaborated, or novel before recovery will be allowed. A written, express contract is by far the best way for a writer to protect an idea.

Contracts for Readings and Lectures

Writers frequently are offered the opportunity to lecture or read before groups interested in their work. The administrative efficiency of the host organization can vary greatly, sometimes leaving the writer with a vexing problem of how to insure receipt of a fee agreed upon beforehand. A good first step to resolve this problem is a written contract detailing not only the amount of the fee and any reimbursements for expenses, such as for travel and lodging, but also the time of payment. A good formula might be for travel expenses to be paid in advance, while the fee and other expenses are reimbursed upon completion of the first day of the engagement. The time which the writer will spend with the group and the nature of the services should be specified. In addition to giving a reading of poetry, for example, the writer might be required to read students' work and sit in on creative writing seminars over a period of several days. If the writer is lecturing or reading, there should be a reservation of the copyrights in any recordings made by the host organization. A contract for a lecture or reading must meet the needs of each occasion, but a simple model contract is shown here for use as a starting point:

Dear Sir/Madam:

I am pleased by your invitation to address your group and would like this letter to serve as our contract with respect thereto. I agree to travel to [specify the location] on [specify the date or dates] and to perform the following services: [specify what is to be done]. In return you promise to pay my round-trip travel expenses in the amount of [specify amount] fourteen days prior to the date of said engagement, and pay me at the end of my first day of services a fee of [specify amount] and additional expenses in the amount of [specify amount and detail the reasons for the expenses, such as lodging and meals]. No recordings of my appearance shall be made without my express, written consent. Recordings shall include any electrical transcription, tape recording, wire recording, film, videotape, or any other method of recording voice or image whether now known or hereinafter developed. In the event permission to record my apperance is given, all copyrights to material contained therein shall be reserved to me and no use of said material shall be made without my written consent thereto and an appropriate placement of copyright notice in my name. If these terms are agreeable to you, please sign this letter beneath the words CONSENTED AND AGREED TO to constitute this a binding agreement between us. Kindly return one signed copy of the letter to me for my records.

Sincerely yours,

Alice Writer

CONSENTED AND AGREED TO:
Municipal University
By: _____
      Authorized Representative

6
Agency Contracts

Writers will often seek the assistance of an agent to facilitate the sale of work. The best agent is the one most suited to the particular writer. Chemistry is as important to the relationship as law. The agent must truly be enthusiastic about selling the writer's work to the relevant markets. If the agent is not enthusiastic, or cannot effectively sell to those markets, the relationship will not be a successful one. Writers weighing the pros and cons of having an agent can request a pamphlet titled "The Literary Agent" from the Society of Authors Representatives (abbreviated as "S.A.R."), 101 Park Avenue, New York, New York 10017. This society, founded in 1928, is a voluntary association of agents who seek to follow ethical business standards. For example, the society advises that the standard practice of the agent is not to advertise and not to charge fees for normal office expenses (such as reading manuscripts). Writers will also be interested in the Independent Literary Agents' Association, a group of independent agents formed in 1977 to exchange information about the trade in order to represent their writers most effectively. Their address is c/o Phyllis Seidel, 164 East 93rd Street, New York, New York 10028.

The beginning writer may be understandably perplexed when trade magazines carry advertisements soliciting unsold manuscripts and promising great sales success. Upon response to such advertisements, the writer discovers that a reading fee will be charged for each manuscript submitted. In return for the reading fee, advice will be given to the writer as to how the work can be made marketable. If the work becomes marketable, the agent promises to undertake placing it.

These fee-charging agencies cannot be completely condemned, although they are understandably in disfavor in the industry. It is true that the neophyte may not be able to obtain an agent at all. The reading fees are alleged to cover the costs of grooming a writer for the time when sales will generate commissions for the agency. At that point, of course, reading fees are no longer charged. Yet charging such fees is suspect, since it alleviates the agent's need to sell the work in order to earn income. The important point is to be aware of what the agency is offering. If it is offering instruction in the craft of writing, the writer seeking instruction may be completely satisfied. If the same writer is seeking to make sales, the instructional activities may seem wasteful of time as well as money. There is absolutely no guarantee that such instruction will ever result in the sale of work. The writer must face this likelihood when considering whether or not to pay a reading fee to an agent.

Each writer must evaluate his or her own unique needs before seeking an agent. It is essential to find out as much as possible about the agent. Is is the agent respected in the field and reputed to be honorable? What markets does the agent sell to? Does the agent run a businesslike office? What kind of personality does the agent have? If a larger agency is involved, the important consideration is the individual who will handle the writer. The writer and agent must interact in such a way that the agent goes to the marketplace praising the writer's work and eagerly trying to sell it.

Many agency agreements are oral, although the larger agencies will generally use written agreements. The fact that the agreement is oral belies the complexity of the relationship between the writer and agent. The writer may well wish to alter an agent's standard contract or, if the agent has no contract, draft a simple letter agreement to resolve the more important issues which might create friction. Needless to say, the advice of a lawyer will be valuable here, despite the apparent simplicity of many of the dealings between writers and agents.

Agency

An agency includes any relationship in which one person is given authority to act for or represent another person. Generally, any competent person of legal age may act as an agent. The agent is a fiduciary who must exercise good faith in dealing with the writer. For example, the agent should keep the writer promptly and regularly informed of the agent's activities and never give confidential information to competitors. The agent must not engage in self-dealing. Thus, the Dramatists Guild specifies that the writer shall not have the same person or firm act as agent to market a play and as producer to produce the play.[1] An agent cannot represent parties with adverse interests unless both parties give an informed consent to the arrangement.[2]

The powers given to an agent can vary greatly. A general agent is usually empowered to do all the acts connected with a particular trade, business, or employment. On the other hand, a special agent can only take limited action in accordance with particular instructions.

S.A.R. indicates that an agent normally can examine contracts, negotiate modifications, and recommend that the writer either reject the contract or approve and sign it. Since the writer will probably wish to be certain that the agent obtain the writer's consent to any contract, a provision is often used stating, "The agent shall submit to the writer any offer obtained, but no agreement shall be binding upon the writer without his or her signature." If the writer does want the agent to be able to make a binding contract for the sale of literary property, a power of attorney can be executed by the writer specifically indicating that the agent is being granted the power of disposition over enumerated rights in a work. A power of attorney is evidence to third parties of the agent's authority to act.

An agent acting within the granted authority obligates the writer. However, agents may sometimes act beyond the scope of their actual authority. Generally there can be no liability for the unauthorized acts of an agent. But if the writer acts in such a way that a third party, such as a publisher or producer, thinks the agent has more authority than the agent actually has, the writer can be bound if the agent concludes a deal based on this apparent authority. For example, the president of a printing company had also been acting as general manager. He contracted to print a book for a publishing house. Under the bylaws, the president lacked the actual authority to do this, although the general manager could have. However, the publishing house was justified in believing the president to have the authority of the general manager. The printing company was obligated by the contract to print the book, despite the fact that executing it was beyond the president's actual authority.[3]

A writer may also consent to the unauthorized acts of an agent, making the acts binding upon the writer by a process known as ratification. An unreasonable delay in repudiating unauthorized acts—or even inaction and silence in some cases—may be interpreted by the courts as a ratification.[4]

Parties to the Agreement

The agreement with the agent will often contain a provision to the effect that "The Agent shall make reasonable and good faith efforts to promote the writer and sell the writer's works." Some contracts may specify particular steps that the agent will take to do this, but specification is difficult and the writer must rely on the agent's acting in good faith. Since the writer must trust the individual agent, it is not uncommon to provide for termination of an agreement with a corporate agency in the event of the cessation of employment or death of that agent. While an agent's delegation of duties to others whom the agent employs may be permitted, assignment of the representation agreement by the agent is prohibited—for example, "This agreement may not be assigned by the agency without the prior written approval of the writer." The agent should maintain as confidential information about transactions executed for the writer.

The agency may, in turn, request assurances of fair dealing on the part of the writer. These might take the form of warranties that the writer has title to the works and the power to enter into the agency agreement.

The agency's duty to the writer requires the agency not to represent adverse or competing interests. But every agent represents numerous writers who can easily be competing with one another. Situations can also arise where the same agent has one client, such as a writer, selling to another client, such as a producer. In normal dealings no problem will arise from the representation of more than one writer by the same agent, although extreme cases can be imagined where one writer might feel the agent abused the fiduciary's responsibilities. In the cases of representing clients negotiating with each other, the agent should make full disclosure. The writer is well advised to have the right to obtain independent representation for that particular transaction and, therefore, not be under an obligation to pay the agent's commission.

Scope of the Agency

The agent will probably want to be the exclusive agent throughout the world for marketing all rights in all the properties created by the writer, including but not limited to publishing, motion picture, stage, radio, television, and recording rights. The writer, of course, may very well wish to limit the scope of the agency.

It is understandable that the agent wants the agency to be exclusive. If it were nonexclusive, nothing would prevent the writer from simultaneously submitting the same work through a number of agents. The duplication of effort and expenditures, not to mention the likelihood of confusion, make this anathema to any agent. But the writer must be aware that the word exclusive has two different meanings. This and other principles of agency law are well illustrated by a case in which an agent took a playwright to the courts in order to recover commissions.

The playwright F. Hugh Herbert finished a new play early in August, 1939. He called up Laura Wilck, an old acquaintance and an agent in Hollywood (although she had not represented Herbert before) to ask her to sell the play. This play, titled *Quiet Please*, was immediately placed with a producer. The playwright was pleased and entered into an agreement dated August 17, 1939, appointing the agent as "sole and exclusive representative for the term of five years (5) years from the date hereof, for any play or plays which (I) may write."[5] The agreement provided that the agent would decide whether or not to represent a play within ten days of receiving it. If she chose not to represent it, the playwright could submit it elsewhere. The agent was entitled to receive a 10 percent commission for monies received "under or by virtue of any contract effected, for which negotiations may have been carried on, within the term of this agreement."[6]

Quiet Please didn't work out as well as had been hoped. The playwright cooled toward the agent and, on January 3, 1942, wrote a letter revoking her authority to act for him. A writer can always revoke an agent's powers. However, the writer must also have the right to terminate the agency or the agent will be entitled to commissions for sales after the revocation.[7] In this case the term of the agency was for five years, so it would not terminate under the agreement until August 17, 1944.

Two months after revoking the first agency, Herbert entered into a two-year agreement with the Sam Jaffe Agency. By November 1942 he had completed a new play titled *Kiss and Tell*. Of course he didn't show it to his old agent, but simply had the Sam Jaffe Agency sell the stage rights. The film rights were also sold, although it was not clear from the testimony whether the sale had been negotiated by Herbert or by the Sam Jaffe Agency. The play had a very favorable reception and earned substantial profits. And the original agent, under the terms of the representation agreement, demanded her 10 percent of the playwright's income.

The court refused to award her 10 percent of the income from the sale of the film rights, unless a jury determined that the sale had been made by another agent and not by the playwright himself. This illustrates the difference between an "exclusive agency" and an "exclusive sale" contract. "A contract to give an 'exclusive agency' to deal with specified property is ordinarily interpreted as not precluding competition by the principal personally but only as precluding him from appointing another agent to accomplish the result. . . . A contract to give the 'exclusive sale' of specified property ordinarily indicates that the agent is to have the exclusive power."[8] The court concluded that the representation was for an exclusive agency, not for an exclusive sale. If the playwright had really sold the film rights by himself, he wouldn't owe his agent a commission. But if he had used another agent to do the selling, he would have violated her exclusive agency and the commission would definitely be owed. This issue was returned to the lower court to be decided by a jury.

So writers should be certain whether their agreement with an agent is an exclusive agency, leaving the writer free to sell work elsewhere as long as no other agent is used, or an exclusive sale arrangement under which a commission must be paid the agent regardless of who sells the work.

Unhappily for Herbert, he had negotiated the stage production through the Sam Jaffe Agency, and the stage production was earning most of the income. But his revocation of the powers of the agent made no difference with respect to his obligation to pay her commission not only on the past profits of the stage production but on a reasonable estimate of the future profits as well (established by expert testimony). One lesson here is that the term of the agency was too long. If an agent wishes to stop representing a writer, it is almost impossible to force the agent to live up to a "best efforts" or "good faith" provision. But if the writer wishes to stop being represented by the agent, the unhappy end result may be the obligation to pay double commissions as Herbert had to do. The writer will usually be well served by an agency which can be terminated at any time upon thirty days notice to the other party. An agreement for longer than one or two years, if all the writer's work is to come within the agreement, seems too restrictive. One possible compromise might be to give the writer a right of termination if the agent fails to generate a specified minimum amount of income over every six-month or one-year period. If the agency is only to represent one or more specified works, the writer may be comfortable in agreeing to a longer term. If no term is agreed upon for the agency, it can be terminated by either party upon giving notice of termination to the other party.[9] The death of the writer automatically terminates the agency, even if the agent is unaware of it.

Agents will sometimes provide that they have an "agency coupled with an interest" for literary property which is sold. This provision may well prevent any revocation or termination of the agency with respect to these contracts, so that the agent would collect monies due even after termination of the writer-agent contract.[10] It is far better for the writer to have the right to receive payments directly from the publisher after termination (although the writer would still have to pay commissions due on contracts entered into during the term of the agency). If the agent insists on having an "agency coupled with an interest," it should be limited to the agent's commission so the writer will definitely be able to receive the balance of payments due directly from the publisher.

The scope of the agency can be limited to specified works. But assuming it is for an ongoing representation of the writer, another kind of limitation would be with respect to different types of work. For example, the agent might represent the writer with respect to fiction, but not nonfiction, or with respect to novels, but not plays. Or the limitation might be with respect to different types of rights. For example, the agent might represent publication rights, but not film, stage, or other rights. The geographic scope of the agency can also be limited. Instead of granting the agent the right to represent the writer throughout the world, the representation could be only for North America.

If the agent is representing all the writer's work, does this include work created prior to the commencement of the agency? What about work created during the agency but sold after the agency has terminated? The agent may want to provide for a commission if, within a limited time period after termination of the agency, the writer sells a work to someone with whom the agent had conducted negotiations during the term of the agency. And will the agent have any claim to commissions if a publisher or producer approaches the writer directly? Or if the writer receives speaking fees, grants, or prizes?

The distinction between an exclusive agency and an exclusive sale agreement is an important one. The writer must also consider limiting the scope of the representation agreement with respect to the types of works or rights covered, duration, and geographic scope. The innumerable details which can crop up in this area indicate that the simplicity of the agent-writer relationship can be singularly deceptive.

Agent's Commissions and Expenses

S.A.R. indicates that the customary practice among literary agencies is to retain a 10 percent commission on domestic sales and up to a 20 percent commission on foreign sales. The

Dramatists Guild stipulates that agents' commissions shall not exceed 10 percent, except for amateur performances in which case the commission shall not exceed 20 percent.[11]

The writer will want to resolve whether the agent is entitled to the full commission if another agent must be used. For example, many agents in New York City will associate with an agent in Hollywood in order to sell works more effectively to the film industry. Presumably the writer should not have to pay double in this situation. But what if the writer sells a work through another agent? Again, if the agency is exclusive, the writer will have to pay the full 10 percent to each agent.

The writer may find that the agent wants to charge for expenses incurred on the writer's behalf, such as telegraph messages, cables, long distance telephone calls, photocopying, manuscript retyping, copies of books for use in the sale of rights, legal fees, and so on. The writer should decide in each case whether such a charge is fair. S.A.R. indicates such practices to be acceptable, but this does not mean the writer should necessarily agree to them. A middle course might be to permit such charges if the writer consents in advance. An agent certainly has no right to threaten to withhold monies collected for the writer in order to force the writer to approve the agent's expenses.[12]

Payments and Accountings

Agents will usually collect monies due to the writer. S.A.R. indicates that the agent's standard practice should be to deduct commissions and expenses, if any, and promptly pay the balance to the writer. This payment should be made from a separate bank account, according to S.A.R., in order to avoid commingling of the writer's funds with the working funds of the agency. The Dramatists Guild goes further by providing that agents may only collect monies due the writer if the agent is the Dramatists' Play Service, Inc., or a member in good standing of S.A.R.[13] Moreover, the guild provides that monies owed the writer by the producer are trust funds, whether or not segregated.[14] This designation as trust funds places an even higher standard of fiduciary responsibility upon the agent and seeks to protect the writer against the agent's creditors. It is a provision which can be included in any agency agreement, if the agent will consent to it.

An accounting is a record of income received during a given period of time. S.A.R. indicates that the agent can be expected to examine royalty statements and, if necessary, obtain corrections from publishers. Of course, royalties may come from other sources as well, and the writer should be able to rely upon the agent to check these accountings.

The writer will usually be satisfied simply with receiving the accountings rendered to the agent from the various income-yielding sources. However, the writer should have the right to receive an accounting from the agent with respect to funds received and, upon reasonable notice, the right to inspect the agent's books. In this way the writer can protect against unscrupulous conduct on the agent's part. And, as S.A.R. advises, the writer can expect the agent to keep the writer's financial affairs confidential.

A sample agent-writer agreement follows, but it must be adapted to the individual writer's unique needs. The relative bargaining strength of the parties will influence the terms of the contract as well. The writer will usually be well served in having the advice of a lawyer when such an agreement must be negotiated.

AGENCY AGREEMENT

Dear Alice Writer:

This letter will confirm your appointment of me as your exclusive agent throughout the world and my acceptance of such appointment to advise you professionally and market all your literary rights, including but not limited to publishing, motion picture, stage, radio, and television rights, in such works as you submit to me during the term of this agreement, including the following works:

_____

_____

I agree to exercise my best efforts in marketing your work and promoting your professional standing.

I agree to collect and receive for you all monies due you from the marketing of your literary rights and hold same as trust funds for you in a bank account segregated from the working funds of the agency. I agree to remit all monies due you promptly as collected, and provide an accounting and permit inspection of my books and records upon your written request. Nothing contained herein shall obligate you to submit all your works created during the term of this agency to me, nor shall you have any obligation to pay commissions to me with respect to works sold by you directly, regardless of whether or not I am representing said works. You agree that I am to retain 10 percent (10%) of monies collected as my full agency commission from the marketing of literary rights in the United States, its possessions, and Canada, and 20 percent (20%) of monies so collected from the marketing of such rights in the rest of the world. I shall not take any reimbursement for expenses incurred on your behalf without your prior written consent. ᵥ

It is mutually agreed that this agreement shall have a term of one (1) year, commencing on the date hereof, and renewing automatically for additional one (1) year terms unless terminated. Either party may terminate the agreement by giving thirty (30) days prior written notice to the other party. In the event that within sixty (60) days after the date of termination an agent representing you enters into a contract for the sale of literary rights with respect to which I had been negotiating prior to said termination, and the terms obtained by said agent are no more favorable than the terms which I could have obtained, the said contract shall be deemed to have been entered into during the term of this agreement.

I agree to submit to you any offers received, and no agreement shall be binding upon you without your consent and signature thereto. It is mutually agreed that this agreement shall not be assigned by either party hereto without the prior written consent of the other party. Modifications to this agreement shall be in writing. The agreement shall be governed by the laws of _____ State.

Your signature beneath the words "CONSENTED AND AGREED TO" shall constitute this a binding agreement between us. Kindly return the duplicate copy enclosed to me for my records.

Sincerely yours,

Catherine Agent

CONSENTED AND AGREED TO:

_____

Alice Writer

7
Marketing Literary Property

The owner of literary property has the powers belonging to any property owner. These include the rights to option, sell, or license the property. The writer marketing literary property may deal in one or more of a number of markets—book, magazine, newspaper, theatre, radio, television, film, and so on. Each of these markets has further subdivisions too numerous to list, but fundamental concepts involved in the marketing of literary property apply to any of these markets. An understanding of these concepts is necessary if the writer is to achieve an agreement fairly reflecting the bargaining strength of the parties. These agreements are often complex, and the writer will benefit from the advice of a knowledgeable lawyer or agent.

The starting point for negotiations is the writer's ownership of literary property. If the writer has worked with a collaborator, a separate collaboration agreement must detail the parties' rights with respect to artistic decisions, control over the property, the sharing of income, authorship credits, and so on. Initially the owner, assumed to be an individual writer, can grant an option to the property, an option being the power within a limited period of time to purchase rights to use the property. The payment for an option is smaller than the payment to be made upon exercise of the option and actual use of the property. Often an option agreement—for example, an option to make a story or novel into a film—will have attached a completed purchase agreement to be used if the option is exercised. Or the writer may sell property outright, such as the sale to a magazine of "all rights" in an article. Far preferable to selling all rights is the practice of licensing certain uses of the property.

The writer giving a license makes a grant of rights to the licensee. This grant will encompass the rights to exploit a work in the medium, territory, time period, and language specified. The writer seeks to narrowly limit this grant, certainly not transferring rights which the licensee cannot effectively exploit. This is because the writer's income from a licensing is usually not a fixed sum, but rather a variable amount which increases based upon the purchaser's success with and use of the property. The measurement of this success will often require carefully drawn definitions of price, profits, or proceeds. The purchaser will try to insist on having both control of and a share in the income from subsidiary rights. Subsidiary rights are simply defined as rights of exploitation in markets not encompassed in the grant of rights to the licensee. For example, film rights would be subsidiary rights in a book publishing contract. And book publishing rights would be subsidiary rights in a film contract. The writer will seek to limit the licensee's interest in subsidiary rights, but the final allocations of control and income will depend on the parties' bargaining strengths. Thus, the interaction of the grant of rights and subsidiary rights provisions must be understood if the writer is truly to know what the licensee has acquired.

The writer will wish to have the work copyrighted in his or her name, but practice varies on this from industry to industry. The licensee will want the writer to give warranties stating that the property is original and does not infringe any copyrights, and also does not contain material which is obscene, defamatory, or an invasion of anyone's privacy. The writer indemnifies the purchaser for losses resulting from a breach or, sometimes, an alleged breach of these warranties. The writer will naturally strive to blunt the impact of any warranty provision.

Artistic control is another important point, although this often does not become obvious until the agreement has been signed and realization of the end product is well under way. If the licensee has full power over artistic decisions, the end product may be so alien to the original concept that the writer would want a right not to be named as author. If the writer is familiar with the reputation and prior work of the licensee, an attempt may be made to restrict the licensee's power to assign the property to others. The writer presumably knows the financial and artistic resources upon which the immediate licensee can draw to guarantee successful completion of the project, while nothing is known about possible assignees of the licensee. Similarly, if the writer is to complete certain work under the agreement, the obligation to do the work cannot be assigned to another writer (although the right to sums due to the writer can be assigned). And the writer, whether marketing subsidiary rights or making a commitment to undertake personally a project, will want to have authorship credit specified in detail.

These typical considerations provide an overview of the marketing of literary property to any market. The bulk of this chapter will be devoted to an examination of the provisions of book publishing contracts.[1] Both the Authors Guild (referred to as "the guild") and the Society of Authors Representatives (referred to as "S.A.R.") have created model contracts. The Authors Guild contract, along with their excellent booklet titled "Guide to the Authors Guild Trade Book Contract," is available to their members. The S.A.R. contract appears on pp. 131–138 by permission of S.A.R. These contracts have not been adopted by publishers, so their value is educational as well as practical. First, the writer must learn which provisions in a publisher's contract are onerous. After learning this, the next step is knowing the form of more favorable provisions which should be sought in negotiation. If this chapter dwells too long upon what is ideal, it is in the hope that the increased awareness and demands of writers will gradually reform the publishers' contracts (which, of course, vary greatly one from another). Realistically, both writer and publisher must recognize that bargaining strength will determine the final form of the contract—assuming equally skilled and knowledgeable negotiators on each side.

Once the thorough discussion of the book publishing agreement is completed, some of the special features of magazine, syndication, theatre, television, and film marketing will be considered. However, the book publishing contract offers a good illustration of the general concerns and concepts present in the marketing of literary property. The numbers of the illustrative clauses in the S.A.R. contract appear in parentheses at appropriate points in the text.

Grant of Rights

After setting forth the names of the parties, their addresses, and the date, a book contract will detail the rights granted by the writer to the publisher (Clause 1). This grant of rights can be limited as to the form of publication, the language, the time during which the work can be used, and the territory in which the book can be sold. The author should never transfer the work itself or title to the work, but only grant rights which are carefully circumscribed. The grant of rights varies between the contracts of different publishers, and often the subsidiary rights provisions must be examined in tandem with the grant of rights in order to be fully aware of the interest which the publisher is acquiring.

The S.A.R. contract limits the publisher to using the work in book form in the English language. The publisher's exclusive right to distribute the book covers the United States, its territories and possessions, the Philippines, and Canada. The exclusive nature of the right means that the writer cannot give any other publisher permission to distribute in these areas. The publisher also receives a worldwide nonexclusive right (except for the British Commonwealth) to sell the English language copies printed in the United States. The publishing rights to the British Commonwealth (except Canada) are not granted so that the writer or the writer's agent can make a direct disposition of such rights to a publisher in the British Commonwealth.

However, the contracts of most publishers provide either in the grant of rights or the subsidiary rights provision for the publisher to participate in distribution or licensing to the British Commonwealth (which may be included in a more general geographic designation, such as "world distribution rights"). Depending on the specific provisions, the publisher may demand the right to sell its editions printed in the United States to the British Commonwealth, license an independent publisher in the British Commonwealth to bring out an edition, or license a subsidiary in the

British Commonwealth to bring out an edition. The writer must determine whether the publisher can more effectively market the book in the British Commonwealth than the writer or the writer's agent working directly with a British publisher would be able to do. Particularly if the writer has no agent capable of marketing abroad, limitations placed on the publisher's right to distribute to the British Commonwealth may be self-defeating.

If the publisher is to have rights with respect to the British Commonwealth, the guild contract recommends giving the publisher the exclusive right to license to the British Commonwealth (and the Republics of Ireland and South Africa) for a limited period of time such as twelve months (definitely no more than twenty-four months) after United States publication. If, after this period elapses, the publisher has not granted a license, the license has terminated, or the license is terminable, the writer has the power to revoke the publisher's rights with respect to the British Commonwealth. In addition, if the publisher does successfully license British Commonwealth rights, the guild suggests that the publisher's share of proceeds be 20 percent and the writer's 80 percent.

The S.A.R. contract reserves translation rights and foreign rights in countries not enumerated to the writer. The guild provides that the publisher shall have the exclusive right to license translations (except into English) in all countries, except that this right can be revoked by the writer after a limited period such as eighteen months (definitely no more than thirty-six months) if the publisher has not licensed the work, such a license has been terminated, or the license is terminable. Again, most publishers will demand translation and foreign rights in either the grant of rights or subsidiary rights provision, so the issue is whether the publisher or the writer's agent can more effectively reach the various markets. If the right to license translations in all countries is given to the publisher, the guild suggests that the publisher receive no more than 25 percent of the licensing proceeds and the writer receive no less than 75 percent.

The guild also limits the duration of the grant of rights to the first term of the United States copyright, whereas most contracts seek to give the publisher rights for the copyright renewal term and any extensions thereof. However, the termination provisions under the copyright revision act will effectively limit the duration of a copyright grant made after January 1, 1978, as explained on p. 39.

Subsidiary Rights

Subsidiary rights will cover many, if not all, of the rights not conveyed to the publisher by the initial grant. First, the writer must determine which subsidiary rights are enumerated in the contract. Next, the control over each of the subsidiary rights must be specified. Will the power to license the right belong to the publisher or writer? Finally, regardless of who has the power to license the right, it must be determined how the publisher and writer will divide between them the proceeds realized from licensing the various subsidiary rights.

Licensings of subsidiary rights can be made for abridgments, book clubs, reprints by another publisher, first and second serializations (which are magazine or newspaper rights before and after book publication), syndication, advertising, commercial uses, films, plays, radio shows, television, and mechanical rendition or recording uses. Foreign and translation rights may also be subsidiary rights, unless included in the grant of rights or reserved entirely to the writer. This illustrates the interplay between the grant of rights and the subsidiary rights provisions, both of which must be examined for the writer to be certain of the interest the publisher is acquiring.

The definition of the different subsidiary rights can vary between contracts. Clarity is essential here, and the writer should scrutinize the definitions to make sure they are precise and sufficient. For example, reprint rights could include mass market paperbacks (for distribution through chain stores and news and magazine wholesalers), cheap hardcover editions, quality paperbacks, and so on. Commercial or novelty rights are often included without definition in the subsidiary rights provision. Commercial rights can be defined to cover the use of the literary work, the title of the work, the names of characters, and characterizations of the characters as a basis for trademarks or trade names for toys, games, clothing, and other products. But these rights may also include the publisher's power to license the use of the writer's name or likeness in connection with such products—an association which the writer may find objectionable, particularly if the merchandise is not of high quality.

The S.A.R. contract allows the publisher to license cheap edition, book club, and postpublication periodical (second serial) publications (Clauses 8[a], [b], [c]), but the publisher must ask the writer for his or her prior approval which is not to be delayed or unreasonably withheld (Clause 8[h]). Also, no cheap edition may be published until one year after the date of initial publication of the trade edition (Clause 8[g]). Assuming the publisher has the power to license subsidiary rights, the time when the exercise of a given power may begin should always be considered. Similarly, the publisher's power to license subsidiary rights can be limited with respect to the geographic extent and duration of each right. For example, the publisher might have the power to license commercial rights in the United States for ten years, but the writer would retain the power to license outside the United States and after ten years would also regain the power to license in the United States.

The publisher should have no right to share in the proceeds from subsidiary rights if the publisher fails to carry through its obligations (especially to publish) under the contract. Publishers will often sell the subsidiary rights prior to publication, so this distinction can be more than academic. It would be anomalous if a publisher never lived up to its obligation to bring out a trade edition, but still shared as a broker in proceeds from book club, paperback, film, and other sales.

The S.A.R. contract permits the publisher to allow excerpts of less than five hundred words to be used in textbooks or anthologies (Clause 8[d]). The work may also be used in its entirety for the blind or handicapped (Clause 8[e]). However, any use in retrieval or storage systems shall be permitted only with the writer's prior written consent which shall not be delayed or unreasonably withheld (Clause 8[f]).

Conspicuously absent from the subsidiary rights provision is any mention of performing (as opposed to publishing) subsidiary rights. The S.A.R. contract follows the recommendation of the guild that the publisher have nothing to do with stage, record, radio, motion picture, television, and audio-visual rights. The rationale here is that the publisher usually does not market to these fields and should not, therefore, control any rights or share in any proceeds. A similar rationale applies to commercial rights. Publishers' contracts, however, do not reflect this reasoning.

Once the subsidiary rights have been enumerated and the issue of control determined (perhaps with the writer effectively having a veto power over certain licensings), the final step is to resolve the division of the proceeds received from licensing the subsidiary rights. Obviously the percentages will be negotiated and vary from contract to contract. The guild has recommended the following percentages as reasonable for the writer to receive: 100 percent of first serialization income (90 percent if the publisher acts as agent), and never any less than 80 percent; for paperback licenses, book club licenses, abridgments and selections, and second serializations, 50 percent of the first $10,000 of income, 60 percent of the next $10,000, and 70 percent of any income over $20,000; 50 percent of income from licensing film strips, microfilm, computer uses, and so on; and 100 percent of income from licensing stage, motion picture, television, and similar rights, unless the publisher is to receive 10 percent for acting as agent, but the writer should never receive less than 80 percent. If the original publication is in paperback, the publisher may sell hardcover rights to another publisher and agree to hold off the paperback publication for a year. In such a case, the writer may receive up to 75 percent of the proceeds, and certainly no less than 50 percent.

The definition of licensing income is critical, since percentages mean little without reference to what they are distributing between the writer and publisher. The S.A.R. and guild contracts permit no reductions at all from licensing gross proceeds prior to payment of the writer's share (Clause 8[i]). Contracts of publishers, however, will generally reduce gross proceeds by various expenses, including agent's commissions. Some contracts simply refer to a term such as "net compensation" without any further definition. This is not satisfactory, since the writer who is to receive a share of something less than gross proceeds should know exactly what is being subtracted to reach the net amount.

The writer should definitely have the right to receive copies of any licensing contracts negotiated by the publisher, as the S.A.R. contract provides (Clause 8[h]).

Reservation of Rights

The grant of rights and the subsidiary rights provisions are likely to cover all the conceivable uses of the writer's work. However, the writer should anticipate unthought of, even uninvented, uses. This is done by insisting on a simple clause stating, "All rights not specifically granted to the publisher are reserved to the writer" (Clause 15).

Delivery of Manuscript, Additional Materials, Permissions

The S.A.R. contract calls for the delivery of "a complete typewritten script of the Work" by a specified date (Clause 3). However, the writer's failure to deliver the manuscript on time does not permit the publisher to terminate the contract and recover any advances. Instead, the publisher must wait three months and, if the manuscript has still not been delivered, give the writer a written notice of termination. After this has been done, the publisher may recover any monies which have been advanced to the writer.

If the publisher's contract specifies that "time is of the essence," the writer should definitely deliver the manuscript on time. If the contract doesn't specify that time is of the essence, the writer should still deliver the manuscript on time, but a late delivery (of perhaps a month or six weeks) may not be a breach of contract which would permit the publisher to terminate the contract and demand the return of the advance. Caution dictates, however, that the writer always request as early as possible a written extension if the delivery date cannot be met.

Publishers' contracts usually require that the delivered manuscript be in "content and form satisfactory" to the publisher. This places the writer in a difficult position, since the publisher's decision can be subjective. If the publisher has seen all or part of the work prior to signing the contract, it should be recited that what was seen was satisfactory. If a practice is followed of submitting portions of the work in progress, it might be provided that the publisher indicate that each portion is satisfactory within a reasonable time after receipt. The writer can also seek to have the word "reasonably" inserted before "satisfactory," so that the publisher's decision cannot be wholly subjective. The contract could also entitle the writer to have a written explanation of the reasons why the work was not satisfactory, with a specified time to make revisions. At the least, the publisher should be required within a limited time, such as a month or six weeks, to make a decision with respect to whether or not the manuscript is satisfactory. The guild has an additional provision granting the writer an automatic extension if any delay is due to military service, illness, or accident, although certain maximum limits are placed on the extensions allowed under this provision.

Most publishers' contracts will require the writer to deliver with the manuscript all photographs, drawings, other illustrations, maps, tables, charts, the index, the bibliography, and permissions. The expenses incurred to obtain these materials will be the writer's. The S.A.R. contract, however, effectively calls to the writer's attention the possibility of dividing these responsibilities and costs with the publisher. Thus, each item indicates whether the publisher or writer is to provide it and, regardless of who must provide it, which party will be responsible for paying for it (Clause 3[a]). If the writer fails to provide any required materials within a reasonable time after submission of the manuscript, the publisher must give the writer thirty days written notice before procuring the necessary materials. This contrasts with the more typical requirement in publishers' contracts that the additional materials be submitted at the time of delivery of the manuscript. And the requirement that the writer approve any materials supplied by the publisher is atypical of publishers' contracts (Clause 3[b]).

The issue of payment for other materials can be especially important for a children's book. If the publisher is to pay for illustrations, this should be specified. The guild advises that the writer who also does illustrations may negotiate for a separate payment as illustrator.

The S.A.R. contract provides that the publisher will obtain any permissions and that the responsibility for payment shall be divided between the writer and publisher (Clause 3[c]). The rationale is that the publisher is better equipped to obtain permissions than the writer. However, publishers' contracts normally require the writer to provide and pay for all permissions. In any case, the guild suggests that if the publisher is to pay for permissions for art books, anthologies, or similar works involving substantial additional materials and permissions, the amount of the payment be stipulated in the contract.

Finally, the S.A.R. contract provides that if the publisher must make payments on behalf of the writer for any additional materials or permissions, these payments shall be advanced by the publisher and deducted only from monies earned under the contract. This is not unusual, except that the publisher is not allowed to deduct the advances from monies earned under other contracts which the writer may have with the publisher. The writer should always seek to have each book be a separate enterprise. No advances or other sums owed on one book should ever be deductible from monies received from another book with the same publisher. Many publishers try to impose this provision on writers, but the best argument against it is that the writer would be in a better position by publishing with another publisher. No question could then arise of deducting sums owed on one book from monies earned by another book. References in any provision to payment of sums owed on one book with monies earned by another book should be stricken from the contract.

Royalties

The S.A.R. contract provides for a percentage scale of royalties, the percentage increasing as more copies are sold (Clause 7[b]). Royalties permit the writer to share in the success of a book and are usually far more desirable than a flat fee. The S.A.R. contract specifies that the percentage of proceeds payable to the writer upon the sale of each copy is based on "retail price." This is an important qualification. If the royalty is based on a net price—that is the price after discounts to wholesalers and book stores—the royalties will be far lower than if based on retail list price. The royalty also should not be a specific amount, such as one dollar per copy, because the publisher invariably has the power to determine the selling price of the book. The guild does, however, recommend an additional provision providing for a specified amount, such as one dollar per copy, as a minimum royalty. This would protect the writer if the publisher set too low a retail price on the book.

Royalty rates vary, so the writer should have the advice of an agent or more experienced writer in trying to determine if an offered royalty is fair. The guild has, however, developed guidelines for royalties in a number of different categories. For example, the writer marketing an adult trade book should receive a minimum of 10 percent of the retail price on the first 5,000 copies, 12½ percent on the next 5,000 copies, and 15 percent on all copies sold in excess of 10,000. The guild recommends that royalties for children's books also start at 10 percent and step up to 15 percent with increasing numbers of copies sold, although the practice varies widely here. This recommendation is based on the results of a 1970 survey of children's book royalties, and the guild is presently working on an update of that report.[2] The writer doing children's books should keep in mind that royalties may have to be divided with an illustrator, if the illustrations compose much of the book. For the publisher's own quality paperback, the guild indicates the royalty should start no lower than 6 percent of retail list price and increase to 7½ percent for sales of more than 10,000 copies (or increase sooner to 7½ percent if fewer than 10,000 copies are printed). On the publisher's own mass market paperback, the guild would have the royalty start no lower than 6 percent and increase to 8 percent when sales exceed 150,000 copies. The guild also provides that no paperback edition may be issued within a year of the original trade publication. After that, the publisher must give the writer 120 days notice of any intended paperback edition, so that the writer can seek a better offer from a paperback publisher. If the writer succeeds in obtaining a better offer, the publisher is bound to accept it. These royalty rates for quality and mass market paperbacks would also apply to books first published in paperback form.

Royalties for professional, scientific, or technical books are customarily based on a net price, instead of retail price.[3] The publisher's discount to bookstores is in the range of 25 percent to 33⅓ percent, so the writer's royalty is calculated against this lower figure. A typical royalty rate might be 15 percent, but the writer should keep in mind that a substantial part of the sales are likely to be mail order, library, or export (which means the writer's royalties will be reduced as discussed later in relation to royalties). For college textbooks, the royalties are also calculated on a net price, and the standard discount to book stores is 20 percent (although some publishers offer as much as 33 percent). On a hardcover textbook, the writer should demand 15 percent of net price on sales up to a specified number of copies (perhaps between 7,500 and 15,000), after which the rate should increase to 18 percent. Publishers are likely to offer 10 percent with an escalation to 15 percent, but this should be resisted, especially if the book is a basic textbook designed for a widely offered undergraduate course. Textbooks often have their best sales in the first few years after publication, so escalation for sales over a given number of copies in any year is another possibility. An original paperback textbook might have royalties in the range of 10 percent to 15 percent of the net price.

Royalties will customarily be reduced for certain sales, such as copies sold at a greater than usual discount from the retail price. The S.A.R. contract, for example, provides that copies sold at a discount of 60 percent or more from the retail price will realize a reduced royalty—15 percent of the publisher's charges for bound copies of the original edition and 18 percent of the publisher's charges for unbound sheets—on sales for export, to reading circles, to book clubs, and to organizations outside the regular book selling channels (Clause 7[c]). The S.A.R. contract stipulates that these royalties are not to be reduced by deductions for discounts or bad debts. The effect of using 15 percent and 18 percent based on a net price (the publisher's charges) is to make certain that royalties cannot fall beneath roughly one half of the regular royalty rates. This is a minimum floor which the writer should always insist upon. If the reductions are based on retail price, the royalty rate should not go below one half of what it would be for a sale which is not at a discount. The guild advises that the writer of children's books give close scrutiny to the discounts for library bound editions sold outside regular book selling channels. The guild also indicates that, if the discount is for a sale in large quantity, all copies in the sale should have to be the same title (to avoid different writers' works being cumulated).

Many publishers' contracts will start cutting royalties when discounts are 48 percent or 50 percent, instead of 60 percent.

The S.A.R. contract provides that the writer will receive 10 percent of the publisher's proceeds on sales made at a discount of 70 percent or more, except that no royalties will be payable to the writer if the publisher is selling at or below the cost of manufacture (Clause 7[h]). It is provided that no sale of overstock may take place until after one year from publication in book form, and that the author must have thirty days notice and the option to purchase the overstock if the sale is to be made at or below the cost of manufacture.

Another common provision cuts royalties on copies made from a small reprinting more than one year after the first publication. The rationale is to allow the publisher to keep the work in print even if demand does not remain strong. The S.A.R. contract allows the royalty to be reduced to three-quarters of the stipulated royalty, but only if sales have fallen below a certain number of copies in the six-month accounting period preceding the reprinting and the reprinting does not take place until two years after the first publication. Also, the reprinting must be less than a given number of copies—one thousand being a figure favorable to the writer.

Finally, the guild indicates that the royalty rate should be reduced to one-half for copies sold by mail order, coupons, or radio or television advertising, but in no case should this figure fall below 5 percent of the retail price. On Canadian sales the S.A.R. contract recommends a royalty at two-thirds of the prevailing royalty rate (although the guild proposes one-half), and this two-thirds figure could be used as well for other export sales. No royalties are payable on copies destroyed or given away without charge to the author or for promotion (Clause 7[i]).

An important provision in the S.A.R. contract indicates that copies sold at a discount or in Canada will be added to the copies sold at regular retail price for the purpose of determining when the royalty rate escalates based upon the number of copies sold. This provision is very advantageous to the writer who should always consider which sales will add to total sales for purposes of escalating the royalty rate.

Advances

An advance is a sum of money paid to the writer which the publisher recoups from royalties earned by the book in the future. The advance may be paid in full at the time of signing the contract, but more commonly is paid in several equal installments. For example, two installments might be paid, one upon signing the contract and the other upon delivery of a satisfactory manuscript. Or three installments might be used, the first on signing the contract, the second on delivery of the manuscript, and the last on publication—although the writer should avoid having to wait until publication.

The amount of the advance varies with the writer's reputation, the success of the writer's previous work, the nature of the book itself, the publisher's expectations with respect to the market, and innumerable other factors which indicate how financially rewarding the book is likely to be. If a writer is uncertain whether an offered advance is fair, it would be wise to consult with an agent or a more experienced writer for advice.

The writer should seek the highest advance which can be negotiated. The writer's time and effort expended on a book can be great, even if the book is not successful on the market. The advance establishes a minimum recompense for the writer's work on the book. Also, the advance increases the publisher's stake. Presumably this will encourage more aggressive promotion and advertising to increase sales. Finally, it is always best to have money as soon as possible, because of the factor of interest. The advance aids the writer in this way as well.

The S.A.R. contract provides that the advance "shall be non-returnable except as provided in Clause 3 above" (Clause 7[a]). Clause 3, as discussed under delivery of the manuscript, indicates that if the writer has not delivered a "complete typewritten script of the work" within ninety days after notice from the publisher with respect to failure to deliver, the publisher may terminate the contract and recover any advances which have been paid. The writer should follow this model and never agree to return an advance except for failure to deliver a satisfactory manuscript (always attempting to qualify the term "satisfactory" as discussed under delivery of the manuscript). The guild goes further by providing that, even if the manuscript is not satisfactory, the publisher may only receive back a portion of the advance (30 percent is suggested) from funds realized by the writer if another publisher brings out the book.

If the advance is nonreturnable except for delivery of an unsatisfactory manuscript or a late delivery (which is also discussed under delivery of the manuscript), it follows that the writer will be able to keep the advance if the publisher rejects the manuscript for any other reason. Thus, the writer must judge the real reason for any rejection. Perhaps the project has become too expensive, a competing book has been issued, or the subject now seems dated. If the publisher in fact is breaching its obligations under the contract, the writer can demand the balance of any advance due and be under no obligation to repay it (even if, for example, another publisher were later to publish the book). These factual questions surrounding the reasons for rejection of a manuscript often lead to arbitration or a compromise of the disagreement.

In any case, the writer should never agree to permit the publisher to recoup the advance on one book by taking royalties from another book. Each book contract, as mentioned earlier, must be considered a separate venture. The guild advises that the publisher should only be able to take a percentage of proceeds from book club, paperback, and other subsidiary publishing rights to pay back advances, and that no proceeds from licensing first serial rights should be applied to the repayment of advances. The guild also indicates that if the writer is to be given funds to cover expenses, the clause should show whether the amounts for the expenses are to be repaid to the publisher from royalties on the book as well as stating whether the amounts given to cover expenses must be repaid in the event the project does not reach fruition. The reasons for the failure of the project would, of course, bear on whether the funds should be refunded. If a publishing contract does not provide for the publisher to recoup monies owed under one contract against monies earned under another contract, the writer should resist any attempts by the publisher at offsetting sums between contracts.[4]

Payments, Statements of Account, Inspection of Books

The S.A.R. contract provides that payments due shall accompany the semiannual statements of account (the guild recommends quarterly statements and payments). A separate statement of account must be issued for each book by the writer, including copies of statements of account from sublicensees to the publisher (Clause 12). The publisher is required to include the following information in these statements: the number of copies printed in each edition, the date of completion of printing and binding, the publication date, and the retail price (Clause 12[a]); for each different royalty rate, the number of copies sold, the number of copies returned, the amount of current royalties, and the amount of cumulative royalties to the date of the statement (Clause 12[b]); the number of copies given away free, remaindered, destroyed, or lost (Clause 12[c]); a description of subsidiary rights sales in which the writer's share is more than $100, including the total amount received by the publisher and the percentage of that total which the writer's share represents (Clause 12[d]); and the amount of reserves held for returns from the two accounting periods following first publication of the work, provided such reserves cannot exceed 15 percent of the royalties received during those first two periods (Clauses 12[e], [g]). If the publisher accidentally makes an overpayment to the writer, this can be deducted from future payments (Clause 9).

An important provision requires that the writer be paid within ten days for subsidiary rights income received by the publisher (Clauses 8[h], 10). This provision is fair, because the publisher is truly acting as an agent with respect to such proceeds. Moreover, the guild proposes that such funds be designated trust funds—as was suggested for funds held by the writer's agent—in order to force separate accounts for these funds prior to payment and provide some protection against the publisher's insolvency or bankruptcy.

The S.A.R. contract gives the writer the power to examine the publisher's books upon written notice (Clause 8[j]). The writer will bear the cost of such an examination, unless errors amounting to 5 percent or more of the total amounts paid to the writer are discovered. Publishers will seek to restrict this right of inspection, but it should be present in every contract, even if in modified form.

The writer who is in a high income tax bracket may wish to spread income forward into future tax years as discussed on pp. 174–175. The S.A.R. contract has a provision for this (Clause 12[e] [ii]). Publishers, however, will rarely pay interest on such withheld royalties. The writer runs the risk of the publisher's bankruptcy as well. Especially with the 50 percent maximum tax on earned income discussed on p. 160, the writer should have the assurance of expert tax advisers that such a provision is necessary before utilizing it. If the provision is used, the guild advises that income from subsidiary licensees should not be declared to be trust funds, since this would jeopardize the tax effect of such a spread-forward provision.

Duty to Publish and Keep Work in Print

The S.A.R. contract requires the publisher to publish the work at an agreed upon retail price within a specified number of months after delivery of the manuscript (Clause 4). The publisher agrees to use best efforts to sell copies of the book and subsidiary rights. In the event of unavoidable delays, the publication date is extended to not more than six months after the end of the reason for the delay. The inclusion of a publication date—the guild suggests the date be no later than one year after delivery of the manuscript—raises the possibility that the publisher will breach the contract by failing to publish. The writer will often find damages difficult to prove in such a case.[5] And many publishers simply place the date of publication within their own discretion. But all rights should revert to the writer if the publisher fails in its obligation to publish within a specified time.

The writer should also have a right to receive back all rights if the work goes out of print (Clause 13).[6] Each contract defines out of print differently, but the S.A.R. contract includes when the publisher has less than fifty copies in stock (Clause 13[a]); when the book is not listed in the general catalog, or when the annual sales fall below one hundred copies (Clauses 13[a], [b]). When the work is out of print, the writer gives notice to the publisher who must declare within thirty days whether there will be a new printing. If the publisher does not respond within thirty days or if a new printing does not occur within six months under the publisher's own imprint, all rights granted under the contract revert to the writer. Any licenses granted continue in effect, but the publisher has no power to renew them. Most out-of-print provisions are far less favorable to the writer. For example, some contracts provide the work is in print if any license for subsidiary rights is in effect. The writer should seek the narrowest possible definition of what will be considered keeping the work in print.

Once a work is determined to be out of print, the S.A.R. contract gives the writer the option to purchase the production materials, such as plates and offset negatives, at scrap value and any remaining copies at either the publisher's cost or remainder price, whichever is lower. This purchase provision exists in most publishing contracts, but the writer is usually required to pay more for the privilege.

Copyright

Copyright should be in the writer's name (Clause 5). This is an accepted practice which should be insisted upon by the writer. A notice in the publisher's name—even if the copyright were held in trust for the writer—could be harmful in such situations as the publisher's bankruptcy, the unauthorized sale of rights by the publisher, the bringing of suits for infringement, or a claim by the publisher that the work is for hire. The publisher should be required to renew the copyright, assuming the contract is still in force. The guild advises the writer to take independent precautions to insure that copyrights are renewed, since after twenty-eight years a publisher may be out of business or simply fail to live up to the obligation to file for renewal. Renewal will not be a problem, of course, for books copyrighted after January 1, 1978, under the new law. The writer should also require the publisher to obtain appropriate copyright notice, preferably in the writer's name, for all exploitations of subsidiary rights.

Warranty and Indemnity

Most publishers' contracts require that the writer give an express warranty to the effect that the work does not infringe any copyright, violate any property rights, contain any scandalous, libelous, or unlawful matter, or invade anyone's privacy.[7] The writer must indemnify the publisher against all claims, costs, expenses, and attorney's fees arising from any breach or alleged breach of the warranty. This means the writer has to pay for the publisher's expenditures even if the alleged breach is completely without merit and never goes to trial. The publisher will have the right to withhold royalties from all contracts with the writer until any suit or threatened suit is settled.

A warranty provision of that kind can be disastrous for the writer, especially since a frivolous claim can take years to resolve in the courts. The S.A.R. contract strictly limits the scope of the warranty clause (Clause 2[a]). The writer's warranty is only that "to the best of his knowledge" the book does not contain libelous matter, does not violate anyone's proprietary rights, is not an infringement of an existing copyright, and has not previously been published in book form in any of the territories covered by the grant of rights. The writer indemnifies the publisher only for claims which are finally sustained, so alleged breaches which never result in a recovery would not be covered. The guild provision is even narrower, since under it the writer only has to pay the publisher after all appeals have been exhausted from a final judgment based on an actual breach of the warranties. The guild further limits the writer's liability by stating that the writer will only pay the lesser of a percentage of sums due under the contract (30 percent is suggested) or a fixed dollar amount. The S.A.R. contract provides that the writer may defend any suit with his or her own lawyers and not be liable for the fees of the lawyers hired by the publisher (Clause 2[c]). Also, the guild would not permit the publisher to set up a reserve to cover possible damages arising from a breach of warranty, or at least would limit such a reserve to no more than 30 percent of sums due the writer (and never more than the damages claimed). The writer should certainly not agree to let sums due under one contract be held in reserve to pay for a breach or alleged breach of the warranty provision under another contract.

The publisher may argue that the warranty provision cannot be changed because the publisher would lose its insurance against such claims. Writers so far have had little success in obtaining insurance similar to that of the publishers. But the writer should not accept this explanation, since the effect of the warranty provision is to make the writer the insurer of the publisher. If money must be paid because of a breach of warranty, the insurance company will pay for the publisher and then sue the writer to recover. Even if the publisher will lose insurance coverage, it is far better for the publisher to play the role of insurer instead of the writer. This is particularly true of a book which is likely to generate claims under a warranty provision. The writer might simply demand that the provision be stricken and the publisher assume all such risks, especially when the risks are clear at the beginning of the project and the publisher is still eager to go forward. It may be better to lose a book if a satisfactory warranty provision can't be negotiated, rather than risk expensive and time-consuming litigation.

Even if the publisher's warranty provision is accepted, the writer should have the power to veto any proposed settlement (after all, it is the writer's money under the typical clause). And the writer should never be liable for material inserted into the book or placed on the jacket by the publisher (Clause 2[a]).

Artistic Control

Most publishers' contracts require that the manuscript be in "content and form satisfactory to the publisher," which means publishers can exert a negative form of artistic control. The writer should insist, however, on the opportunity to make any necessary changes in the work and to approve any changes done by other persons. The S.A.R. contract provides that the publisher has the right only to copy edit the manuscript in the customary manner and that the writer shall not unreasonably withhold approval of such copy editing (Clause 4). If the publisher wants major changes (for example, changing more than 10 percent of the manuscript), the contract might provide for additional payments to the writer, especially if the book is being done for a flat fee.

However, the writer who chooses to change the manuscript after production has started will sometimes be liable for the cost of the changes. The S.A.R. contract provides that the writer shall be charged for any changes in the galleys or page proofs in excess of 15 percent of the original cost of composition (Clause 6). Many publishers make the cutoff figure 10 percent. But the S.A.R. contract also requires the publisher to promptly give an itemized statement of the extra expenses as well as showing the corrected proofs to the writer. Of course such changes should only be deductible against income earned under the contract for the particular book, not other contracts the writer may have with the publisher.

Most publishers' contracts give the publisher the power to fix the book's retail price, title, form, type, paper, and similar details. The S.A.R. contract differs in that a minimum retail price is established (Clause 4), the title may only be changed if the writer consents in writing (Clause 1), and the publisher agrees to consult with the writer about the format and style of the text, graphic material, and the dust jacket (Clause 4). Since the dust jacket presents the book to the public, the writer may wish to have a voice in its content. Particularly with children's books, the writer may want to be able to approve rough and final illustrations and the accompanying captions. The writer's controls here will have to be added into the usual contract, as will any prohibition against advertisements appearing on the cover or in the text. Such advertising can demean a book, and the S.A.R. contract forbids it unless the writer consents in writing (Clause 4). This advertising prohibition applies as well to licensees, such as book clubs or paperback publishers. Since the writer is also given the power to approve any condensations or abridgments (Clause 8[k]), the publisher must require licensees to obtain the writer's consent to such changes (Clause 4). If the publisher can license translation rights, the writer may seek to have control over the choice of a translator and the final form of the translation. A writer with great bargaining power might even insist that the final form of a film script accurately reflect the original book. Artistic control should be recognized as an issue in every publishing contract.

If the publisher has the right to revise the book in the future, the writer should have the right of first refusal. If the writer cannot do the revisions, however, another writer may be chosen by the publisher under most contracts. The guild advises that the publisher should have the right to revise the book only at intervals of several years, subject to the writer's approval which cannot be unreasonably withheld. The use of such a clause will vary, of course, depending on the subject matter. The writer's royalties will be reduced if another writer does the revisions, so the guild recommends placing a minimum base (perhaps two-thirds of the original royalties) below which royalties may not be reduced. Regardless of whether the writer who revises the book is paid a flat fee or given royalties, any charges made against the original writer on account of the revisions should only be deductible from income earned from the book being revised. Also, assuming the writer cannot have a veto power over revisions by someone else, the guild advises the writer to reserve the right to remove his or her name from the book in the event the revisions prove unsatisfactory.

Credits

The exact nature of the writer's credit should be specified, including size and placement, especially if another writer or editor has also worked on the book. If the book may be revised in the future, the credit to be given to the reviser should also be specified.

Original Materials

The publisher should be required to return the original manuscript to the writer along with any other materials, such as art work. The S.A.R. contract requires return of the original manuscript, galley proof, page proof, and any graphic material within one year after publication (Clause 6). The publisher will usually not agree to either insure the work or pay if valuable materials included in the manuscript (such as transparencies) are damaged or lost, although the writer might demand this if the work is of great value.

Competing Works

The publisher may try and restrict the writer from creating competing works. The S.A.R. contract contains no such provision and the guild indicates the writer should not agree to this. If the writer publishes a work too closely similar to that already licensed to the publisher, the publisher will be able to sue the writer for copyright infringement. If the publisher insists on such a clause, however, the writer should narrowly restrict its scope with respect to subject matter, audiences, forms of publication, duration, and geographic extent.

Options

Another common provision gives the publisher the option to publish the writer's next work (see the option clause drafted by S.A.R., but not included in their contract). Such a provision may well be unenforceable unless the terms of the future publication are made definite. In any case, the writer should insist that the option provision be deleted from the contract. If the writer and publisher are satisfied with one another, they will want to contract for future books. If they are not satisfied, there is no reason why the writer should have to offer the next book to the publisher. If an option provision is agreed to, the writer should not give an option for more than one work and should require the publisher to make a determination with regard to that work (perhaps based on an outline) within a reasonable time period after submission.

Free Copies

Most publication contracts will provide for the writer to receive five to ten free copies of the regular edition and any subsequent cheap edition (Clause 11). Additionally, provision is made for the writer to purchase unlimited copies for personal use at a substantial discount, such as 40 percent to 50 percent from retail list price. The writer should be certain the contract has such a clause.

Assignment

It is not uncommon to require the written consent of either party to an assignment by the other (Clause 16). Presumably the publisher would not wish to have another writer substituted under the contract, but neither should the writer have to accept a different publisher. Nothing should prevent the writer from assigning to another person money due or to become due under the contract (Clause 16). The publisher may require a provision permitting assignment to a new publisher taking over the entire business.

Infringement by Others

If the book's copyright is infringed by someone else, the contract must specify each party's obligations and rights to any sums recovered. The S.A.R. contract provides that the publisher and writer can both participate in bringing an infringement suit. In that case the parties would split the expenses of the suit. If monies were recovered, the expenses would first be recouped, after which the balance of the recovery would either be divided equally or, with respect to the subsidiary rights in Clause 8, divided according to the specified percentages. If one party chooses not to participate in the suit, the other party may proceed and recoup all expenses from any recovery before the balance of the recovery is divided as if the parties had both participated. The writer should retain the exclusive right to sue for infringement of rights retained by the writer.

Termination

The S.A.R. contract provides for termination by the writer if the book is out of print as discussed earlier in the chapter (Clauses

13[a], [b]). However, the writer is also given the right to terminate if the publisher fails to provide the semiannual statements of account or fails to accompany the statements with the required payments (Clause 13[c]). And the writer may terminate if royalties fall below a minimum amount (which must be written into the contract), but this provision can only be invoked ten years or more after the initial trade publication (Clause 13[d]).

The writer should also require a termination power in the event of the publisher's failure to fulfill the material terms of the contract, including a failure to publish within ninety days of the writer's notice stating the publisher is past the specified publication date (Clause 14[a], [b[). There should be an automatic termination if the publisher has become bankrupt or insolvent (Clause 14[b]). In the event of termination for any reason, the S.A.R. contract gives the writer the option to purchase the production materials and remaining copies as discussed with respect to the out-of-print provisions (Clause 13[e]).

Arbitration

The writer will generally benefit from an arbitration provision, because disputes under the contract can be quickly and easily resolved.[8] Many contracts will provide for arbitration before the American Arbitration Association, but the writer should be satisfied as long as unbiased arbitrators will hear the dispute. The disadvantage of arbitration is that an arbitrator's adverse decision is very difficult to appeal to the courts, so the writer should feel certain the arbitration will be fairly conducted. The writer may choose to reserve the right to sue if the dispute relates to royalties due under the contract (Clause 17).

Agency

The S.A.R. contract gives the agent authority to act on behalf of the writer in all matters arising from the contract (Clause 21). If, in fact, the agent's powers are limited, it would be wise to strike this provision and append a copy of the writer-agent contract to the publishing contract. Also, as discussed on p. 91, the writer should always have the right to receive payment directly from the publisher of a minimum of 90 percent of sums due if the writer wants direct payment once the writer-agent contract has terminated. This can be accomplished by the use of a clause to the effect that "The authorization of the agent to act on behalf of the writer and to collect sums due the writer shall continue in effect until the publisher shall otherwise be instructed in writing by the writer." The exact language of the agency clause will have to be negotiated in the writer-agent contract.

Collaborators

The writer may collaborate with another writer, an editor, an illustrator, a technical expert, or a well-known person.[9] In some cases the collaboration may be with someone the writer never meets, but who merely contributes material for the book. In any case, the writer and any collaborator must have a contract between them which divides up all the rights (especially of control and to income) contained in the publishing contract. In the absence of a provision giving control over uses of the work to one party, all collaborators will normally have the power to authorize nonexclusive licenses and the income will be shared among the collaborators.[10] The contract must include a method for resolving disputes, such as a disagreement over publishers to which the completed work should be submitted. Thought must be given to what will happen if one party became disabled or dies during the collaboration. Artistic control—and an orderly plan to progress the work—must be decided upon. Authorship credit will require elaboration. It must be determined who will own the copyright and what will be the form of copyright notice. If each collaborator can sell his or her interest in the work, the other parties may wish a right to have first opportunity to purchase the interest on the same terms being offered by outsiders. Consideration should also be given to whether the collaborators should have a separate or a joint contract with the publisher. For example, is the writer to be liable for breaches of a warranty by a collaborator? These and similar questions will depend on the contractual relationship of the collaborators to one another and the publisher. And if the collaboration fails to reach fruition, a determination must have been made as to the rights each collaborator will have in the incomplete work.

Advertising

Some writers of works which are potentially very profitable to publishers may be able to require the designation of an advertising budget. If this is done, the budget should only be expendable for the single title, not group ads including other titles. A further breakdown into the categories of advertising is difficult prior to publication, although in special cases it may be possible to pinpoint markets in which advertising should later take place. The writer risks limiting the publisher's flexibility, however, and perhaps also having the publisher cease advertising once the stipulated amount has been expended. The more usual approach is to request the highest possible advance, and leave the publisher to its own ingenuity with respect to advertising and promotion.[11]

Most contracts require that the writer allow the publisher to use the writer's name, likeness, or photograph in advertising and promotion for the work. This clause is desirable, but the writer might want an assurance that a suitable decorum will be maintained.

Security Interest

Some publishers' contracts contain a provision granting the publisher a security interest in the work. This secures the publisher for any sums due under the contract, including advances not recouped, by giving the publisher the power to attach the manuscript and all related materials and, upon demand, take immediate possession of these properties. The writer is required to execute such documents as are necessary to perfect the security interest. Needless to say, any situation in which a publisher can seize a writer's work to pay monies owed is highly undesirable. Mechanisms for payment back of advances and other sums owed are provided in most contracts, including a right to monies received under a subsequent publishing contract for the same book, and should be sufficient to protect the publisher.

Other Provisions

Some publishers' contracts will permit withdrawal of the contract offer if the writer does not return the signed contract within a limited period of time, such as sixty days. The S.A.R. contract includes the same right for the writer (Clause 20). Contractual modifications will have to be written. The state whose laws govern the contract will be specified (Clause 22). The contract may state that heirs, legal representatives, successors, and assigns are bound by its terms, although the S.A.R. contract omits this provision. Waivers and defaults under one provision will be restricted so as neither to permit future waivers or defaults nor affect obligations under other provisions of the contract (Clause 19). The manner in which notice can be given—to whom and at what address—will be indicated (Clause 18).

This concludes the examination of the book publishing contract. The general principles described apply to the licensing or selling of literary property to other markets, and the balance of the chapter will be devoted to a brief examination of some points of special interest in these other markets.

Magazines

Sales to magazine publishers involve the same considerations as sales to book publishers, except that the contracts will be much simpler. The grant of rights to the magazines is the writer's main concern. Some magazines purchase all rights (sometimes called exclusive world rights in perpetuity) which means the writer retains no rights to the work. Magazines may purchase all rights with the understanding that the copyright will be held in trust for the writer and transferred back after publication (subject, perhaps, to certain rights retained by the magazine). In such a case, a written contract should set forth precisely the rights to be retained and those to be transferred back.

Many magazines purchase only first serial rights (sometimes called first rights), the right to be the first magazine to publish the work. After such publication, the writer is free to sell the work elsewhere. A variation of first serial rights would be first North American serial rights whereby the writer conveys to the magazine the right to be the first publisher of the work in North America. Another grant of rights would be second serial rights: the right to publish work which has appeared elsewhere—for example, in a book. This is sometimes more generally referred to as reprint rights: the right to publish work which has appeared elsewhere. A different grant of rights would be one-time rights: the right to use the work once but not necessarily first. Another way of expressing this could be the grant of simultaneous rights: granting the right to publish to several magazines at once. The writer should keep in mind the possibility of limiting the grant of rights with regard to exclusivity, types of uses, languages, duration, and geographical scope. The writer who wishes can define exactly the nature of the permitted publication.

The writer should be certain what credit will be received for work. If any changes can be made in the work, the writer should seek the right to approve such changes. If expenses are to be reimbursed, this should be agreed upon in writing. The writer can expect a warranty provision and a deadline for delivery of the work. The writer should anticipate that the work may never be used and request a provision transferring back all rights in such event. If the magazine has paid on acceptance, the writer should require a provision stating no part of the payment need be returned if the magazine fails to use the work. If the magazine pays on publication, the writer should stipulate a fee, known as a "kill fee," be paid in the event the magazine does not use the work within a specified time period. The writer may reasonably ask for several free copies of the issue containing the work. Generally, the writer should consider the refinements of the book contract when negotiating the simpler licensing or sale to a magazine.

The protection of the copyrights in contributions to collective works is discussed on pp. 13–14 and pp. 34–35.

Syndication

A syndicate gathers marketable features and columns for distribution on a regular basis to markets such as newspapers and magazines.[12] Some syndicates purchase single articles much as magazines would, while others enter into an ongoing relationship with the writer. For a continuing series, the writer will normally be recompensed on the basis of the success of the syndicated material, rather than by payment of a flat fee.

A syndication contract involves a grant of rights, which the writer should restrict as narrowly as possible. The writer should keep the copyright and all other literary property rights in the material. Beyond the grant of rights, of course, will be the issue of subsidiary rights. The syndicate should not be given rights over or income from subsidiary rights in media which it cannot directly exploit. And the writer should weigh whether the syndicate's requests for control or a given percentage of income are reasonable with respect to each subsidiary right. Consultation with an agent or more experienced writer will help here, although the guild guidelines for books can provide an idea of how to approach the problem.

The duration of the contract is particularly important and should be fairly short, probably no more than two years. This enables the writer to negotiate a better contract if the syndication is a success or stop working on an unpopular venture. Since any kind of automatic renewal option would defeat the purpose of a short term, such a provision should be refused. Also, the writer might consider reserving a right of termination if proceeds from the syndication fall below a specified level. This would permit entering into a new contract with a syndicate capable of more vigorous exploitation. In any case, the writer should not agree to either noncompetition or option provisions which might prevent dealing with others. If the syndicate insists, these provisions should be narrowly restricted in their application.

Payment is based on the receipts from the syndication, which in turn depend on how many publications carry the feature or column and what each publication pays for it (although the writer should demand as well the guaranteed minimum payment discussed in the next paragraph). The writer can expect to receive 40 percent to 60 percent of the syndication receipts. But care must be taken that the percentage is of gross receipts, not net receipts (which might also be phrased as "gross receipts less expenses"). If gross receipts are to be reduced prior to calculating the share due the writer, the reductions must be set forth and carefully defined. Package deals, where several features or columns are sold together, should be forbidden. Otherwise the writer won't know what would be paid if his or her own material were separately purchased. And, in fact, a more successful series may be carrying a less successful one, with both writers receiving the same income. If the syndicate is part of a newspaper chain, it must be specified that special discounts may not be given to newspapers in the chain. There should be a right to periodic accountings showing the source of all receipts and the exact nature of any expenses. The writer should also be able to inspect the books of the syndicate.

The syndicate should promise to use its best marketing efforts. In appropriate cases, the writer might even insist in advance upon an advertising and promotional plan and budget. A very important provision, however, is a minimum payment guaranteed to the writer regardless of the amount of receipts. The writer should seek this in every contract, both to insure that the writing will not go unrecompensed and to give the syndicate a greater stake in the enterprise.

The writer should seek control over the final form of the material. At the least, however, there should be a right of approval over any interpolations or changes by the syndicate. Warranties with respect to the material will invariably have to be given, although the writer should as always seek to limit their scope. Also, prior written consent should be required for any assignment of the contract, so the writer will always be able to choose the organizations and people with whom dealings take place.

The discussion of book publishing contracts should provide guidelines for the other provisions and considerations which may be relevant to the writer creating a feature or column for syndication.

Dramatic Productions

The Dramatists Guild, Inc. (referred to as "the guild") has developed a number of contracts for use by their members, including a minimum basic production contract for first-class dramatic plays and musicals (which would be used for productions on Broadway and at other leading theatres across the country) and a minimum basic production contract for off-Broadway dramatic plays and musicals. The guild countersigns its contracts when used by members to insure compliance with the required minimum provisions. This being the case, every writer marketing a dramatic play or musical should join the guild for both advice and a firm stance from which to start negotiations.

Producers initially take an option to produce a dramatic play or musical. An advance against future royalties is paid for the option, which is typically for six months (perhaps renewable for additional six-month terms if certain conditions are met). If the producer successfully previews and opens the play before the expiration of a time period specified in the option or extensions of the option, the writer's compensation is then based on a percentage of the box office's weekly receipts (receipts being carefully defined). However, the producer who mounts a production which runs beyond a stipulated number of performances gains additional rights—for example, a right to do first-class tours, to do an English production, to move from off-Broadway to Broadway, to reopen the show after it has closed, to have a bargaining position with respect to motion picture rights, and to have a monetary interest in specified subsidiary rights. However, the producer acquires no control over the subsidiary rights, merely a right to share in proceeds if the original play or musical has a long enough run. For example, the subsidiary rights can include worldwide motion picture rights and the following rights in the continental United States and Canada: radio, television, second-class touring performance, foreign language performance, concert tour versions, condensed and tabloid versions, commercial uses, play albums or records, stock and amateur performance, and musicals based on the play. The producer's right to a percentage of subsidiaries (that is, the income from these subsidiary rights) applies only to contracts executed within a specified number of years after the close of the production. Control over disposition of subsidiary rights is retained by the writer.

The guild has established the writer's control over the written script. The writer does agree to perform reasonably necessary services to do revisions, but has a power of approval over additions, omissions, or alterations in the script. The writer agrees to assist in selecting the cast, offer advice generally as to production problems, and attend rehearsals and previews unless a reasonable excuse can be given for not doing so.

The fact that a dramatic play or musical is a group endeavor necessitates a greater specification of billing credit. Must the writer's name be used on advertising, promotional materials, programs, or houseboards? Insofar as the name must be used, what size must it be relative to the play's title and other names and what placement must it have relative to other collaborators, the producer, the director, and the leading performers?

The guild's involvement in the contracts of its members insures minimum terms which are fair to writers. Conceptually, many of the terms in a contract for production of a dramatic play or musical can be understood from the discussion of similar terms in the book publishing contract. The first-class and off-Broadway minimum basic production contracts have been discussed extensively in other sources.[13] And the writer negotiating with respect to a dramatic play or musical should definitely look to the guild for assistance.

Films and Television

Film and television production companies must draw together the financial and creative elements necessary to create a finished product. Ownership of literary property is a necessity, whether optioned or purchased from other media or written by an employee of the company. The production company will be especially interested in gaining literary property rights not necessarily considered in a book publication contract. These are the exclusive rights to characters, characters' names, characterizations, locales, themes, incidents, and similar elements of the literary property which might be used in sequels, series, spin-offs, specials, or remakes. If rights in a novel about a fictional detective are sold to a film production company, will this include the right to use that detective in other movies or a television series not based on the specific novel and not using the novel's title? This actual case arose involving Dashiell Hammett's *The Maltese Falcon*. In that case, the court decided that the right to use the characters in the book for a series or sequel had not been acquired by the motion picture company.[14] But acquisition of those rights is an issue which is negotiated in every sale of a literary property for television and films. In television, for example, a minor character on one series may be excised and used as the generative force in an entirely new series. If the writer is going to grant such rights, adequate reimbursement must be specified for such additional uses. The production company may also try to tie up the writer's right to create new works based on the same characters, or at least have an option to purchase any such works. Insofar as the writer reserves rights, the exercise of these rights may be restricted to a number of years in the future in order not to compete with the television or film production. The writer, of course, has to weigh whether the purchase price offered is worth such concessions.

The grant of rights will usually be quite extensive, although distinctions have to be made between television and film which reach different markets. The practice with respect to artistic control is exactly the opposite from that with respect to dramatic plays and musicals. The writer can expect to have no control over changes in the property and the final form which it takes. Also, the writer will invariably have to give the production company the power to assign the contract (although the production company may remain liable if the assignee fails to fulfill its obligations), since the financing arrangements require this. If the writer is to share in receipts from a film distribution, it must be specified whose receipts (the producer's or the production company's) and how the receipts are defined. Billing credit will also require specification, because of the number of people and companies involved in creating the end product.

The complexities of television and film contracts require that the writer obtain the assistance of a lawyer or agent.[15] In any case, it is rare for literary property to be marketed to the television or film industries without an agent, lawyer, or other representative acting as intermediary. And writers who are employed in the creation of television or film scripts will usually be required to join the Writers Guild of America, a union which periodically negotiates revisions of the collective bargaining agreement it has with numerous production companies. The terms of the collective bargaining agreement are beyond the scope of this book, but can be obtained from the Writers Guild of America, West or the Writer's Guild of America, East (which together form the Writers Guild of America).

AGREEMENT made this   day of   19   ,

between   (hereinafter called the Author),

whose residence address is

whose citizenship is: Social Security Number...............................

and   (hereinafter called the Publisher);

whose principal place of business is at

WITNESSETH:

In consideration of the mutual covenants herein contained, the parties agree as follows:

The Grant and the Territory.

1. The Author hereby grants and assigns to the Publisher the exclusive right to publish in the English language in book form in the United States of America, its territories and possessions, in the Philippine Islands, and in Canada, a Work provisionally entitled

(hereinafter called the Work) which title may be changed only by mutual consent in writing. All other territory (except the British Commonwealth and Empire as politically constituted at the date of this agreement) shall be a non-exclusive territory for the sale of English language copies of the Work published hereinunder in the United States.

The Warranty.

2. (a) The Author represents that he is the sole proprietor of the Work and that the Work to the best of his knowledge does not contain any libelous matter and does not violate the proprietary rights of any person or persons, does not infringe any existing copyright, and has not heretofore been published in book form in the territories hereinabove defined. The Author shall hold harmless and indemnify the Publisher from any claims, demands, or recovery finally sustained, by reason of any violation of copyright or other property or personal right; provided, however, that the Publisher shall with all reasonable promptness notify the Author of any claim or suit which may involve the warranties of the Author hereunder; and the Author agrees fully to cooperate in the defense thereof. The warranties contained in this Article do not extend to drawings, illustrations, or other material not furnished by the Author.

(b) If any rights granted to the Publisher or which the Publisher is authorized to license are infringed, the Author and the Publisher shall have the right to participate jointly in an action for copyright infringement. If Author and Publisher both participate, they shall share the expenses of the action equally and shall recoup such expenses from any sums recovered in the action; the balance of the proceeds shall be divided equally between them, except that with respect to any rights specified in Clause 8 below, the said balance shall be divided in the proportions provided in said Clause. Each party will notify the other of infringements coming to its attention.

(c) If either party declines to participate in such action, the other may proceed; the party maintaining the action shall bear all costs and expenses which shall be recouped from any damages recovered from the infringement; the balance of such damages shall be divided between them as provided in (a) and (b) above. The Author may, if he chooses, defend such suit with counsel of his own choosing, at his own expense; provided that if he does, the Publisher may nonetheless participate in the defense with counsel of its choosing and at its own expense. If the Author shall defend such suit, he shall not be responsible for the Publisher's attorney's fees or costs.

3. The Author agrees to deliver to the Publisher not later than _____ 19___ , a complete typewritten script of the Work. If the script shall not have been delivered within three (3) months after the Publisher notifies the Author of failure to deliver on time, the Publisher may, at its option, terminate this agreement by notice in writing posted or delivered to the Author and may recover from the Author all monies which it may have advanced to the Author upon the Work.

(a) The following additional materials shall be provided and paid for as indicated below:

	Provided by (insert "Publisher" "Author" or "none")	Costs and Fees paid by Publisher	Author
photographs	_____	_____%	_____%
drawings	_____	_____%	_____%
maps	_____	_____%	_____%
tables	_____	_____%	_____%
charts	_____	_____%	_____%
index	_____	_____%	_____%
other illustrations	_____	_____%	_____%

Photographs, drawings and maps shall be in form suitable for retouching and reproduction by Publisher; tables and charts shall be in a form from which type can be set.

(b) If the Author does not submit additional materials to be provided by him within a reasonable time after submission of manuscript and prior to publication, the Publisher shall, after thirty (30) days written notice to the Author, provide such materials, the costs of which shall be divided as scheduled above. Materials so provided shall be subject to the Author's approval.

(c) Any permissions required to use material copyrighted by others shall be obtained by Publisher and any fees for such permissions shall be paid as follows: %

by Publisher,   % by Author.

(d) Any share of costs or permission fees payable by the Author under (a), (b) or (c) above shall be advanced by Publisher and deducted from royalties or other earnings payable to Author hereunder.

4. The Publisher agrees to publish the Work at its own expense at a catalogue retail price of not less than _____ Dollars ($) per copy within _____ (   ) months of the delivery of the completed Work. The Publisher will use its best efforts to promote the sale of copies of the Work, and to exploit the rights therein which Publisher is authorized by this Agreement to license.

No one except the Author may make any changes in the Work, except that the Publisher shall have the right, after consultation with the Author, to copy edit the Work (to conform the style of the Work to customary form and usage). The Author shall have the right to approve the finally copy edited manuscript and such approval shall not unreasonably be withheld or delayed.

Publisher will consult in advance with the Author concerning the format and style of all trade editions, and concerning the text, graphic material, and style of the dust jacket.

In the event of a sale of periodical rights for publication prior to book publication, book publication shall be delayed until such periodical publication is completed.

If publication is delayed beyond the agreed publication date because of acts or conditions beyond the control of the Publisher or its suppliers or contractors, including (by way of illustration and not by way of limitation) war, shortages of material, strikes, riots, civil commotions, fire or flood, the agreed publication date shall be extended to a date not more than six (6) months following removal of the cause of the delay.

Advertisements may not be inserted or printed in any edition of the Work, whether issued by the Publisher or its licensee, without Author's written consent. Such consent may be withheld in Author's sole discretion, and he may require that a share of the advertising proceeds be paid to him, as a condition for his consent, if he so elects.

Any license granted by the Publisher to reprint the Work in book club or paperback editions, or in any other medium except newspapers and periodicals, must explicitly prohibit the licensee from inserting advertisements in its edition of the Work without the written consent of the Author as provided above. The Publisher must also explicitly prohibit the licensee from causing any alterations in the text from the original hardcover version without first obtaining the written consent of the Author.

The Copyright.   **5.** The Publisher, upon first publication of the Work, agrees duly to copyright it in the name of the Author in the United States of America and under the Universal Copyright Convention in the other exclusive territory specified in Paragraph 1 above, and to imprint the copyright notice required by law in each copy of the Work. The Author agrees to furnish the Publisher promptly with any authorization or other document necessary to carry out the provisions hereof. The Publisher shall, prior to the termination of the first term, make timely application for renewal of copyright under existing United States Copyright Law, provided this contract shall, at that time, be in force and effect.

Printer's Proofs.   **6.** The Publisher shall furnish the Author with galley proof and page proof of the Work which, except for such reasonable copy editing as is provided for in Clause 4, shall conform to the completed manuscript as submitted by the Author. The Author agrees to return such proof to the Publisher with his corrections within thirty (30) days of the receipt thereof by him. The cost of alterations in the galley proof or page proof required by the Author, other than corrections of printer's and/or editor's errors, in excess of fifteen (15%) percent of the original cost of composition, shall be charged against the earnings of the Author under this agreement; provided also, however, that the Publisher shall promptly furnish to the Author an itemized statement of such additional expenses, and shall make available at the Publisher's office the corrected proof for inspection by the Author or his representatives. Publisher shall return the original manuscript, galley proof and page proof, and any graphic materials forming part of the Work, to the Author within one (1) year after publication.

Advances and Royalties.
•
•
   7. The Publisher shall pay to the Author the following advances and royalties:

     (a) An advance of $ against all sums due the Author under this agreement, payable

which advance shall be non-returnable except as provided in Clause 3 above:

•
•
•
•
     (b) A royalty upon the regular edition sold in the United States of:
         percent of the retail price thereof on the first   copies sold
         percent on the next   copies sold
         percent on all copies sold in excess of

     (c) A royalty of fifteen percent (15%) of the amount of the Publisher's charges for bound copies of the original edition of the Work and eighteen percent (18%) for unbound sheets, sold for export and to reading circles, to recognized book clubs, and to organizations outside the regular book selling channels, provided that such sales are made at a discount of sixty percent (60%) or more from the retail price. Such royalties shall be payable without deduction for discounts or bad debts.

     (d) Two-thirds (⅔) of the prevailing United States royalty on all Canadian sales.

•
     (e)   percent of the retail price of each copy sold of any reprint edition issued by the Publisher at a retail price not more than two-thirds (⅔) of the original retail price.

(f) In determining the royalty rate in (b) above, all copies sold under (b), (c), and (d) shall be included as total sales under (b).

(g) Three-quarters (¾) of the stipulated royalty on all copies sold from a reprinting of   copies or less made after two (2) years from the date of the first publication hereunder and provided that the regular sales in the six-month period preceding such reprinting did not exceed   copies; the reduction of royalties provided for in this sub-division is to enable the Publisher to keep the Work in print and in circulation as long as possible.

(h) Ten percent (10%) of the amount of the Publisher's charges for copies of overstock which the Publisher sells at a discount of seventy percent (70%) or more; provided that if such sale is made at or below cost of manufacture, no royalty shall be paid. If the purchaser is a firm owned or affiliated in any way with the Publisher, the Author will be paid ten percent (10%) of the price at which copies are resold by the purchaser. If the Publisher determines to sell any of its overstock, it shall give the Author thirty (30) days notice in advance thereof, and give the Author first option to purchase such overstock at or below cost of manufacture. No sale of overstock may take place before the expiration of one (1) year from the first publication of the Work in book form.

(i) No royalties shall be payable on free copies furnished to the Author or on copies for review, sample, or other similar purposes, or on copies destroyed.

Share of Proceeds; examination of Accounts.

8. The Publisher shall make the following payments to the Author for the subsidiary rights indicated below:

(a) An amount equal to   % of the first $;   % of the next $; and   % thereafter of proceeds derived from the sale or licensing to any other Publisher of the right to issue or distribute a cheap edition of the Work.

(b) An amount equal to   % of the first $;   % of the next $; and   % thereafter of proceeds derived from the sale or license granted a book club to publish the Work in whole or in part for distribution to its members.

(c) An amount equal to   % of the gross amount paid for post-publication periodical rights, unless such rights are held by the purchaser of the pre-publication periodical rights.

Subsidiary Rights Accountings.

(d) The Publisher may permit others to reprint selections from the Work in textbooks or anthologies, and payments made for such permission shall be equally divided between the Author and Publisher. The Publisher may grant permission to publish extracts of the Work containing not more than five hundred (500) words of prose without compensation therefor.

(e) The Publisher is authorized to permit publication of the Work in Braille, or photographing, recording and/or microfilming the Work for the physically handicapped without payment of fees and without compensation to the Author, providing no compensation is received by the Publisher. In case compensation is received, the Publisher shall pay the Author fifty percent (50%) of the proceeds.

Notices regarding Licenses.

(f) Anything to the contrary herein notwithstanding, the Publisher shall grant no license without the prior written consent of the Author (such consent not to be unreasonably withheld or delayed) with respect to the following rights in the work: use thereof in storage and retrieval systems, whether through computer, mechanical, or other electronic means now known or hereafter invented, and ephemeral screen flashing or reproduction thereof, whether by print-out, photo-reproduction or photocopy, including punch cards, microfilm, magnetic tapes, or any like processes attaining similar results. Proceeds thereof shall be divided   % to the Author and   % to the Publisher. However, such license shall not be deemed keeping the Work in print once the Work has gone out of print in all editions.

(g) No cheap edition in any category may be published earlier than one (1) year from the date of the original publication.

(h) The Publisher shall submit to the Author for his prior approval (such approval not to be unreasonably withheld or delayed) the terms of any proposed license for book club distribution, cheap edition publication, or post-publication periodical rights. Copies of contracts shall be furnished by the Publisher to the Author or his representative and the Author's share shall be paid within ten (10) days of the Publisher's receipt thereof [subject to the conditions of Clauses 7 (a), 12 (e), (ii)].

(i) No deduction for attorneys' fees, agents' commissions, duplicate plates, or other expenses, shall be made from the proceeds of licenses granted by the Publisher before payment of the Author's share.

(j) The Author shall have the right upon written request, to examine the books of account of the Publisher insofar as they relate to the Work; such examination shall be at the cost of the Author unless errors of accounting amounting to five (5%) per cent or more of the total sum paid to the Author shall be found to his disadvantage, in which case the cost shall be borne by the Publisher.

(k) Any license granted by the Publisher for condensation or abridgement of the Work shall provide that the Author will have approval of any such condensation or abridgement.

9. Whenever the Author receives an overpayment of monies under the terms hereof, the Publisher may deduct such overpayment from any further sums payable to the Author in respect to the Work; provided, however, that the term "overpayment" shall not in any event apply to unearned advances, nor to returns or payments relating to other books.

10. With respect to licenses made by the Publisher which do not require the approval of the Author, the Publisher agrees promptly to advise the Author of the terms of any contracts entered into for any grant or license permitted under this agreement whenever the Author's share of the proceeds or royalty is One Hundred ($100) Dollars or more. Copies of contracts shall be furnished by the Publisher to the Author or his representative and the Author's share shall be paid within ten (10) days of the Publisher's receipt thereof [subject to the conditions of Clauses 7 (a) and 12 (e), (ii)].

11. The Publisher agrees to present to the Author ten (10) free copies of the regular edition of the Work and five (5) copies of any cheap edition published, and the Author shall be permitted to purchase further copies for his personal use at a discount of fifty (50%) per cent from the retail price. The Publisher further agrees to present to the Author's representative two (2) free copies of the regular edition of the Work and five (5) free copies of any cheap edition published. The representative shall be permitted to purchase additional copies at the same discount as the Author.

12. The Publisher agrees to render semi-annual statements in duplicate including copies of statements of sub-licensees on   and   in each year following the publication hereof, showing an account of sales and all other payments due hereunder to   and preceding said respective accounting dates.

The Publisher shall not combine statements for other works with the statements for this Work. Payments then due shall accompany such statements. Statements shall include the following information:

(a) The number of copies printed and bound in the first printing and in all subsequent printings of each edition, the dates of completion of the printing and binding, the date of publication, and the retail price.

(b) For each royalty rate listed in Clause 7, the number of copies sold, the number of copies returned, the amount of current royalties and the cumulative totals.

(c) The number of copies distributed gratis for publicity purposes, subsidiary rights purposes, or other purposes, the number remaindered, destroyed, or lost.

(d) A description of all subsidiary rights payments in which the Author's share amounts to one hundred ($100) dollars or more, including the gross amount received for each license granted by Publisher, together with a statement of the percentage of the total payment which the Author's share represents.

(e) The amount of reserves withheld in the current statement, and the amount of reserves withheld as of the previous statement, in accordance with Clauses 12 (e) (i) and 12 (e) (ii).

    (i) The Publisher may set up a reserve which in its opinion will allow for returns during the two royalty accounting periods following first publication of the Work. This reserve shall not exceed fifteen percent (15%) of earnings due the Author in the respective royalty periods.

    (ii) In no event, however, shall the Author be entitled to receive more than $ during any one calendar year. If in any one calendar year the sums accruing to the Author hereunder shall exceed such amount, he shall be entitled to receive the excess amount in any succeeding calendar year in which the sums accruing to him hereunder do not exceed the maximum herein stated, provided that the total amount to which the Author may be entitled in any succeeding year shall not exceed the maximum herein stated. Should the Author die, his executors or administrators may, by notice in writing to the Publisher, terminate this provision.

*Out of Print
Provisions
and Default;
termination
and reversion
of rights.*

13. (a) In the event that the Work shall at any time be out of print (whenever the Publisher shall have fifty (50) copies or less in stock, or when the Publisher fails to list the Work in his general catalogue), the Author or his representative may give notice thereof to the Publisher, and in such event the Publisher shall declare within thirty (30) days in writing whether or not he intends to bring out a new printing of the Work under the Publisher's own imprint within six (6) months. Failure to give such thirty (30) days notice or to reprint the Work within six months shall cause all rights herein granted to revert to the Author at the expiration of either of said periods without further notice or procedure.

(b) When annual sales of the Work fall below one hundred (100) copies, and/or the stock of the Work falls below fifty (50) copies, the Work shall be deemed out of print. In that event, the Author, or his representative, may give notice thereof to the Publisher and the Publisher shall declare within thirty (30) days in writing whether or not he intends to bring out a new printing of the Work under the Publisher's own imprint within six months. Failure to give such thirty-day notice or to reprint the Work within six (6) months shall cause all rights herein granted to revert to the Author at the expiration of either of said periods without further notice or procedure. Any license heretofore granted by the Publisher to others shall continue in effect until such license terminates or is terminated and the Publisher shall continue to account to the Author. However, such license may not be renewed by the Publisher once the Publisher's hardback edition has gone out of print.

(c) If the Publisher shall, during the existence of this agreement, default in the delivery of semi-annual statements, or in the making of payments as herein provided, and shall neglect or refuse to deliver such statements or make such payments, or any of them, within thirty (30) days after written notice of such default, this agreement shall terminate at the expiration of such thirty (30) days without prejudice to the Author's claim for any monies which may have accrued under this agreement or to any other rights and remedies to which the Author may be entitled.

(d) Anything to the contrary in (a) or (b) above notwithstanding, if during any calendar year following the tenth full calendar year after the publication date of the trade edition, the royalties payable to the Author under Clauses 7 and 8 above do not exceed $, the Author may terminate this agreement by written notice given within thirty (30) days after he receives the last statement covering payments due for such calendar year. Upon such termination all rights granted herein shall automatically revert to the Author, but the Publisher shall have the right to dispose of existing stock.

(e) Upon any termination, the Author may, within thirty (30) days of notification of such termination, purchase the plates, offset negatives or computer drive tapes (if in existence) at their scrap value and any remaining copies at cost, or at the remainder price, whichever is lower; otherwise, the Publisher may dispose of said materials, subject to the royalty provisions of this agreement.

14. (a) If publication of the Work is delayed beyond the publication date called for under the provisions of Clause 4, the Author shall have the option to give the Publisher a notice in writing, stating that if the Publisher fails to publish the Work within ninety (90) days after the date of such notice, then all of the Publisher's rights in and to the Work shall terminate at the end of such ninety (90) day period; and if, in such event, the Publisher shall fail to publish the Work within such ninety (90) day period, all of the Publisher's rights in and to the Work shall terminate and revert to the Author.

Bankruptcy.   (b) If the Publisher shall otherwise fail to comply with or fulfill the terms and conditions hereof, or in the event the Publisher is adjudicated a bankrupt or makes an assignment for the benefit of creditors, or liquidates its business, this agreement shall terminate and the rights herein granted to the Publisher shall revert to the Author. In such event all payments theretofore made to the Author shall belong to the Author without prejudice to any other remedies which the Author may have, subject to the provisions of Clause 13.

Reserved rights.   **15.** All rights in the Work now existing, or which may hereafter come into existence, not specifically herein granted, are reserved to the Author for his use at any time. Reserved publication rights include, but are not limited to, the right to publish or cause to be published in any form, excerpts, summaries and novelizations of dramatizations and motion pictures of the Work, thereof, not to exceed seventy-five hundred (7500) words in length, to be used for advertising and exploitation of motion pictures and televised motion pictures, or dramatizations based upon the Work.

Assignment.   **16.** No assignment of this contract, voluntary or by operation of law, shall be binding upon either of the parties without the written consent of the other; provided, however, that the Author may assign or transfer any monies due the Author or to become due the Author under this agreement.

Arbitration.   **17.** Any controversy or claim arising out of this agreement or the breach thereof shall be settled by arbitration in accordance with the rules then obtaining of the American Arbitration Association, and judgement upon the award may be entered in the highest court of the forum, State or Federal, having jurisdiction. Such arbitration shall be held in the City of New York unless otherwise agreed by the parties. The Author may, at his option, in case of failure to pay royalties, refuse to arbitrate, and pursue his legal remedies.

Notices.   **18.** Any written notice required under any of the provisions of this agreement shall be deemed to have been properly served by delivery in person or by mailing the same to the parties hereto at the addresses set forth above, except as the addresses may be changed by notice in writing; provided, however, that notices of termination shall be sent by registered mail.

Waiver.   **19.** A waiver of any breach of this agreement or of any of the terms or conditions by either party thereto, shall not be deemed a waiver of any repetition of such breach or in any way affect any other terms or conditions hereof; no waiver shall be valid or binding unless it shall be in writing, and signed by the parties.

20. This agreement shall not be binding upon either the Publisher or the Author unless it is signed by both parties and delivered to the Publisher within a period of sixty (60) days from the date of the agreement.

Agency.
•   **21.** All sums of money due the Author under this agreement shall be paid to the Author's agent,

New York, New York
and the receipt of the said agent shall be a good and valid discarge of all such indebtedness; and the said agent is hereby empowered by the Author to act on his behalf in all matters arising from and pertaining to this agreement. For services rendered and to be rendered, the Author does hereby irrevocably assign and transfer to said agent and said agent shall retain a sum equal to ten (10) percent, as an agency coupled with an interest, out of all gross monies accruing to the account of the Author under this agreement, prior to deductions from or charges against such monies for any reason whatsoever.

22. Regardless of the place of its physical execution, this contract shall be interpreted under the laws of the State of New York and of the United States of America.

IN WITNESS WHEREOF the parties hereto have duly executed this agreement the day and year first above written.

In the (seal)

Presence of:

_____
Publisher

By_____

( )

In the Presence of:

_____

_____

_____
Author

Society of Authors' Representatives, Inc.
Page Eight

[The following clause has been drafted by S.A.R., but is not included in their contract:]

Option.   The Author hereby agrees that the Publisher shall have the first option to publish the Author's next full-length book on terms to be arranged. It is agreed and understood that any such option shall automatically be cancelled if the Publisher merges with another or is bought by another. In the case of a Work of non-fiction such option shall be exercised on submission of an outline or reasonably representative sample material describing the book. The Author shall, nevertheless, be free to accept from another publisher a commission to write a book based on that publisher's own idea. The Author agrees to notify the Publisher when he accepts such a commission.

8

Self-Publication and Vanity Presses

Commercial publishers cannot possibly print and market all the books submitted to them. Of necessity, many books make the rounds of the publishing houses only to return without being placed. The writer must not only wait for this slow process of disappointment to play itself out, but must face the fact that his or her work may never find an audience. And the verdict of the editors will frequently not be that the work lacks merit, but rather that there is an insufficient likelihood of earning a profit to justify underwriting the investment necessary for publication, distribution, and promotion.

If rebuffed, the resourceful writer will seek alternatives to commercial publishing. These exist in the form of university presses, small presses, writers' cooperatives, self-publishing, and vanity presses. University and small presses require the same submission procedure as commercial publishers, while writers' cooperatives require joining a group and contributing money for publication. The most direct route for the writer is to pay for either self-publication or publication by a vanity press.

Self-publication encompasses a number of different methods of bringing out a book. Many valuable insights with respect to self-publication can be found in *The Publish-It-Yourself Handbook: Literary Tradition & How-To*, a self-published book which has had great success (and is listed in the selected bibliography). The writer may buy a printing press, following the examples of Anais

Nin for *Winter of Artifice* and Virginia Woolf for "The Mark on the Wall." An easier alternative is that taken by Stephen Crane for *Maggie: A Girl of the Streets* and by D. H. Lawrence for *Lady Chatterley's Lover.* They contracted with printers to publish a specified quantity of the bound book. Here, of course, the writer's concern must be with the quality, price, and promptness of the printing job. Once the book is in the writer's hands, the hurdle of distribution must be overcome. The ingenious writer will find many avenues open to promote and distribute the book, but the cost of these endeavors may be substantial. In any case, there should be a realistic appraisal of what the total cost of self-publication will be before any project is undertaken. Most writers who self-publish probably do not earn back their investment, yet the experience of reaching an audience can still be rewarding. And if others criticize a book because it is self-published, their ignorance of the venerable history of self-publication makes silence the only polite response.

Vanity presses, on the other hand, usually undertake to distribute books which they have published at the writer's expense. This raises the risk that the distribution and promotion will be a passive affair, since the publisher has already made its profit. Moreover, vanity presses are scorned by most people who have ever published in another way. Yet vanity presses could offer to the public a heterogeneity of style and subject matter which is beyond the ability of commercial publishers. But these presses must repair their image before they can be accepted as a valid publishing vehicle. An excellent appraisal of the vanity presses is contained in "Vanity Press: Stigma or Sesame?", an article by Nelson Richardson which first appeared in *Coda: Poets & Writers Newsletter*. It is published here by permission of Poets & Writers, Inc.

Vanity Press: Stigma or Sesame?
By Nelson Richardson

Vanity publishing is big business. The top vanity presses issue between 150 and 500 books each per year. The founder of one of them, Edward Uhlan of Exposition Press, claims that his firm took in the sixth highest revenue of any U.S. publisher for fiscal

1974–75. Martin Littlefield, vice president of Vantage Press, Exposition's chief competitor, disputes this claim but still ranks Vantage and Exposition "probably in the top twenty-five in number of titles." The total number of books issued each year by all vanity houses is at least 2,000, or one-sixteenth of the total 1975 U.S. output of 32,000.

Yet for poetry and fiction of quality, vanity is hardly used at all. Most writers have a very low opinion of it and rank it last among the six major types of publishing currently used. These six types are listed below:

	Who Pays Publication Costs	Who Owns & Distributes the Books
Trade	Publisher	Publisher
University	Publisher & Grant Agencies	Publisher
Small Press	Publisher & Grant Agencies	Publisher
Author's Co-Op	Authors & Grant Agencies	Authors or Distributor
Self-publishing	Author	Author or Distributor
Vanity Press	Author	Publisher

In one way, the vanity press is like a printer; it finds out what you want and tries to provide it at an agreed fee. But the fee covers more than printing and binding. It also includes design, proofreading, promotion, advertising, distribution, and bookkeeping costs, plus the vanity house's profit. It may or may not cover editing, depending on the particular house. At any rate, editing is minimal, and taste and style are not discussed.

As in all types of publishing, the author hopes that the money will come back as royalties or a percentage of sales. But sales rarely occur, except for a few copies purchased by friends. According to most vanity publishers, only 10% of their authors get their investment back from sales. It's not unusual for a vanity book to sell less than 25 copies.

For poetry and fiction, the low sales are due in part to a general lack of literature audiences. Sales of under 500 copies for poetry are common for all types of publishing. But in the case of vanity publishing, low sales may be further depressed by the vanity publisher's weak sales motivation. The average vanity publishing house doesn't need sales any more than a printer does, since its profit has already been made from the fee paid by the author. In addition, the quality of the writing in vanity books is generally abysmal, so there can be no prestige motive for promoting the books. *Kirkus Reviews* won't mention them, they never appear in *Publishers Weekly's* "Forecasts," and book stores and libraries ignore them after one look at the name on the spine. Vanity imprints are treated the same way vanity press editors treat their manuscripts—with indifference. A reviewer for a major magazine says, "they come in four at a time, and when I see the imprint, I throw them immediately in the wastebasket. I wouldn't even give them away."

Coda got in touch with twelve vanity presses which are now in operation:

Standard Vanity Presses *(The Author Pays All Costs)*	*Approximate #* *of Books/Year*
CARLTON PRESS* 84 Fifth Ave., New York, NY 10011, (212) 243-8800	300
CRESCENT PUBLICATIONS* 5410 Wilshire Blvd., Suite 400, Los Angeles, CA 90036, (213) 934-3054	12
DORRANCE & CO. 35 Cricket Terr., Ardmore, PA 19003, (215) 642-8303	150
EXPOSITION PRESS 900 S. Oyster Bay Rd., Hicksville, NY 11801, (212) 895-0081	300
FRANKLIN PUBLISHING* 2047 Locust St., Philadelphia, PA 19103, (215) 563-3837	25
HYPERION BOOKS 131 Townsend St., San Francisco, CA 94107, (415) 957-1277	8
MOJAVE BOOKS 7040 Darby Ave., Reseda, CA 91335, (213) 342-3403	65

PAGEANT POSEIDON PRESS*   165
155 W. 15 St., New York, NY 10011, (212) 929-5956

VANTAGE PRESS   500
516 W. 34 St., New York, NY 10001, (212) 736-1767

WILLIAM-FREDERICK PRESS   65
55 E. 86 St., New York, NY 10028, (212) 722-7272

"Guaranteed Sales" Vanity Presses
(The Author Buys Books from the Press)

GOLDEN QUILL PRESS*   25
Francestown, NH 03043, (603) 547-6622

WINDY ROW PRESS*   10
Peterborough, NH 03458, (603) 924-3334   _____
                                           TOTAL   1,625

*NOTE: Golden Quill and Windy Row also published commercially under the same imprints until 1974 but are now exclusively "guaranteed sales" vanity publishers. Crescent, Franklin, and Pageant Poseidon issue both vanity and non-vanity titles under the same imprints. Carlton publishes vanity books under two other imprints as well, Lyceum Books and Geneva Books. This list does not include British vanity publishers, of which the largest are Mitre Press, Regency Press, and Stockwell & Co.

The vanity presses listed above are full-service publishers. They are not to be confused with book manufacturers, which also make money from authors' fees. Some book manufacturers use an author's imprint, but some have imprints of their own., like Harlo, Sol III, RVK, J. Marks, Heritage, Hallmark, Thom Henricks, Nimrod, Port City Press, and Publication Press. These only print and bind books for a fee and then hand them over to the author. Use of their services is part of self-publishing. The vanity presses, on the other hand, not only manufacture but also distribute the books. In most cases, the author does not own the books and must buy them just like anyone else.

It is also important not to confuse vanity publishing with co-op and small press publishing, in which the author pays directly in cash or contributed labor or indirectly by foregoing advances and royalties. The difference lies in editorial control: co-ops and small presses exercise subjective literary judgment, while vanity presses leave literary decisions to the author.

SEVEN POSSIBLE ADVANTAGES OF VANITY PRESSES

Despite their bad reputation, vanity presses offer seven possible advantages:

• Their books are usually bigger and better-produced than those of the small presses, co-ops, or hired manufacturers, and they are mainly hardcovers. Hardcover binding is essential for sales to libraries, and just as important as a reputable imprint for getting reviews. Furthermore, printing quality is often excellent. Exposition and William-Frederick, for example, use letterpress printing routinely for small print runs of 1,000 copies, instead of the less attractive photo-offset method which most publishers use, trade included.

• The chances of your manuscript being rejected are small. Unsolicited work is profitable to the vanity publisher and is welcomed. While a trade publisher usually wants to see only a summary or sample, the vanity publisher wants your whole manuscript right away—the cost can't be estimated without it.

• Vanity publishers work fast. A trade publisher or small press editor may hold a manuscript in limbo for over a year, but the vanity publisher can have it in book form in as little as three months after the contract is signed. If there is any editing to speak of, it certainly won't involve the massive rewriting or deletions that a traditional literary editor might demand.

• Promotion, distribution, bookkeeping, and royalty payment, though rarely used to the full, are nonetheless available. Ads can be purchased, flyers mailed. All vanity books which are selected for the research collection of the Library of Congress are automatically listed in Bowker's *Weekly Record of Books* and *Books in Print,* the most widely used book-buying reference works. Most of the vanity books which get on these lists are from Exposition Press, according to one Bowker editor, but the other imprints (except for Carlton and Windy Row) show up from time to time on the Bowker lists. Sales potential is exploited where it exists—for some cookbooks, technical books, or local histories, for example. In 1974–75, Exposition Press billed book stores for more than a million dollars for sales of such books, according to Edward Uhlan. 40% of Exposition's revenue, he claims, come from sales. William-Frederick Press claims to have about 50 standing orders from libraries for its "William-Frederick Poets Series." About 10% of William-Frederick's revenue comes from sales. Franklin Publishing claims that a third of their books have sold over 1,000 copies each, including about five books of poetry.

Furthermore, a minimum of $300 is usually spent on promotion and advertising, if only to fulfill the publisher's contract obligations. $300 is clearly inadequate, but it's about all a book of poetry ever gets—even from a top trade publisher. With cooperation from a knowledgeable author, it can be spent effectively.

• Royalties are an impressive 40% on the first printing of vanity books, contrasted with a 12% or 15% royalty from a trade publisher's books or payment in free copies of the book, which is customary from small presses. When a first printing sells out, the subsequent printings are published at the vanity house's expense. Royalties then go down to about 20%.

• Royalties are usually tax-free until the original investment is regained. Or, in some cases, losses may be deducted. According to Hank Krell of Pageant Poseidon Press, tax treatment varies with the Internal Revenue District in which the author lives, but it is usually favorable if an author can demonstrate a business motive.

• When vanity books are good they do get reviewed. This has happened frequently for books on technical subjects, like Pageant Poseidon's *Success in Commodities* by Eugene Nofri, which was reviewed in the "Business and Finance" section of *The New York Times* for November 3, 1975. Reviews have been extremely rare for poetry and fiction, however, largely because these books are generally a vanity press's worst.

BEGINNERS CAN'T KNOW HOW BAD THINGS REALLY ARE

Among almost a thousand poetry and fiction titles listed in vanity catalogues, *Coda* could identify only four by poets who later went on to non-vanity publishers. The four poets are A. R. Ammons, Dan Gerber, Charles Ghigna, and Alex Kuo. Ammons, Gerber, and Ghigna published first books of poetry with Dorrance & Co., founded in 1920 by a member of the Campbell Soup family. Alex Kuo published his first book of poetry with Windy Row Press, a "guaranteed sales" vanity press in New Hampshire.

All four poets were unaware at the time that their books were in bad company and none consulted a lawyer. Kuo was already widely published and was referred to his vanity publisher by another poet. The other three were typical beginners attracted by vanity press ads.

Vanity presses thrive on the same fantasy of sales that other publishers thrive on, but at a much greater financial cost to the author. For beginners the fantasy of sales is stronger and ads can be irresistible. Vanity presses advertise regularly in *Writer's Digest*, *The New York Times Book Review*, literary quarterlies, daily papers, and on radio and television. The following ad is typical:

FREE TO WRITERS SEEKING
A BOOK PUBLISHER:

Two fact-filled, illustrated brochures tell how to publish your book, get 40% royalties, national advertising, publicity and promotion. Free editorial appraisal. Write Dept. STM-3. Exposition Press, 386 4th Ave., N.Y., N.Y. 10016.

Those who answer such ads are very frequently complimented. Elizabeth McCall of Orlando, Florida, received the following comments from Exposition Press:

My editor and I have given your poetry manuscript a thorough reading; I can tell you that we, too, feel you have a firm command of the poetic idiom. You write by the line and, I must add, a lyric line. Your determination to place the correct word in the right place is absolute, and this is a commendable quality that's lacking in contemporary poetry. I was particularly impressed by the fact that you can create both humorous verses and poems that contain a fine blending of emotion and thought, as evidenced by the poem, "The Downfall of Superman."

The letter concluded with an estimate of $3,550 for publication of a 64-page hardcover edition with illustrations or $1,800 for a 32-page hardcover without illustrations. To return Mrs. McCall's investment, at 40% royalties on a $5 cover price, Exposition would have to sell 1,770 copies of the 64-page version of her book, or 900 copies of the 32-page version—sales which would put her on the same level with many well-established poets.

Mrs. McCall had begun to write poetry only a year before. Even though the letter promised nothing, she didn't know that most poetry doesn't sell unless the poet sells it. Nor did she know that the stigma of a vanity imprint can lower a writer's standing. Like most beginners, she sought advice. She called a teacher at a local college who urged her not to purchase Exposition's services.

Besides placing ads, vanity publishers also sell their services in person through sales representatives. An announcement is published in a local paper, stating that a "representative of a large New York publishing firm" will be available for interviews with prospective authors on such-and-such a date. Appointments are made by mail, and prospective authors wait eagerly for their big chance. Poet Peggy Simpson Curry of Wyoming recalls an example dating back about 15 years. A young German student in her creative writing class went to such an interview and contracted, without the help of a lawyer, for a book of poems from Vantage Press. Later, when the hoped-for sales didn't materialize, sympathetic friends bought extra copies to lessen his loss. Curry says that she still gets many calls from students inquiring about the same type of ad.

WHEN IS AN AD "MISLEADING"?

There is a widespread feeling among writers that vanity presses trick or mislead authors. In part this feeling is due to the fact that the ads sound positive but fail to convey the expense and risks of publishing or the bleak prospects for sales. But can the vanities be faulted with anything more substantial?

In 1961 suspicions led to an investigation by the Federal Trade Commission. Eventually it focussed on the Exposition Press ad quoted previously. The F.T.C. felt that by mentioning royalties, the ad misled authors into thinking that the press, not the author, would be paying for publication. Hearings were held on nine separate days, in New York and in Richmond, Virginia. The F.T.C. accumulated a transcript 1,100 pages long and numerous exhibits.

Not a single actual victim could be found. Those who had answered the ad stated that it had been clear to them that they would have to pay for publication, and that the 40% royalties would probably not offset their investment. None felt deceived or dissatisfied. Still, a court ruled against Exposition, forcing deletion of the term "royalties" from its advertising and the advertising of all other vanity houses. Is anyone really being misled?

Perhaps greater abuses existed at one time but have now abated. One probable cause of improvement is F.T.C. surveillance. Another is stricter advertising policies on the part of periodicals like *Writer's Digest*, which sells space to vanities only on condition that their ads mention the availability of *Writer's Digest*'s free reprint, "Does It Pay to Pay to Have It Published?" The pamphlet explains the danger, expense, and limits of vanity publishing and the necessity of consulting a lawyer. "We still get complaints about them from readers, but far fewer than we used to," says *Writer's Digest*'s advertising manager, Colleen Dowling. "Substantial complaints," she adds, "should be reported to a Better Business Bureau or state attorney general's office."

TWO POETS WHO KNOW FROM EXPERIENCE

In 1966, poet Dan Gerber answered a Dorrance ad and contracted for an edition of 1,000 copies of his first poetry book, *The Waiting*. At the time, he did not know that Dorrance was a vanity press, or that it carried a stigma. He didn't even consult a lawyer before signing. The cost to him was about $900, he recalls, and the job was well done.

"They were quite up-front with me. Given who and where I was at the time, I had no reason to be disappointed," he recalls. Dan pushed the book himself in his home town in Michigan and made sure that copies were displayed in the local book store. The first edition sold out and, at royalties of $1 a copy, paid for itself completely. Yet Gerber won't use a vanity press again and won't recommend them. "Go to your local printer instead," he advises. "He can print your book for less, give you more control, and save you the stigma." Gerber is now the editor of Sumac Press, which has published his own books as well as books by Jim Harrison, George Oppen, Charles Simic, and several other highly respected poets. Apparently the stigma of his first book hasn't haunted him.

Charles Ghigna's first book, *Plastic Tears*, was issued in 1973, also by Dorrance. It is now in its second printing and is listed in *Books In Print*. Ghigna paid $1,680 for the book, and, like Gerber, he signed without consulting a lawyer. He was very pleased with the book's design, production quality, and distribution. "I don't think I've gotten all of my investment back," he reflects, "but the royalty checks come in regularly and I expect to break even before long."

Ghigna himself helped sales by suggesting names for the promotional mailings and by placing a notice in the *English Journal*, of which he was editor at the time. Steps like these must be taken by any poet who wishes to see his book sold, no matter who the publisher is. Despite the vanity imprint on *Plastic Tears*, Ghigna went on to publish in *Southern Poetry Review*, *Harpers*, *Texas Quarterly Review*, *Mississippi Review*, and several other distinguished periodicals.

VANITY FEE IS LIKE A CHURCH TITHE

Yet Ghigna too is now against vanity publishing. One of his reasons is the lack of real editorial guidance; he feels that *Plastic Tears* was premature and should have been withheld. Another is that vanity houses can't help but encourage unrealistic hopes. He compares them to "rich churches where poorer members tithe in hopes of reserving a place in heaven."

A third poet who published through a vanity press is Alex Kuo. *The Window Tree*, his first book of poems, was issued by Windy Row Press, a "guaranteed sales" press, in 1971. It is still listed in *Books In Print*.

Kuo was not a beginner; he had been publishing poetry in little magazines for ten years, and his manuscript for *The Window Tree* had been making the rounds of trade and university publishers for about six years. One publisher kept it for three years, promising constantly to call him with a decision "next week," before rejecting it. Meanwhile, self-publication was out of the question because Kuo was too busy writing and coordinating a minority program at Northern Illinois University. He finally sent the manuscript to Windy Row on the advice of a friend, unaware that it was a vanity press. Windy Row was at this time difficult to identify as a vanity press, since it printed both vanity and trade books, and the two kinds of books looked identical.

Windy Row offered Kuo a "guaranteed sales" contract.

"Guaranteed sales" means that the author must be responsible for selling enough books within several months to cover manufacturing costs, or else buy them himself. "Advertising and distribution were terrible," recalls Alex. "I ended up buying about $800 worth of books which I simply gave away." After this period, about 400 books were sold gradually by the press, partly by using Kuo's mailing list. But the contract didn't provide for royalties on these sales, and Kuo received nothing back. If his contract had allowed more time for the initial "guaranteed sales," Kuo might have fared better. Poetry is traditionally a backlist item; at best it sells slowly over a period of two to three years.

In spite of his disappointment with the lack of sales and royalties, Kuo is pleased with the editing and production for *The Window Tree.* He can't tell whether the vanity imprint hurt the book, but it didn't prevent it from getting good reviews in a few literary magazines. Kuo continued to publish his poetry in *Yardbird, New Letters, Poetry Northwest,* and other magazines, and in 1974 Greenfield Review Press issued his second book: *New Letters from Hiroshima and Other Poems.*

From the standpoint of prestige, the second book was a step up: the imprint is respectable and Kuo didn't have to subsidize the costs. But editing and production, as with most small presses, were a step down from vanity. Distribution was no better. *New Letters from Hiroshima* sold fewer copies than *The Window Tree,* and not only were there no royalties—there wasn't even a contract. Contracts are still very rare in small press publishing. "In the last analysis, I'm more pleased with my vanity publishing experience than with my small press experience," states Kuo. "I'd say that if you don't have time to publish yourself and there aren't any other alternatives, vanity publishing is a reasonable choice."

"I'D DO IT AGAIN" SAYS A. R. AMMONS

A. R. Ammons published his first book, *Ommateum,* with Dorrance in 1954, while he was employed at a biological and laboratory glass manufacturing firm in New Jersey. There is no telling how long Ammons might have waited for a book if he hadn't gone ahead and published it through a vanity press. He was too busy and too inexperienced to launch a career by self-publishing, and other types of publishing were not available to him.

For nine years following *Ommateum* he continued in the glass business and had nothing but this one book to show for his career as a poet. When an offer finally did come, in 1964, it was through sheer luck. A friend tipped him off about a new poetry series being started by Ohio University Press, and Ammons got there at the head of the line. His career then skyrocketed to the National Book Award in 1973 and the $5,000 Bollingen Prize in 1975 and he is now one of the most distinguished poets published in America. Copies of his Dorrance book are worth $500 to $1,000 on the rare book market.

Ammons neither consulted a lawyer nor supervised distribution when he published *Ommateum*. Sales were disappointing. "The royalty checks usually were two 4¢ stamps," he recalls. (Ammons was not aware that he could compensate his losses through income taxes and did not attempt it.) Production quality, however, pleased him very much and he is still proud of the book. He would use a vanity publisher again if he had to, in spite of the stigma.

Ammons and Kuo are alone. Other poets are much less sanguine. Says poet Harold Witt: "Try everything else before vanity." Says poet Jim Weil, "Editorially it does only harm. Better to invent your own imprint and publish the work yourself." "I refuse to pay for publishing my own work," states poet Lewis Turco. Turco published his *First Poems* on a standard contract with Golden Quill before financial pressures forced it to become exclusively a vanity imprint.

VANITY OFFERS PUBLISHING, NOT JUST PRINTING

Poet Charles Levendosky is totally against vanity publishing. He recommends self-publication through a local print shop, which he feels is both cheaper and more respectable than vanity.

Recently, a friend of Levendosky took this advice and hired a local printer for under $1,000 for an edition of 1,000 copies in hardcover. But this price was for book manufacturing only. It did not include design, proofreading, promotion, advertising, storage, distribution, and bookkeeping, which he had to do himself. These are the services that make a vanity press more than a mere manufacturer, and because of them, vanities charge more.

The ten standard vanity presses contacted by *Coda* won't publish a hardcover for under $1,800. $1,800 would pay for a 32- or 40-page book of poetry with no illustrations in an edition of at least 1,000 copies. Books of over a hundred pages may easily cost authors $4,000. For this much money, authors should make sure that promotion and advertising are effective. If they aren't effective, authors should make sure that they can acquire the unsold books, in bound form, to distribute themselves.

These assurances aren't easy to come by. Only one vanity press, William-Frederick, binds the entire first printing immediately and gives the author control of all unsold copies at any time. The other presses store the books as flat sheets and bind only a few hundred at a time, or as many as they think they can sell, just as do many trade publishers. If the books aren't sold by the expiration date of the contract—usually two years—they may not be bound at all and may therefore have no second chance.

But more important, is effective promotion and advertising even possible, given the stigma attached to the vanity imprints? Apparently it was possible for poets Gerber, Ghigna, and Kuo; but without the vanity stigma, would their books have sold even more? These problems were faced realistically by poet Jose-Angel Figueroa, when he approached Vantage Press in late 1975 with his manuscript, *Noo Jork.*

FIRST SHREWD ATTEMPT AT VANITY PUBLISHING

Unlike Ammons, Gerber, Ghigna, and Kuo, Jose-Angel Figueroa chose vanity publishing warily and with enough experience to know its limitations and potential value. His previous book, *East 110th Street,* had been published in 1972 by Broadside Press, a respectable small press in Chicago whose authors include Pulitzer Prize-winner Gwendolyn Brooks and National Book Award nominee Audre Lorde. Like most small press editions, it was a paperback and therefore could not be sold to most libraries. Furthermore, the manuscript was cut from its original 120 pages down to 45 and distribution was poor.

Jose-Angel had also tried self-publishing. Using his own imprint, TalkaTive TypeRiter Publications, he had published 200 copies of a 50-page paperback anthology, *Unknown Poets from the Full-Time Jungle.* At $2 a copy it had sold out returning twice his investment. But for *Noo Jork* Jose-Angel wanted a full 96-page hardcover edition, with better design and production, and with promotional literature and a mail-order campaign. He knew that the cost and the risk would be too high for a small press and he hesitated to attempt it on his own. At the same time, he had received the usual rejections from trade publishers. He wasn't about to wait a decade to be accepted by them, as Ammons had.

Jose-Angel picked Vantage because it is one of the largest vanity publishers and is probably capable of doing a good job. He found that the production quality of Vantage's books varied greatly, however, and the jacket designs were poor. Jose-Angel therefore commissioned the cover himself from Walter Velez, a freelance illustrator and former art director of *Latin N.Y.* magazine. He also roughed out the book's overall design.

Vantage offered to do the book for $3,900. The contract specified that publication would take place no later than eight months from signing. 400 copies would be bound to be used for publicity and initial sales.

At least 75 copies would be mailed to reviewers, and Jose-Angel would get 50 copies free. The royalty rate would be the standard vanity rate of 40%. The retail price—$4.95—would yield royalties of $1.98 per copy. If Jose-Angel wanted additional copies, he could buy them at an author's discount of 45%, or for $2.72 each. He could resell these copies if he wished and keep all proceeds. This much was acceptable to Jose-Angel and his lawyer, but several problems remained.

First, the contract left design decisions to Vantage. This gave Vantage the right to reject Jose-Angel's commissioned cover art or to charge him extra for using it. Jose-Angel protested, and Vantage then agreed to a contract amendment stating that the Velez cover would be used. It still wasn't clear, however, whether Jose-Angel could control other design aspects.

Second, Jose-Angel and his lawyer foresaw possible problems with record album rights, in case sections from the book were recorded. Since the contract mentioned nothing concerning album rights, another amendment was added stating that Vantage would have no claim to any recording income.

VAGUE PROMOTION CLAUSES

Third, Jose-Angel was unsatisfied with the advertising and promotion clauses, which were vague and weak. At $2 a copy royalty, Jose-Angel would have to sell about 2,000 copies to gain back his investment. This would require a big effort. Yet, while various types of promotion were "suggested" or "recommended" with hypnotic frequency in the contract's accompanying litera-ture, nothing definite was stated in the contract itself.

Furthermore, Jose-Angel would need to direct the promotional efforts himself. He alone knew how to reach his poetry audience: through Spanish-speaking disc jockeys, the editors and publishers of Hispanic cultural arts magazines, the "Puerto Rican New York" TV series on Channel 11, the "Latin N.Y." series on Channel 9, and community arts and educational agencies serving the His-panic community, such as ASPIRA, Puerto Rican Forum, Puerto Rican Heritage House, and the Museo del Barrio. For non-Hispanic audiences and audiences outside New York, he would have to mail announcements and coordinate promotion with a reading tour. Jose-Angel had to be sure of Vantage's cooperation. But no agreement could be reached. Finally, Jose-Angel decided that $3,900 was too much to risk.

Jose-Angel still feels that vanity publishing might be turned to advantage, however, provided that an author first investigates carefully and consults a lawyer. Jose-Angel would be willing to discuss his experiences further with any author who is interested. His address is 320 West 22 Street, 1C, New York, New York 10011, (212) 242-6278.

In the meantime, it is easy to obtain a contract, an estimate, and sample books by sending a manuscript to any of the twelve vanity presses listed in this article.

CONTRACTS: WHAT TO LOOK FOR

If quality writing and vanity publishing ever make friends, part of the process will be learning how to avoid treacherous contracts. The points below are summarized from several sources, including the *Writer's Digest* reprint, "Does It Pay to Pay to Have It Pub-lished?"; comments by vanity publishers; and warnings from poets. It would be wise to go over these points carefully with a lawyer before signing any vanity contract.

• What does the contract mean by the term, "first edition"? Make sure that binding and jacketing are included, not just print-ing. A minimum number of completed copies is usually made available for sale by a certain date. As with most publishers, the remaining copies are not bound and jacketed until more orders are received.

• An exception to this, as mentioned earlier, is the procedure followed by William-Frederick Press, which prints and binds the entire first edition of 1,000 and gives the author complete control of the books. William-Frederick limits its other services, however, to fulfillment of orders and royalty payment. For promotion and advertising, a separate contract must be negotiated, and the author pays an additional fee.

• How many free copies do you get?

• Can you resell your copies? (You may wish to assign them to a class you are giving or sell them at readings.)

• Or, can you get copies to sell at readings or in classrooms on a commission basis?

• After the first printing is sold out, will additional copies be produced at the publisher's expense, or will you have to invest your money again?

• Exactly how much promotion and advertising will your book receive? Vantage, Exposition, and Pageant Poseidon claim that about $300 is spent on promotion and advertising for each of their books. $300 could pay for a substantial mailing. If your book needs more, your fee may have to be raised, or you may have to buy advertising and mail promotion independently.

• Can you direct the advertising and promotion yourself? This is a crucial question not just for vanity but for all types of publishing. With vanity publishing, however, you are paying for these services yourself and ought to have some say in the matter. If you leave it up to the vanity house, they may do a bad job. But even if they do a good job, the stigma attached to the imprint may hurt your book rather than help it.

WHY NOT REPLACE THE VANITY IMPRINT WITH YOUR OWN?

The most frequently cited drawback of vanity houses is the stigma. To reduce it, why couldn't the vanity house substitute a writer's own imprint? The new imprint could be used on the book and promotional literature. The vanity imprint would still appear on invoices and labels used in fulfillment, to save the cost of reprinting these, but only as the book's "distributor." This is currently done by trade publishers for authors' co-ops such as the

Fiction Collective, whose books are distributed by Braziller, and Inwood Press, whose books are distributed by Horizon.

"No one ever approached us with a request for a new imprint," says Roy Sandstrom of Dorrance & Co. "We would be willing to consider it." "Sure, we'll do it," says Edward Uhlan of Exposition. "We did it for Alan Truscott, a bridge commentator for *The New York Times*, who published a book with us under his Yarborough Press imprint." "We've substituted an imprint whenever anyone has asked," says Alvin Levin of William-Frederick.

"We've never done it for a poetry book, but we published a chemistry book under a private imprint," says Irving Tannenbaum of Mojave Books. Carlton, Franklin, Pageant Poseidon, and Vantage, however, have never met with a request for imprint substitution.

Perhaps we will see more imprint substitutions in the future. With publishing outlets shrinking, this and other concessions to authors may win the vanity presses a new clientele among authors of quality poetry and fiction who know what they want.

POST-SCRIPT: WHITE ELEPHANT LIBRARY

There is only one place in the U.S. where vanity books, the white elephants of the book world, are welcome: Beloit College Library, Beloit, Wisconsin 53511, (608) 365-3391. The Beloit library contains a large collection of important contemporary poetry in which vanity books were not originally included. Its vanity holdings began when Marion Stocking and Clyde Peterman, former editors of the *Beloit Poetry Journal*, began saving the free review copies sent by vanity publishers. They rarely reviewed the books but were eager to preserve them as artifacts of cultural history. If you have copies of vanity press books and would like to give them away, why not pack them up and send them to Beloit?

9
Income Taxation

The writer's professional income—for example, from sales of work, advances, royalties, and wages—is taxed as ordinary income by the federal government and by the state and city where the writer lives, if such state or city has an income tax. The business expenses of being a writer, however, are deductible and reduce the income which will be taxed. Both income—as gross receipts—and expenses are entered on Schedule C, *Profit or (Loss) from Business or Profession*, which is attached to Form 1040. A sample Schedule C is reproduced on pp. 168–169. The writer must also determine whether other state or local taxes, such as New York City's unincorporated business tax, must be paid in addition to the personal income tax.[1] These taxes vary with each state and city, so guidance must be obtained in the writer's own locality.

General guides to federal taxation are IRS Publication 17, *Your Federal Income Tax*, for individuals and IRS Publication 334, *Tax Guide for Small Businesses*, for businesses. These and the other IRS publications mentioned in the income tax chapters can all be obtained free of charge from any IRS office. The writer should keep in mind, however, that these publications represent the views of the IRS and are sometimes inconsistent with precedents already decided by the courts.

Record Keeping

All income and expenses arising from the profession of being a writer should be promptly recorded in a ledger regularly used for that purpose. The entries should give specific information as to dates, sources, purposes, and other relevant data, all supported by checks, bills, and receipts whenever possible.

LEDGER

Date	Category	Description	Income	Expense
9/21	Office supplies	Manilla envelopes (paid by check no. 694)		7.95
9/21	Book review	Review of *Law Today* for *Barrister's News*	15.00	
9/22	Telephone	Call to *New Jersey Hunter Magazine* re article on Hemingway (201-776-1776)		1.93
9/22	Transportation	Cab to *Daily Star* to leave "Elks Heaven" article		2.35

Monthly items, such as rent, can be posted to the ledger at the end of each month. This ledger can be supplemented by a breakdown of categories drawn from Schedule C, in order to make the entries on Schedule C easier at the end of the year. Thus, each item of expense or income would be entered twice—once in the ledger and once in a specific account such as those below.

Transportation		*Office Supplies*		*Rent*	
DATE	*AMOUNT*	*DATE*	*AMOUNT*	*DATE*	*AMOUNT*
9/22	2.35	9/21	7.95	9/30	75.00

It is advisable to maintain business checking and savings accounts through which all professional income and expenses are channeled separate from the writer's personal accounts. IRS Publication 552, *Recordkeeping Requirements and a Guide to Tax Publications,* and 583, *Recordkeeping for a Small Business,* provide details as to the "permanent, accurate and complete" records required.

Accounting Methods and Periods

Like any other taxpayer, the writer may choose either of two methods of accounting: the cash method or the accrual method. The cash method includes in income all income actually received during the tax year and deducts all expenses actually paid during the tax year. The accrual method, on the other hand, includes as income all that income which the writer has earned and has a right to receive in the tax year, even if not actually received until a later tax year, and deducts expenses when they are incurred instead of when they are paid. Since most writers operate on the simpler cash method, the chapters on income taxes will assume that the cash method is being used.

Income taxes are calculated for annual accounting periods. The tax year for the vast majority of taxpayers is the calendar year: January 1 through December 31. However, a taxpayer could use any fiscal year (for example, July 1 through June 30). Since most writers use the calendar year as their tax year, the income tax chapters will assume the use of a calendar year.

The cash method of accounting in a few cases, however, may include income not actually received by the writer, if the income has been credited or set apart so as to be subject to the writer's control. For example, income received by an agent for the writer will be taxable to the writer when received by the agent unless substantial limitations or restrictions exist as to how or when the agent will make payment.[2]

One valuable tax-saving device for the cash basis, calendar year writer is to pay expenses in December while putting off receipt of income until the following January when a new tax year has begun. The expenses reduce income in the present tax year while the income is put off until the new tax year.

Further information on accounting methods and periods can be obtained in IRS Publication 538, *Tax Information on Accounting Periods and Methods.*

Types of Income

The writer must be aware of the different types of income.

The first distinction is between ordinary income and capital gains income. Ordinary income is realized from all the income-producing activities of the writer's profession. Ordinary income is taxed at the regular income tax rates, which go up as high as 70 percent. Capital gains income is realized upon the sale of capital assets, such as stocks, real estate, or silver bullion. Capital gains from assets owned more than six months are classified as long-term gains and receive preferential tax treatment (by basically being reduced in half before being taxed).[3] The Tax Reform Act of 1976 extends the holding period necessary for long-term gains to nine months in 1977 and one year thereafter.

The substantial tax discrimination in favor of long-term capital gains as compared to ordinary income will cause the writer to wonder why a copyright or a manuscript is not an asset which receives favorable capital gains treatment. Congress, when enacting the tax laws, specifically stated that "a copyright, a literary, musical, or artistic composition, a letter or memorandum, or similar property, held by the taxpayer who created it" cannot be an asset qualifying for capital gains treatment.[4] And if the writer gives a copyright or a manuscript to someone else, that person will own the work as the writer did—as ordinary income property rather than an asset qualifying for capital gains treatment.

Another distinction to be kept in mind is between ordinary income which is earned and that which is unearned. The professional income of the writer is considered earned income, but income from stock dividends, interest, rent, and capital gains, for example, is treated as unearned income. Personal service income, which is earned income plus pension or annuity or deferred compensation income, is never taxed at a rate of more than 50 percent.[5] But ordinary income which is not personal service income may be taxed at a rate as high as 70 percent as mentioned earlier. Writers will also be concerned about earned income in such areas as retirement (discussed on pp. 172–174) and income earned abroad (discussed on pp. 179–182).

Basis

The cost of creating a work is called its "basis" for tax purposes. The cash basis writer, who deducts expenses currently when paid for, must remember that such expenses cannot be deducted again as the basis of the works when sold. In other words, if the writer deducts expenses currently, then the work has a zero basis and the entire amount of the proceeds from sales will be taxable. If the work is given to someone else, that person will have the same zero basis of the writer and, as mentioned earlier, realize ordinary income upon sale.

Grants

Grants to writers for scholarships or fellowships to further their education and training are excluded from gross income as long as the grants are not compensation for services and are not given primarily for the benefit of the grant-giving organization.[6] Amounts given to cover related expenses are also excludable from income if the expenses are specifically designated and are spent for the purpose of the grant. A degree candidate has no limit on the grant amounts which may be excluded as long as teaching, research, or other employment under the grant is required for all candidates for the particular degree.

A writer who is not a degree candidate may only exclude up to $300 times the number of months to which amounts received from the grant are attributable, but for no more than a total of thirty-six months, consecutive or otherwise, during the writer's lifetime. After the thirty-six months are exhausted, the full amount of any grants and related amounts for expenses are fully includable in income. A writer who is not a degree candidate can only exclude the grants at all if the grants are paid by certain governmental, non-profit, or international organizations. More information on the taxation of grants can be obtained in Chapter 7, "What Income is Taxable," IRS Publication 17, *Your Federal Income Tax.*

Prizes and Awards

Prizes and awards to writers are, in most cases, taxable, even if they are given in the form of goods or services. The sole area in which tax can be avoided is when prizes and awards are given in recognition of past achievements in the field of writing without application or services on the part of the writer (for example, the Pulitzer Prize or Nobel Prize). Once the writer is selected as a candidate, however, filling out application forms or appearing for an interview will not cause the prize or award to be includable in gross income.[7]

Professional Expenses

Deductible business expenses are all the ordinary and necessary expenditures the writer must make professionally. Such expenses, which are recorded on Schedule C, include, for example, writing materials and supplies, work space, office equipment, certain books and magazines, repairs, travel for business purposes, promotional expenses, telephone, postage, commissions of agents, and legal and accounting fees.

Writing Supplies and Other Deductions

Writing materials and supplies are generally current expenses, deductible in full in the year purchased. These include all items with a useful life of less than one year, such as paper, ink, pens, erasers, typewriter rentals, mailing envelopes, photocopying, file folders, stationery, paper clips, and similar items. Moreover, the sales tax on these and other business purchases is a deductible expense and can simply be included in the cost of the item. Postage is similarly deductible as soon as the expense is incurred. The cost of professional journals is deductible, as is the cost for books used in preparation for specific works. Dues for membership in the writer's professional organizations are deductible, as are fees to attend workshops sponsored by such organizations. Telephone bills and an answering service are deductible in full for a business telephone. If, however, use of the telephone is divided between personal and business calls, then records should be kept itemizing both long-distance and local message units expended for business purposes, and the cost of an answering service should also be prorated. Educational expenses are generally not deductible, unless the writer can establish that such expenses were incurred to maintain or improve skills required as a writer (but not to learn or qualify in a new profession). IRS Publication 508, *Tax Information on Educational Expenses,* can be consulted here.

Repairs to professional equipment are deductible in full in the year incurred. If the writer moves to a new house, the pro rata share of the moving expenses attributable to professional equipment is deductible as a business expense. More substantial deductions for reasonable moving expenses can be taken if the self-employed person's new work location is at least thirty-five miles further from the former residence than was the old job location and certain other requirements are met. This deduction is explained in IRS Publication 521, *Tax Information on Moving Expenses.*

Work Space

If the writer rents work space separate from where the writer lives, all of the rent and expenses in connection with the work space are deductible. However, the Tax Reform Act of 1976 places limitations on business deductions which are attributable to an office or studio at home.[8] Such deductions will be allowed if the writer uses a part of the home exclusively, and on a regular basis, as the writer's principal place of business. The exclusivity requirement means, for example, that a room that has personal as well as professional use will not qualify for a deduction. Even though the writer may have another profession, the business deductions may be taken if the studio at home is the principal place of the business of being a writer (although complete certainty with respect to this will require waiting for the appropriate regulations). Also, the writer who maintains a separate structure used exclusively, and on a regular basis, in connection with the business of being a writer (even if not as the principal place of the business) is entitled to the deductions attributable to the separate structure. A provision less likely to apply to the writer allows deductions when a portion of the home is used exclusively, and on a regular basis, as the normal place to meet with clients and customers.

To determine what expenses are attributable to an office or studio, the writer must calculate how much of the total space in the home is used as work space. If one room comprising a fifth of the apartment area is used as work space, 20 percent of the rent is deductible. A homeowner makes the same calculation as to work-space use. However, capital assets, those having a useful life of more than one year, must be depreciated. A house has a basis for depreciation (only the house, land is not depreciated), which is usually its cost less its salvage value at the end of its useful life. This basis is divided by the useful life of the house to determine the amount of depreciation of the house each year. Thereafter, the percentage of the house used professionally is applied to the annual depreciation figure to reach the amount of the depreciation which is deductible for the current year. IRS Publications 529, *Other Miscellaneous Deductions*, and 534, *Tax Information on Depreciation*, are of aid in the determination of basis, salvage value, and the calculation of depreciation. These publications also describe more rapid methods of depreciation than the straight-line method which is described above, but the writer should consult an accountant to determine whether such methods can and should be used. IRS Publication 587, *Tax Information on Operating a Business In Your Home*, can also be consulted with respect to deductions for or related to work space.

The portion of expenses for utilities, insurance, and cleaning costs allocable to the work space are deductible. Repairs to maintain the house or apartment are also deductible on this pro rata basis. Property taxes and mortgage interest are deductible in full regardless of whether or not the writer's home is used for work purposes, provided the writer itemizes personal deductions on Schedule A of Form 1040. If personal deductions are not itemized on Schedule A, the portions of property taxes and mortgage interest deductible as business expenses would be entered on Schedule C.

The Tax Reform Act of 1976 also limits the amount of business expenses which may be deducted when attributable to a home office. This provision does not, however, in any way limit business expenses not attributable to the home office. Assuming the writer qualifies to take the home office deduction under one of the tests described earlier, the deductions for work space cannot exceed the writer's gross income from writing minus deductions which would be allowed whether or not connected with a business or trade (such as real estate taxes and mortgage interest which can be itemized and deducted on Schedule A). For example, a writer earns gross income of $1,500 in a year from writing, while exclusively, and on a regular basis, using one-quarter of the writer's home as the principal place of the business of being a writer. The writer owns the home, and mortgage interest is $2,000 while real estate taxes are $1,600, for a total of $3,600 of deductions which could be taken on Schedule A regardless of whether incurred in connection with a business. Other expenses, such as electricity, heat, cleaning, and depreciation, total $8,800. A one-quarter allocation would attribute $900 of the mortgage interest and real estate taxes and $2,200 of the other expenses to the writer's business. The writer's gross income of $1,500 is reduced by the $900 allocable to the mortgage interest and real estate taxes, leaving $600 as the maximum amount of expenses relating to work space which may be deducted. Since the remaining expenses, in fact, total $2,200, the writer will lose the opportunity to deduct $1,600 because the income from writing was not large enough to match against the expenses. A writer who rents will make a simpler calculation, since the expenses attributable to a home office or studio will simply be subtracted from gross income from writing and any excess expenses will not be deductible. This provision of the Tax Reform Act of 1976 will work a hardship on the many writers who sacrifice to pursue their writing despite not earning large incomes.

Professional Equipment

The cost of professional equipment having a useful life of more than one year cannot be fully deducted in the year of purchase but must be depreciated. Again, IRS Publication 534, *Tax Information on Depreciation*, will aid in the computation of depreciation.

The useful life of professional equipment will vary, but a good faith estimate based on the personal knowledge and experience of the writer (or upon the guidelines of the more complex Class Life Asset Depreciation Range System described in Publication 534) will be acceptable. The salvage value of an asset (other than a house) having a useful life of three years or more may be reduced by 10 percent of the asset's original cost for depreciation calculations, and thus a salvage value of less than 10 percent will not affect the depreciation computation at all. Bonus depreciation of 20 percent of original cost may be added to the first year depreciation of an asset (other than a house) having a useful life of at least six years—as computed in Publication 534. If an asset becomes worthless before expiration of its estimated useful life, the remaining basis is claimed as depreciation in the year of worthlessness.

Travel, Transportation, and Entertainment

Travel, transportation, and entertainment expenses for business purposes are deductible, but must meet strict record keeping requirements. Travel expenses are the ordinary and necessary expenses, including meals, lodging, and transportation, incurred for travel away from home in pursuit of professional activities.[9] Such expenses would be deductible, for example, if the writer traveled to another city to conduct interviews and do research for an article and stayed several days to complete the work. If the writer doesn't have to sleep or rest while away from home, transportation expenses are limited to the cost of travel (but commuting expenses are not deductible as transportation expenses). Entertainment expenses, whether business luncheons or parties or similar items, are deductible as long as the expense is incurred for the purpose of developing business. Business gifts may be made to individuals, but no deduction will be allowed for gifts to any one individual in excess of $25 during the tax year. Accurate records detailing business purpose, date, place, and cost are particularly important for all these deductions. The writer should also get into the habit of writing these details on copies of bills or credit card charge receipts. IRS Publication 463, *Travel, Entertainment and*

Gift Expenses, gives more details, including the current mileage charge should the writer own andd use a car. Also, self- promotional items, such as advertising, printing business cards, or sending Christmas greetings to professional associates, are deductible expenses.

Commissions, Fees, and Salaries

Commissions paid to agents and fees paid to lawyers or accountants for business purposes are tax deductible, as are the salaries paid to typists, researchers, and others. However, the writer should try to hire people as independent contractors rather than employees, in order to avoid liability for social security, disability, and withholding tax payments. This can be done by hiring on a job-for-job basis, with each job to be completed by a deadline, preferably at a place chosen by the person hired. Record keeping expenses and taxes will be saved, although Form 1099, *Statement for Recipients of Miscellaneous Income*, must be filed for each independent contractor paid more than $600 in one year by the writer.

Schedule C

The completion of Schedule C—by use of the guidelines in this chapter—finishes much, but not all, of the writer's tax preparations. The next chapter discusses other important tax provisions—not reflected on Schedule C—which can aid the writer or which the writer must observe.

SCHEDULE C (Form 1040)

Department of the Treasury
Internal Revenue Service

Profit or (Loss) From Business or Profession
(Sole Proprietorship)
Partnerships, Joint Ventures, etc., Must File Form 1065.

► Attach to Form 1040. ► See Instructions for Schedule C (Form 1040).

1976

Name of proprietor	Social security number
Alice Writer	000 ¦ 00 ¦ 000

A Principal business activity (see Schedule C Instructions) ► Writer ; product ► writing

B Business name ► .... C Employer identification number ► ....

D Business address (number and street) ► 125 Epistle Street
City, State and ZIP code ► Hollywood, Florida

E Indicate method of accounting: (1) [X] Cash (2) ☐ Accrual (3) ☐ Other ► ....

F Were you required to file Form W-3 or Form 1096 for 1976 (see Schedule C Instructions)? . . . . | Yes |
If "Yes," where filed ► ....

G Was an Employer's Quarterly Federal Tax Return, Form 941, filed for this business for any quarter in 1976? . . . . .

H Method of inventory valuation ► NA .... Was there any substantial change in
the manner of determining quantities, costs, or valuations between the opening and closing inventories? (If "Yes," attach explanation) . . .

Income

1 Gross receipts or sales $........... Less: returns and allowances $........... Balance ►	1	15,592
2 Less: Cost of goods sold and/or operations (Schedule C–1, line 8)	2	0
3 Gross profit	3	15,592
4 Other income (attach schedule)	4	0
5 Total income (add lines 3 and 4)	5	15,592

Deductions

6 Depreciation (explain in Schedule C–3)	6	420
7 Taxes on business and business property (explain in Schedule C–2)	7	
8 Rent on business property	8	2,400
9 Repairs (explain in Schedule C–2)	9	
10 Salaries and wages not included on line 3, Schedule C–1 (exclude any paid to yourself) .	10	1,556
11 Insurance	11	
12 Legal and professional fees	12	727
13 Commissions	13	1,250
14 Amortization (attach statement)	14	
15 (a) Pension and profit-sharing plans (see Schedule C Instructions)	15(a)	
(b) Employee benefit programs (see Schedule C Instructions)	(b)	
16 Interest on business indebtedness	16	
17 Bad debts arising from sales or services	17	
18 Depletion	18	

19 Other business expenses (specify):

(a) Advertising	75	
(b) Entertainment	157	
(c) Postage	92	
(d) Professional dues	45	
(e) Stationery	35	
(f) Telephone	341	
(g) Telephone Answering Service	120	
(h) Travel	82	
(i) Utilities	359	
(j) Miscellaneous	143	

(k) Total other business expenses (add lines 19(a) through 19(j))	19(k)	1,449
20 Total deductions (add lines 6 through 19(k))	20	7,802

21 Net profit or (loss) (subtract line 20 from line 5). Enter here and on Form 1040, line 29. ALSO enter on Schedule SE, line 5(a)	21	7,790

SCHEDULE C–1.—Cost of Goods Sold and/or Operations (See Schedule C Instructions for Line 2)

1 Inventory at beginning of year (if different from last year's closing inventory, attach explanation) . . .	1	
2 Purchases $........... Less: cost of items withdrawn for personal use $........... Balance ►	2	
3 Cost of labor (do not include salary paid to yourself)	3	
4 Materials and supplies	4	
5 Other costs (attach schedule)	5	
6 Total of lines 1 through 5	6	
7 Less: Inventory at end of year	7	
8 Cost of goods sold and/or operations. Enter here and on line 2 above	8	

Did you claim a deduction for expenses of an office in your home? . . . . [X] Yes ☐

SCHEDULE C-2.—Explanation of Lines 7 and 9

No.	Explanation	Amount	Line No.	Explanation	Amount
		$			$

SCHEDULE C-3.—Depreciation (See Schedule C Instructions for Line 6)

If you need more space, use Form 4562.

a. Description of property	b. Date acquired	c. Cost or other basis	d. Depreciation allowed or allowable in prior years	e. Method of computing depreciation	f. Life or rate	g. Depreciation for this year
Total additional first-year depreciation (do not include in items below)		20% of $300.00				60
Other depreciation: File Cabinets	1/2/76	240.00		straight line	8	30
Home Office Improvements	1/25/74	3,300.00	660.00	straight line	10	330
3 Totals		3,540.00				420
4 Less amount of depreciation claimed in Schedule C–1, page 1						0
5 Balance—Enter here and on page 1, line 6						420

SCHEDULE C-4.—Expense Account Information (See Schedule C Instructions for Schedule C-4)

Enter information with regard to yourself and your five highest paid employees. In determining the five highest paid employees, expense account allowances must be added to their salaries and wages. However, the information need not be submitted for any employee for whom the combined amount is less than $25,000, or for yourself if your expense account allowance plus line 21, page 1, is less than $25,000.

	Name	Expense account	Salaries and Wages
Owner	. . . .		
1			
2			
3			
4			
5			

Did you claim a deduction for expenses connected with:

(1) Entertainment facility (boat, resort, ranch, etc.)? . . ☐ Yes ☐ No (3) Employees' families at conventions or meetings? . . ☐ Yes ☐ No

(2) Living accommodations (except employees on business)? ☐ Yes ☐ No (4) Employee or family vacations not reported on Form W–2? ☐ Yes ☐ No

10
Income Taxation: II

The writer must also be aware of a number of other tax benefits and obligations in order to be able to make rational choices and to seek professional advice when necessary. These provisions, while not gathered neatly in one place as income and expenses are on Schedule C, are of great significance to the writer.

Self-Employment Tax

The social security system of the United States creates numerous benefits for those who have contributed from their earnings to the federal social security system. It provides benefits for a person's family in the event of death or disablement as well as providing a pension and certain medical insurance. Writers, whether employees or self-employed, are covered by the system. Since the payments for social security are not automatically withheld for a self-employed writer, as they are for one who is an employee, the self-employed writer must file, with the Form 1040, a Schedule SE, *Computation of Social Security Self-Employment Tax*, and pay the self-employment tax shown on the Schedule SE. Self-employment income is basically the net income of the writer reported on Schedule C, subject to certain adjustments. If a writer and spouse both earn self-employment income, each must file a separate Schedule SE. If a writer has more than one business, the combined earnings should be totaled on Schedule SE for purposes of calculating the self-employment tax.

Social security coverage to gain the various benefits is created by having a certain number of years during which a worker makes payments for social security. A self-employed writer must, in any case, make social security payments for each year when net self-employment income is more than $400, but when the writer does so a year of work credit is recorded for social security benefits. If a minimum number of years of work credit is established, the writer qualifies for benefits. Some benefits require the writer to be "fully insured" (that is, have at least ten years of work credit), while other benefits only require that the writer be "currently insured" (that is, have at least six quarters of coverage in the thirteen-quarter period ending when benefits are to begin). The amount of benefits is based on average yearly earnings covered by social security. Therefore, the writer benefits by paying self-employment tax each year on the maximum permissible amount of self-employment income. The maximum amount of income on which tax must be paid has been increasing constantly over the years: for example, from $15,300 in 1976 to $16,500 in 1977.

Calculation of the self-employment tax is done by first taking all income from employers from which the social security tax has already been withheld and subtracting that from the maximum amount of income on which tax must be paid to determine how much tax must be paid on the remaining self-employment income. In 1977 the social security tax rate was 7.9 percent for the self-employed, but these rates are scheduled to increase. For 1977 the maximum self-employment tax is $1,303.50, payable if the income to be taxed, as shown on Schedule SE, is $16,500 or more.

Further information as to the computation of the self-employment tax can be found in IRS Publication 533, *Information on Self-Employment Tax*. Additional information as to the benefits available under social security to either the writer or the writer's family is available from the local office of the Social Security Administration, including pamphlets titled "Your Social Security" and "If You're Self-Employed. . . Reporting Your Income for Social Security."

A retired writer's monthly social security benefits may be reduced if the writer has "excess income" from self-employment and wages. If such an excess exists, however, it only reduces benefits in those months when the writer did a substantial amount of work (at least fifteen hours of writing during the month). A writer receiving $75 per month in benefits might have $600 in excess income for the year, but if the writer did less than fifteen hours work for seven months of that year, then only five months of benefits would be lost ($375) rather than the total of the excess earnings ($600). For this reason, the writer receiving benefits should keep a record of time spent writing each month. Also, royalties attributable to works created and copyrighted prior to the taxable year in which the writer turns sixty-five will be excluded from the calculations of excess income if such royalties are received between ages sixty-five and seventy-two. Upon reaching age seventy-two the benefits are not reduced even if excess income is earned.[1]

Estimated Tax

Employers withhold income and social security taxes from the wages of their employees. However, the self-employed writer must pay income and social security taxes in quarterly installments computed on Form 1040-SE, *Estimated Tax Declaration Voucher*, and mailed on or before April 15, June 15, September 15, and January 15. In most cases, Form 1040-SE is required if the writer estimates that the total of income and self-employment taxes for the next tax year will exceed any withheld taxes by $100 or more. IRS Publication 505, *Tax Withholding and Declaration of Estimated Tax*, gives more detailed information regarding the estimated tax.

Retirement Plans

Keogh plans now permit a self-employed person like a writer to contribute the lesser of 15 percent of net self-employment income or $7,500 to a retirement fund and to deduct the amount of the contribution from gross income when computing income taxes. The writer will be allowed a minimum deduction of the lesser of

$750 or 100 percent of self-employment income (but, to qualify for this minimum, the writer's adjusted gross income must not exceed $15,000 computed on an individual basis). However, the deduction is allowed in any year only if the writer places the amount to be deducted in one of the following retirement funds: a trust, annuity contracts from an insurance company, a custodial account with a bank or other person, special U.S. government retirement bonds, or certain face-amount certificates purchased from investment companies. Even if the writer is employed by a company with a retirement program, the writer still may have a Keogh plan for self-employment income from the writing career. Originally a contribution to a Keogh plan had to be made before December 31 to be deductible in that tax year. But with an appropriate election, such a contribution can now be made before the filing date of the tax return, which is usually the following April 15 or any extensions of the filing date, as long as the Keogh plan was in existence during the tax year for which the deduction is to be taken. Because the money contributed to a Keogh plan is deductible, there are penalties for withdrawal of monies from a plan prior to age 59½ unless the writer becomes permanently disabled. Distributions are taxed when made, and must begin no later than age 70½. The writer's tax bracket then, however, may be much lower than when contributions are made. It should be kept in mind that employees will probably have to be covered if the writer begins a Keogh plan. More information about Keogh plans can be obtained from the institutions, such as the local bank or insurance company, which administer them. Also helpful are IRS publications 560, *Retirement Plans for Self-Employed Individuals,* and 566, *Questions and Answers on Retirement Plans for the Self-Employed.*

Separate from the Keogh plan, the writer can begin an Individual Retirement Account. This account is for persons who do not have a Keogh plan and whose employers do not provide any retirement plan. By creation of such an account, the writer may contribute into a retirement fund up to $1,500 per year (or only 15 percent of wages and professional fees, if that is less than $1,500). A married writer with a nonworking spouse may be able to contribute $1,750 to benefit both spouses. The amount of the contribution is a deduction from gross income. Again the funds contributed must be taken out of the writer's hands and placed in a trust, a custodial account with a bank or other person, annuity contracts with a life insurance company, or special U.S. Government retirement bonds. The payment, to be deductible, must be made not more than forty-five days after December 31 of the tax year in which the deduction will be taken. More information can be obtained from the institutions administering Individual Retirement Accounts, as well as IRS Publication 590, *Tax Information on Individual Retirement Savings Programs.*

Keogh plan contributions are claimed on Form 1040, line 40a, and Individual Retirement Account contributions are claimed on Form 1040, line 40b. The writer should consult with the Keogh Plan or Individual Retirement Account administrator to determine what additional forms may have to be filed.

Income Averaging

Income averaging might be a valuable tax saving device for the writer when there is a large increase in the writer's taxable income for one tax year as compared to the previous years. The effect of averaging, which is computed on Schedule G of Form 1040, is to treat a certain amount of the extra income realized in the current tax year as if it had actually been received over the preceding four years. Substantial savings result because of the progressive nature of the tax structure. IRS Publication 506, *Computing Your Tax Under the Income Averaging Method*, should be consulted for details.

Deferred Payments and Installment Sales

Any writer, especially one who is highly successful financially, may wish to defer income until the future.[2] This can be done by agreeing in a contract for the sale of literary property that royalty payments will not be greater than a certain amount in any year. Excess royalties are carried over to be paid to the writer in the future. For this strategy to save on taxes, of course, the writer must be in a lower tax bracket when the deferred amounts are finally paid. Also, the writer will usually not receive interest on the deferred payments and must face the risk of the publisher becoming insolvent. And if the writer should suddenly need the deferred payments, they will not be available.

An amateur writer—someone who earns a living in another occupation, such as sports or politics—may sell literary property on an installment basis if the sale price is greater than $1,000 and no more than 30 percent of the sale price is received in the year in which the sale occurs (that is, when the manuscript is delivered and assigned to the publisher).[3] Gains from the sale will be taxed as the installment payments are received by the writer. The proportion of the total gain taxed each year will be based upon the proportion of installment payments received during that year to the total sale price.

The writer considering either a deferred payment contract or an installment sale will be well advised to seek the advice of a lawyer.

Investment Credit

Apart from depreciation, another significant tax consideration for the writer's equipment (but not applicable to buildings) is the investment tax credit. This gives a tax reduction equal to 7 percent of the investment in new or used (if used, only to the amount of $50,000) depreciable property. The amount of the credit hinges on the length of the asset's useful life, and the useful life for purposes of computing the investment credit must be the same as the useful life for depreciation purposes. The basis for depreciation is not, however, reduced by the amount of the investment credit. To get the full 7 percent, the asset must have an expected useful life of seven years or more. The 7 percent credit is only allowed on two-thirds of the investment if the useful life is five to seven years, and on one-third of the investment if the useful life is three to five years. No investment credit is available for assets having useful lives of less than three years. Form 3468, *Computation of Investment Credit*, is used for the computation and sets forth some limitations on such credit. Early disposition of the asset causes recapture of part of the investment credit on Form 4255. The final entry from Form 3468 is made on Form 1040, line 29.

The Tax Reduction Act of 1975 increased the investment tax credit to 10 percent (and, in the case of used property, increased the permissible amount to $100,000), but only for equipment placed in use after January 22, 1975. The Tax Reform Act of 1976 extended these increases through 1980. IRS Publication 572, *Tax Information on the Investment Credit,* contains additional information regarding the investment credit.

Net Operating Losses

The writer who experiences a business loss as determined on Schedule C will carry the loss to Form 1040 where it is eventually subtracted from gross income in the calculations to reach taxable income. However, if the loss is large enough to wipe out other taxable income for the year, the excess loss can first be carried back to reduce taxable income in previous taxable years and then carried forward to reduce taxable income in future taxable years. This is quite likely to happen when a professional writer is changing over from being employed to devoting all working time to writing. The result is that the writer will be entitled to a tax refund (if taxable income in previous years is reduced) or will save on taxes in future years. IRS Publication 536, *Losses from Operating a Business,* describes the net operating loss, but the writer will probably need an accountant's help for the computation of a net operating loss.

Bad Debts

A common error is the belief that if a writer (on the cash basis) sells a work for $1,000, and the purchaser never pays, the writer can take a bad debt deduction. The writer cannot, since the $1,000 purchase price has never been received and included in income. As stated in Publication 334, *Tax Guide for Small Businesses,* "Worthless debts arising from sales, professional services rendered . . . and similar items of income will not be allowed as bad debt deductions unless the income from those items has been included in gross income in the return for the year for which the deduction is claimed or for a previous year."

A cash basis taxpayer can, however, gain a tax benefit from either business or nonbusiness bad debts of the proper kind. In almost all cases, the writer's bad debts will be nonbusiness. For example, if the writer makes a loan to a friend who never repays the loan, the amount of the loan will be a nonbusiness bad debt. The loan cannot be a gift, however, and must be legally enforceable against the borrower. The nonbusiness bad debt deduction is taken in the year the debt becomes worthless. It is reported as a short-term capital loss on Schedule D.

Contributions

Contributions to qualified organizations are deductible if personal deductions are itemized on Schedule A. Since the writer's own copyrights, manuscripts, and similar property usually have a tax basis of zero (or, at most, a basis of those costs which were attributable to the work but were not deducted as current expenses when incurred), the writer's deduction is limited to such basis. Numerous bills have been proposed to rectify this inequitable treatment, and perhaps the writer will soon be able to deduct either part or all of the fair maket value of contributions.

Gifts

The writer can avoid paying income taxes by giving away the writer's creations. If the family member or other person who receives the gift is in a lower tax bracket than the writer, the recipient will pay less in taxes than the writer would have. Gifts over certain amounts, however, are subject to the gift tax. The making of gifts and the gift tax are discussed on pp. 206–207, but careful planning is a necessity if gifts are to be effectively used in tax planning.

Child and Disabled Dependent Care

The Tax Reform Act of 1976 changed the deduction for child or disabled dependent care into a tax credit. The amount of the credit is 20 percent of the employment related expenses which a writer pays in order to be gainfully employed. Basically, this credit is available to the writer who maintains a household including either a child under age fifteen or a disabled dependent or spouse for the care of whom it is necessary to hire someone so the writer can gainfully pursue employment, self-employment, or the search for employment. The amount and availability of this credit are subject to limitations which are described in greater detail in IRS Publication 503, *Child Care and Disabled Dependent Care.*

Employee Expenses

Often writers who work as employees will find that they are required to incur expenses in the performance of their duties. The nature of the expenses is the same as the expenses which a self-employed person could deduct—supplies, work space, equipment, travel, telephone, and so on. These expenses, if ordinary and necessary, will be deductible. However, the employee can deduct certain of these expenses from gross income in the calculation to reach adjusted gross income, while other of the expenses can only be deducted if the taxpayer uses Schedule A for itemized deductions in the calculation to reach taxable income from adjusted gross income.

The expenses which are deductible from gross income are: (1) expenses for travel, meals, and lodging while away from home in the performance of services as an employee; (2) expenses covered by a reimbursement or other expense allowance arrangement by the employer; (3) expenses for business transportation (commuting, of course, is not included); or (4) an employee's moving expenses. Moving expenses are entered on Form 3903, *Moving Expense Adjustment,* and the other expenses appear on Form 2106, *Employee Business Expenses.* College professors, for example, are usually expected to undertake lecturing, writing, and independent research as part of their contribution to the advancement of knowledge. If a professor incurs travel or transportation expenses in order to give a reading, such expenses would be entered on Form 2106 and taken as a deduction from gross income.

Other employee expenses, unless reimbursed, are deductible

only if itemized deductions are taken on Schedule A. For example, the cost of professional journals, postage, photocopying, and so on would be taken as deductions on Schedule A under line 33 which reads "Other (itemize)." The itemization can be done on a separate page or Form 2106 can again be used with the entries made under Part II for "Employee Business Expenses which are Deductible if You Itemize Deductions on Schedule A." Employees will find it difficult after the Tax Reform Act of 1976 to take a home office deduction, since the stringent standards applicable to the self-employed must be met and, in addition, the home office must be maintained for the employer's convenience.

American Writers Living Abroad

American citizens, whether or not they live in the United States, are taxable by the United States government on all of their income from anywhere in the world. However, a tax benefit for many American citizens living abroad has been the exclusion from American taxable income of either $20,000 or $25,000 of earned income from foreign sources.[4] The Tax Reform Act of 1976 reduces the exclusion to $15,000 for taxable years beginning after December 31, 1975. The exclusion can result in tax benefits where the tax rates of the foreign country—such as Ireland, where a qualified writer can live tax free (discussed on pp. 217–218)—are lower than the tax rates in the United States.

Publication 54, *Tax Guide for U.S. Citizens Abroad*, generally explains the guidelines for eligibility for these exclusions. The basic requirement is either a one-year residence or a physical presence in a foreign country and earned income created from work done in the foreign country. Residence is a flexible concept based on the circumstances of each individual. While the residence must be uninterrupted (for example, by owning or renting a home continually), remaining abroad for all of the taxable year in question isn't necessary. Brief trips to the United States do not affect the tax status as a resident abroad. However, the length of each visit and the total time spent in the United States must be watched carefully. Physical presence requires the taxpayer to be present in a foreign country or countries for at least 510 days during a period of eighteen consecutive months. Regardless of which test is met, the income to be excluded must be received no later than the year after the year in which the work was performed which generated the income.

Assuming the writer met either the residence or physical presence test, the requirement that the income to be excluded had to be earned income often proved fatal to the writer's attempt to benefit from the exclusion. The reason for this was the definition, still found in Publication 54, of certain types of writer's income as unearned:

> If you write a book and sell the manuscript outright. . . , the proceeds you receive are not earned income any more than the proceeds from the sale of your car or any other item of property would be . . .
>
> If, on the other hand, you enter into a contract to write a book or series of articles. . . , for a flat amount in cash or a certain amount of cash plus a commission on the sale of your literary or musical works, your renumeration is earned income . . .

Since many writers work independently, this definition made the income received by such writers unearned income which was not eligible for the exclusion from United States taxable income.

This unjust situation has been substantially rectified, however, by a case involving a painter, Mark Tobey, while he was a resident of Switzerland. Artists had been subjected to a rule identical to that applied to writers. In *Tobey* v. *Commissioner*[5] the issue before the Tax Court was whether Mark Tobey, all of whose "works were executed . . . without prior commission, contract, order, or any such prior arrangement," had earned income such that he could avail himself of the $25,000 exclusion from United States taxable income. The court, noting that *earned* generally implies a product of one's own work, reasoned:

> The concept of the artist as not "earning" his income for the purposes of Section 911 would place him in an unfavorable light. For the most part, the present day artist is a hardworking, trained, career-oriented individual. His education,

whether acquired formally or through personal practice, growth and experience, is often costly and exacting. He has keen competition from many other artists who must create and sell their works to survive. To avoid discriminatory treatment, we perceive no sound reasons for treating income earned by the personal efforts, skill and creativity of a Tobey or a Picasso any differently from the income earned by a confidence man, a brain surgeon, a movie star or, for that matter, a tax attorney.

This rationale necessarily led to the conclusion that Tobey's income was earned. Unfortunately, this decision can be relied upon only with the following warning. The Internal Revenue Service has not acquiesced in *Tobey* v. *Commissioner*, which means the Service reserves the right to challenge each person claiming the exclusion. This procedure may ultimately bring the different United States Circuit Courts into conflict, thus creating the groundwork for a definitive determination by the Supreme Court. Keeping this in mind, however, *Tobey* v. *Commissioner* is at present persuasive as to the writer's income being earned regardless of whether the income is derived from contractual commitments or independent sales. In fact, the Authors League has successfully challenged an IRS determination that a nonresident writer's royalties were unearned income, but that case is not a precedent binding on the IRS.[6]

Each writer hoping to benefit from the exclusion for income earned abroad must, of course, consult with a lawyer or an accountant to determine the effect of the foregoing legal provisions on each unique situation. Writers already living abroad should also inquire at their American consulate to determine whether any treaty regarding taxation between the United States and the country in which they live might affect their tax status. Then, noting the refusal of the Internal Revenue Service to acquiesce in *Tobey* v. *Commissioner*, writers satisfying either the residence or physical presence test may legitimately claim the benefits of the exclusion for earned income created during their stay abroad.

The writer living abroad should also consider whether any income taxes paid to a foreign government may be taken as either a deduction or tax credit. However, the Tax Reform Act of 1976 provides that no credit or deduction will be allowed on foreign income taxes paid on earned income excluded from United States taxation.[7] IRS Publication 514, *Foreign Tax Credit for U.S. Citizens and Resident Aliens*, explains these provisions further.

Foreign Writers in the United States

Foreign writers who are residents in the United States are generally taxed the same as United States citizens. Foreign writers who are not residents in the United States should seek legal advice with respect to their taxes, since they are taxed under special and complex rules.[8] A foreigner who is merely visiting or whose stay is limited by immigration laws will usually be considered a nonresident. A foreigner who intends, at least temporarily, to establish a home in the United States and has a visa permitting permanent residence will probably be considered a resident. Treaties may also affect the income tax treatment of a foreign writer. IRS Publication 519, *United States Tax Guide for Aliens*, should be consulted by foreign writers for a more extensive discussion of their tax status.

Forms of Doing Business

Depending on the success of the writer, various forms of doing business might be considered. There may be both business and tax advantages to conducting the writer's business in the form of a corporation or partnership, but there may be disadvantages as well.[9]

Generally, the nontax advantages of incorporation are limited liability for the stockholders (which means that a judgment in a lawsuit can affect only the assets of the corporation but not the personal assets of the writer), centralized management, access to capital, transferability of ownership, and continuity of the business. Two types of corporations exist—the regular corporation and the Subchapter S corporation. The tax treatment, however, differs significantly between the two types of corporations.

The Tax Reduction Act of 1975 and the Tax Reform Act of 1976 have temporarily lowered the tax rates for regular corporations, so that net corporate income is taxed at 20 percent to $25,000, 22 percent from $25,000 to $50,000, and 48 percent over $50,000. Usually the tax on the corporation can be substantially avoided by the payment of a salary to the writer, which creates a deduction for the corporation. Such an arrangement can effectively average the writer's income from year to year. The Subchapter S corporation is not taxed at all, but the income is credited directly to the accounts of the stockholders and they are taxed as individuals. Both types of corporations permit the writer to take certain business deductions which would not be possible as an individual proprietor. Thus, it is a deductible business expense for either type of corporation to maintain $50,000 worth of life insurance as well as medical insurance for the writer. However, while the regular corporation may deduct more for a pension plan than a contributor to a Keogh plan, the Subchapter S corporation may only create a retirement plan based on the same limitations as a Keogh plan would have. Some of the disadvantages of incorporation are additional record keeping, meetings, and paper work, as well as significant expenses both for the initial incorporation and for any ultimate dissolution.

A partnership is an agreement between two or more persons to join together as co-owners of a business in pursuit of profit. Partnerships are not subject to the income tax, but the individual partners are taxable on their share of the partnership income. Partners are personally liable for obligations incurred on behalf of the partnership by any of the partners. A partnership offers to the writer an opportunity to combine with investors under an agreement in which the investors may gain tax advantages by being allocated a greater share of partnership losses. A variation of the usual partnership often used in raising runds for theatrical productions is the "limited partnership," in which passive investors have limited liability (but the general partner, running the business actively, is still personally liable). Another variation is the "joint venture," which can simply be described as a partnership created for a single business venture.

Another form of organization is the nonprofit corporation or association. This would not be a relevant form for an individual writer, but could serve as a vehicle for an organization designed to serve writers. Such an organization could qualify for tax exemption if "organized and operated exclusively for religious, charitable, scientific, testing for public safety, literary, or educational purposes . . ."[10] The advantage of being tax exempt is that contributions made to the organization are tax deductible. The activities of the organization must be for exempt purposes. Merely publishing a magazine will often not be an exempt purpose, but the publication of a magazine in conjunction with other services such as workshops, panels, seminars, grants, and competitions should be sufficient.[11] Many magazines benefit by coming within the umbrella of a larger tax-exempt organization, such as a university. Tax-exempt status is obtained by a time-consuming process of application to the IRS, but the exemption letter given by the IRS is retroactive if the organization's activities have been consistent with the basis of its exemption.[12]

The writer contemplating doing business as a corporation or partnership should consult a lawyer for advice based on the writer's unique needs.

11
The Hobby Loss Challenge

Often the writer sufficiently dedicated to pursue a writing career despite year after year of losses on Schedule C will face a curious challenge from the IRS: that the losses incurred by the writer cannot be deducted for tax purposes because the writer was only pursuing a hobby and did not have the profit motive necessary to qualify the writing career as a business or trade.[1] A hobbyist in any field may deduct the expenses of the hobby only up to the amount of income produced by the hobby. For example, if a hobbyist makes $500 in a year on the sale of writing, only up to $500 in expenses can be deducted. On the other hand, a writer actively engaged in the business or trade of being a writer—one who pursues writing with a profit motive—may deduct all ordinary and necessary business expenses, even if such expenses far exceed income from writing activities for the year.

A Test: Two Years out of Five

But how can a writer determine whether the requisite profit motive is present to avoid being characterized as a hobbyist by the IRS? At the outset, there is an important threshold test in favor of the taxpayer.[2] This test, which was introduced in the Tax Reform Act of 1969, provides a presumption that a writer is engaged in a business or trade—and hence is not a hobbyist—if a net profit is created by the activity in question during two of the five consecutive years ending with the taxable year at issue. Thus, many writers who have good and bad years need not fear a hobby loss challenge to a loss in one of the bad years. A writer who has not been engaged in writing for five consecutive years may elect to have the determination as to profit motive suspended until after five consecutive years have passed. The disadvantage of this, however, is that if the writer is then determined to be a hobbyist, the IRS can collect on taxes owed for each of the five years.[3]

If a hobby loss problem is anticipated, writers on the cash basis may be able to create profitable years by regulating the time of receipt of income and the time of incurrence of expenses. For example, instead of having five years of small losses, a writer is far better off having two years where a small profit is earned and three years where larger than usual losses are incurred.

Profit Motive: The Nine Factors

But even if a writer does not have two profitable years in the last five years of activity as a writer, the contention by the IRS that the writer is a hobbyist can still be overcome if the writer can show a profit motive. The regulations to the Internal Revenue Code specifically provide for an objective standard to determine profit motive based on all the facts and circumstances surrounding the activity. Therefore, statements by the writer as to profit motive are given little weight. But the chance of making a profit can be quite unlikely, as long as the writer actually intends to be profitable.

The regulations set forth nine factors used to determine profit motive.[4] Since every writer is capable, in varying degrees, of pursuing writing in a manner which will be considered a trade or business, these factors can create an instructive model. The objective factors are considered in their totality, so that all the circumstances surrounding the activity will determine the result in a given case. Although most of the factors are important, no single factor will determine the result of a case. The writer should be aware that many IRS auditors are unfamiliar with these factors— both from a lack of familiarity with the regulations and because the regulations do not adequately reflect how the courts evaluate these factors with respect to writers. In particular, the auditors will often use a simplified guide titled "Tax Audit Guidelines and Techniques for Tax Technicians" which discusses the hobby loss factors only with reference to farmers. Such a guide is completely inadequate where writers are concerned. The nine factors follow:

1. *Manner in which the taxpayer carries on the activity.* The writer must establish effective business routines. Most importantly, there should be accurate bookkeeping procedures to record all receipts and expenses. A regularized system for correspondence, submissions, follow-ups, contracts, deadlines, and similar business matters will also be significant in showing profit motive.

2. *The expertise of the taxpayer or his advisors.* One important indication of expertise can be study. However, expertise can also be shown by publication credits, encouragement by agents or publishers, awards of prizes, memberships in professional organizations, recognition in critical publications, and the use of business advisors such as lawyers and accountants. Teaching, if the position is at least partially based on success as a writer, also shows expertise.

3. *The time and effort expended by the taxpayer in carrying on the activity.* Employment in another occupation does not mean the writer lacks a profit motive. But a reasonable amount of time—such as several hours each day—must be devoted to writing, preferably on a regular basis.

4. *Expectation that assets used in activity may appreciate in value.* This factor seldom has relevance to writers.

5. *The success of the taxpayer in carrying on other similar or dissimilar activities.* Past literary successes, either financial or critical, are relevant to present profit motive despite the fact that some period of inactivity may have occurred. This factor would not be relevant if a writer were just starting a career.

6. *The taxpayer's history of income or losses with respect to the activity.* Past income from writing is a very helpful factor. Also, increases in receipts from year to year would support having a profit motive. Losses may not be overly significant in showing the absence of a profit motive, unless expenses are vastly greater than receipts, income is being received from sources not related to writing, and the losses continue for a long period of time.

7. *The amount of occasional profits, if any, which are earned.*
Here receipts are contrasted with expenses, but disproportionate
expenses will be important only if the writer is wealthy enough to
gain tax benefits from taking losses. If such expenses are an
economic strain, such a disproportion will not have as great
weight.

8. *The financial status of the taxpayer.* The need for additional
income or the inability to support a hobby would show that the
pursuit of writing had a profit motive. However, wealth or other
substantial sources of income are factors which would be considered to make a profit motive less likely.

9. *Elements of personal pleasure or recreation.* This factor is
aimed more at gentlemen farmers than writers. The writer need
only be wary of this if the writing has involved substantial travel.
Otherwise writing is as difficult and demanding as any profession.

The Cases

A look at some typical hobby loss cases will illustrate the approach of the courts to these factors.

Case I: No Profit Motive

Charles Nemish began writing in high school.[5] During college
he wrote guides and articles and, after serving in the Naval Air
Corps during World War II, he wrote short stories based on his
wartime experiences. His gross receipts from writing in the 1940s
amounted to about $2,000. In 1951 he began working as a pilot
for United Air Lines, but he had sufficient free time to continue
writing and had gross receipts of about $2,500 in the 1950s. From
1958 to 1965 he wrote at least fourteen short stories which were
submitted—sometimes through literary agents—to the major
magazine markets, but a sale in 1958 was his sole success during
this period. Starting in the early 1960s, Nemish had two novels in
progress—*Orion* and *Mr. Gus.*

The IRS denied him any deductions in 1964 and 1965 for his
writing expenses, which had appeared as follows on the returns:

	1964	1965
Automobile expense....................	$ 972.00	$ 487.00
Travel expense and writing materials.....................	840.00	980.00
Home expense	418.00	289.00
Total	$2,230.00	$1,756.00

The tax court agreed with the IRS. Although Nemish had earned about $4,500 between 1940 and 1958, he had made no sales after 1958, while deducting an average of $1,500 per year for expenses (the court assumed that expenses prior to 1958, even if not claimed on the returns, had probably averaged about $1,500 per year). Thus, over a twenty-five-year period, expenses had been greatly in excess of income. Nemish, however, explained that he believed "sooner or later I am going to make a killing—it will be tremendous, these days a novel will go for hardly less than one hundred thousand dollars."[6]

The court stated, "Giving consideration to petitioner's adequate income from his full-time job as a pilot, to his enthusiasm for writing evident ever since he was a child, and the lack of profits over a 25-year period, we do not think he did his writing for financial gain."[7]

The lack of a profit motive means that losses will be disallowed, but the court also pointed out that the automobile and travel expenses had been incurred on trips to vacation areas such as Lake Tahoe and Reno. Even if Nemish had been found to have a profit motive with respect to his writing, the court would have denied a deduction for the travel expenses since, "We do not think the record justifies a finding that the expenses of his holiday excursions were incurred for business purposes."[8]

Case II: No Profit Motive

John Baltis graduated from college in 1948 and commenced work in the newspaper field.[9] In 1967 and 1968 he was a copy editor for the *San Francisco Chronicle*. During the same two years, he took deductions as a free-lance writer—$1,968 in 1967 and

$1,974 in 1968. Between 1948 and 1968 he had sold only three articles for a total of $550. Also, many of the claimed items of expense were for family visits. The tax court agreed with the IRS that no profit motive could be shown since the trips were "undertaken primarily for personal reasons . . . whatever free lance writing petitioner did either on these trips or as a consequence thereof was of such relatively minor significance that it did not constitute the carrying on of a trade or business."[10] The court also pointed out that "there was almost complete failure to substantiate the specific items which the Commissioner disallowed."[11] Accurate record keeping is essential for the substantiation of deductions.

Case III: No Profit Motive

John Chaloner, a wealthy individual, wrote and published books over a twenty-year period.[12] Little effort was made to sell the books and the receipts from sales were negligible. Chaloner claimed a deduction for the salaries of his secretaries, but their duties were not specified. The court concluded that no profit motive could be found and disallowed the deductions claimed for writing and publishing.

Case IV: No Profit Motive

Corliss Lamont, a philosopher who taught at Columbia University, lectured across the country on such topics as philosophy, civil liberties, and international affairs.[13] He also wrote numerous books and pamphlets about these subjects. He had independent wealth, so he could afford the continuous losses from his writing over a thirty-year period. The court concluded, "Although continuity and efficiency of operations are criteria which would tend to support the existence of a trade or business . . . the totality of circumstances surrounding Lamont's background, his interest in the wide dissemination of his ideas, his activities and financial status justifies the conclusion of the Tax Court, that a profit motive was lacking."[14]

Case V: A Profit Motive

Seymour Stern, a resident of Los Angeles, spent three hundred and thirty-five days in New York City during 1965.[15] He had been writing since 1926 and his credits included numerous articles and screenplays. Stern, an expert on the film director D. W. Griffith, had spent the time in New York researching and arranging D. W. Griffith's papers located at the Museum of Modern Art. The results of this work provided the basis for an issue of *Film Culture Magazine* published in 1965, and the contents of the magazine were then to be used in a hardcover book scheduled for future publication. Stern received no income from the magazine, but had a contract providing for standard author's royalties on the hardcover book.

The IRS sought to deny $6,040.00 of travel expenses claimed in 1965 in relation to the work done in New York City. It was argued that Stern was not in the business or trade of being a writer in 1965 and, also, that the expenses should be capitalized and recaptured. The court found in favor of Stern on both issues. Despite the lack of an immediate profit, the court concluded that Stern had "participated in that endeavor with a good faith expectation of making a profit."[16] The expense, therefore, was deductible as a business expense. Moreover, the court disagreed with the capitalization argument. Capitalization would have basically allowed Stern to deduct the $6,040.00 of expenses only when income from the book was received in the future. The court indicated capitalization might be required if the writer were a hobbyist or if the payments were for securing a copyright and plates which were to belong to the person making the payments. For Stern, however, the expenses were ordinary and necessary business expenses which could be fully deducted in 1965 when they were incurred.

Case VI: A Profit Motive

Cornelius Vanderbilt, Jr., commenced his career as a writer in 1919 and pursued it with great success for two decades.[17] Although his wealthy family took him off his allowance early in his writing career, he persevered and published numerous books and articles in addition to founding newspapers and a news service syndicate. Motion picture producers purchased a number of his stories, and he began a successful lecturing career in 1929. During World War II, active military duty in the army interrupted Mr. Vanderbilt's civilian activities. In 1942 he inherited substantial wealth, but suffered several heart attacks which required hospitalization and, eventually, caused his discharge from the service.

He resumed his writing and lecturing career after the war. The lectures often dealt with travel and current foreign affairs topics, and much of Mr. Vanderbilt's writing—including several books —was devoted to these same topics. His business activities involved a substantial amount of travel, causing the following imbalance between receipts and deductions from writing:

Year	Income from Trusts and Dividends	Receipts from Business	Business Deductions	Net Profit (or Loss) from Business
1949	$39,671.93	$ 3,800.00	$26,010.63	($22,210.63)
1950	39,354.60	4,852.00	23,239.30	(18,387.30)
1951	41,082.67	6,702.67	30,175.90	(23,473.23)
1952	40,088.35	9,512.58	33,179.45	(23,666.87)
1953	57,377.67	1,794.16	38,394.00	(36,599.84)
1954	44,145.49	17,828.31	64,126.17	(46,297.86)
1955	36,865.95	48,850.43	39,523.27	9,277.16

The IRS sought to disallow the entire amount of business deductions claimed in 1951—$30,175.90—on the rationale that Mr. Vanderbilt was not in the business or trade of being a writer in that year as shown by the following factors: "(1) petitioner's large losses over a number of years with no indication from the record of a possibility of profit, (2) his background of inherited wealth as a guardian against financial disaster while engaged in his writing and lecturing activities, (3) his inattention to practical business details of his venture . . . and (4) his general propensity towards engaging in this field of endeavor whether it resulted in profit or not. . . ."[18] The court disagreed with the IRS's characterization of Vanderbilt's career as bearing "a strong resemblance to that of a romanticist and adventurer."[19] Instead, the court noted that Vanderbilt had worked at writing with great commercial success prior to the war and continued to take his work seriously when he was able to resume working. Despite the losses after the war, the court believed Mr. Vanderbilt had a profit motive in 1951 and was engaged in the business or trade of being a writer. The court allowed all ordinary and necessary expenses, including expenses for travel to gather material, legal expenses incurred in negotiating sales, and an outlay in 1951 to pay part of a libel judgment rendered against Vanderbilt in 1924. However, the court concluded that Vanderbilt's wife lacked a bona fide business purpose in accompanying her husband abroad and her travel expenses were not deductible.

Case VII: A Profit Motive

Marian Crymes lived in Washington, D.C., in 1966 and 1967 and worked as a proofreader for the Bureau of National Affairs.[20] Since 1960 she had been working on two booklets—"Component Good" and "Integral Spirituality"—which she wished to have reach a teen-age reading public. In 1967 she paid $1,288.97 to print one hundred copies of each of the booklets. She copyrighted the booklets and offered to sell the books to a foundation, while writing letters to others who might wish to sell the books more widely.

The court agreed with the IRS that she was not in the trade or profession of being a writer in 1967. Thus, her expenses could not be deducted as the ordinary and necessary business expenses of a writer. But the court did believe that she had a profit motive, as shown by her attempts to sell the booklets, despite her lack of success. The expenses of producing the booklets were, therefore, deductible under a section of the Internal Revenue Code permitting the deduction of ordinary and necessary expenses incurred for the production of income. The court pointed out that "the proper test is not the reasonableness of the taxpayer's belief that a profit will be realized, but whether the enterprise is entered into and carried on in good faith and for the purpose of making a profit . . ."[21]

An Overview

Writers with wealth and independent incomes, whose writing expenses are large relative to their receipts over a lengthy period, are most likely to be found to be pursuing a hobby. Writers who devote much time to their work, who have the expertise to receive some recognition, and for whom the expenses of writing are burdensome will probably be found to be engaged in a business or trade rather than a hobby. Younger writers, who are making the financial sacrifices so common to the beginning of a writing career, should be found by the courts to have a profit motive even if other employment is necessary for survival during this difficult early period. As the tax court stated in a notable decision in favor of an artist, "It is well recognized that profits may not be immediately forthcoming in the creative art field. Examples are legion of the increase in value of a painter's works after he receives public acclaim. Many artists have to struggle in their early years. This does not mean that serious artists do not intend to profit from their activities. It only means that their lot is a difficult one."[22]

Each case where a writer is challenged as a hobbyist requires a determination on its own facts, but an awareness on the part of the writer as to what factors are relevant should aid in preventing or, if necessary, meeting such a challenge. It is advisable to have the professional assistance of an accountant or lawyer as soon as a hobby loss issue arises on an audit. Such professional advisors can be particularly helpful in effectively presenting the factors favorable to the writer. The presence of a lawyer or accountant at the earliest conferences with the IRS can aid in bringing a hobby loss challenge to a quick and satisfactory resolution.

12
The Writer's Estate

Estate planning should begin during the writer's lifetime with the assistance of a lawyer and, if necessary, an accountant, a life insurance agent, and an officer of a bank's trusts and estates department. Writers, like other taxpayers, seek to dispose of their assets to the people and institutions of their choice, while reducing the amounts of income taxes during life and estate taxes at death. This chapter cannot substitute for consultation and careful planning with professional advisors, but it can at least alert the writer to matters of importance which will enable more effective participation in the process of planning the estate.

Written Works

Written works are unique because they are the creation of the writer and possess aesthetic qualities not found in other assets which pass through an estate. The writer may wish to exert posthumous control over a number of artistic decisions. For example, should unpublished works be published after the writer's death? If such works are published, may they be edited and, if so, by whom? If works are incomplete, can someone else finish the works so they can be published? If this is permitted, who will do the additional writing and how shall the authorship credits appear? The manner of publication—for example, hardcover or paperback—can be an issue as well. And is the writer willing to have works exploited as films, on records, or as the genesis for novelty items? Each of these artistic decisions will also have financial implications for the writer's estate.

Related issues involve the writer's personal papers. Who will be allowed to publish letters written by the writer? In what manner must the publication be undertaken? Who will have permission to look at the writer's rough drafts, notebooks, and diaries? Who will have access to letters received by the writer? And if the writer wishes to designate an official biographer, how will this affect the estate's willingness to make information available to other researchers and the public at large?

The writer who donates manuscripts and personal papers to a university or museum may wish to know in advance the treatment which will be accorded the donated materials. For example, Frances Steloff had been active in the literary world for over fifty-five years. She accumulated letters from such writers as Ezra Pound, Gertrude Stein, Bertrand Russell, and Thornton Wilder. This collection was given to New York University on the understanding that it be kept in a James Joyce room to be created in the new library. When Miss Steloff found that no James Joyce room had been provided for by the university, she took back her collection and donated it to the Berg Collection of the New York Public Library.[1] But what if a writer's executors are faced with a similar situation? How are they to know what the writer would have wished? If they do know, will they have the power to rectify such a breach of promise by a cultural institution? And can heirs be required to obey the writer's wishes with respect to the work?

In 1945 Eugene O'Neill entrusted the original manuscript of *Long Day's Journey into Night* to his editor, Bennett Cerf, at Random House. A written agreement between O'Neill and Random House provided that the play should only be published twenty-five years after O'Neill's death. At that time an advance of $5,000 would be paid to his estate's executors or administrators. Within two years of O'Neill's death in 1953, however, his widow Carlotta demanded that Random House publish the play. Cerf felt honor-bound not to do so, but his desire to follow O'Neill's wishes simply resulted in Carlotta withdrawing the manuscript from Random House and having it published by the Yale University

Press. She had the power to do this as executrix under O'Neill's will. O'Neill also left in his estate an unfinished manuscript of *More Stately Mansions.* He had told Carlotta shortly before his death that, "Nobody must be allowed to finish my play. . . . I don't want anybody else working on my plays." On a flyleaf placed in the manuscript of *More Stately Mansions* he had written, "Unfinished work. This script to be destroyed in case of my death!" Despite these admonitions, Carlotta permitted *More Stately Mansions* to be revised and eventually published and produced on Broadway as a new play by Eugene O'Neill.[2]

These examples could be multiplied, but their import for the writer is that lifetime planning is a necessity to ensure correct posthumous treatment of work passing through the estate.

The Will

A properly drafted will is crucial to any estate plan. Such a will is a written document, signed and witnessed under strictly observed formalities, which provides for the disposition of the property belonging to the maker of the will upon death. If the maker wishes to change the will, this can be done either by adding a codicil to the will or by drafting and signing a completely new will. If no will is made, property passes at death by the laws of intestacy. These laws vary from state to state, but generally provide for the property to pass to the writer's spouse and other relatives. An administrator, often a relative but sometimes not, is appointed by the court to manage the estate.

A will offers the opportunity to distribute property to specific people. Manuscripts and copyrights can, of course, be willed. For example:

> I give and bequeath all my right, title, and interest in and to my copyrights [describe which copyrights] and any royalties therefrom and the right to a renewal and extension of the said copyrights in such works to my daughter, JUNE.

A bequest means a transfer of property under a will, while a gift is used to mean a transfer of property during the life of the person who gives the property. It should be noted that the renewal right granted under the Copyright Act of 1909 cannot be willed if the writer's spouse or children are surviving, since in that case the renewal right would automatically pass to the spouse or children.[3]

Use of a will permits: (1) the payment of estate taxes in such a way that each recipient will not have any taxes assessed against bequests received, (2) the uninterrupted maintenance of insurance policies, and (3) the payment of storage and shipping costs so the recipient need not pay to receive bequests. The estate taxes are usually paid from the residuary of the estate, the residuary being all the property not specifically distributed elsewhere in the will.

The will allows a writer to choose the executor or executors of the estate. Since the executors must act as the alter ego of the writer and make all the decisions the writer would have made, the importance of choosing suitable executors cannot be emphasized too strongly. The executor, especially for a small estate, will often be a spouse or close relative. The writer must be certain that such a person is capable of making the necessary artistic and financial decisions for the estate. Joint executors, particularly when one is an expert with respect to writing and the other is a financial expert, would seem well suited to run the estate. When individuals serve as executors, consideration must be given to their age and health. Corporate executors offer the advantage of continuity, although their artistic insight may not satisfy the writer and the expense to the estate is usually greater.

Artistic and financial decisions are often closely intertwined. For example, the determination to sell film rights in a novel is a decision with both artistic and financial implications. The extent to which the writer may safely restrict the discretion of executors as to artistic matters may depend upon other aspects of the estate, such as whether funds are available to pay estate taxes and meet the immediate needs of the estate. If the writer absolutely bars the sale of film rights in a novel, will the funds available to the estate be sufficient? Restrictions of this kind conflict with the usually desirable practice of giving to the executor the maximum powers for management of the estate.

Each estate, whether large or small, will require a decision by the writer as to executors and executors' powers, based on the unique facts of the writer's own situation. At the least, however, clear and complete written instructions should be left for executors and heirs, detailing the treatment of work which the writer would consider ideal. Whether these instructions are in a letter or a will—and whether the instructions, if in a will, are binding or nonbinding on the executors—must depend on decisions made by the writer after consultation with expert advisers.

The will also provides the opportunity to anticipate and control the amount of taxes to be levied by the state and, more importantly, federal governments. A writer who lives in more than one state may risk having a so-called double domicile and being taxed by more than one state, but careful planning can parry such a danger. The writer will also wish to benefit from a number of deductions, discussed later, which can substantially reduce the estate if planned for properly. But tax planning is especially necessary for the writer because copyrights and manuscripts are valued at fair market value in computing the value of the writer's gross estate.

Trusts

Trusts are a valuable estate-planning device whereby title to property is given to a trustee to use the property or income from the property for the benefit of certain named beneficiaries. Trusts can be created by the writer during life or, at death, by will. Trusts can also be revocable, subject, that is, to dissolution by the creator of the trust, or irrevocable, in which case the creator cannot dissolve the trust. Trusts are frequently used to skip a generation of taxes, for example, by giving the income of a trust to children for their lives and having the grandchildren receive the principal. In such case the principal would not be included in the estates of the children for purposes of estate taxation. The Tax Reform Act of 1976, however, severely restricts the effectiveness of generation-skipping trusts and other transfers for a similar purpose.

The Gross Estate

The gross estate includes the value of all the property in which the writer had an ownership interest at the time of death.[4] Gifts made within three years of death (if greater in amount than the $3,000 gift exclusion discussed later in the chapter), as well as gift taxes paid on such gifts, are also added to the gross estate. Complex rules, depending on the specific circumstances of each case, cover the additional inclusion in the gross estate of such items as life insurance proceeds, property over which the writer possessed a general power to appoint an owner, annuities, jointly held interests, and the value of property in trusts.

Valuation

The property included in the writer's gross estate is valued at fair market value as of the date of death or, if so chosen on the estate tax return, as of an alternate date six months after death.[5] Fair market value is defined in the Regulations to the Internal Revenue Code as "the price at which the property would change hands between a willing buyer and a willing seller, neither being under any compulsion to buy or to sell and both having reasonable knowledge of relevant facts."[6]

Expert appraisers are used to determine the fair market value of copyrights and manuscripts. But whether the estate is large or small, the opinions of experts can exhibit surprising variations. For example, Gabriel Pascal's estate included the right to produce a musical based on George Bernard Shaw's *Pygmalion*, the right to make a motion picture of the musical of *Pygmalion*, and the right to make a motion picture of *Devil's Disciple*.[7] Shaw had refused to give his motion picture rights to anyone but Pascal, who had produced the film versions of *Major Barbara*, *Androcles and the Lion*, *Caesar & Cleopatra*, and *Pygmalion*. Shaw's estate continued this preference. However, Pascal died in 1954 without finalizing arrangements for the production of either of these works. Pascal's estate then realized great profits when *My Fair Lady* achieved a singular success as a musical and motion picture.

The issue became the fair market value of these rights as of the date of Pascal's death. In order to gain a higher basis for income tax purposes (a possibility ended by the Tax Reform Act of 1976, as explained later in the chapter under carry-over basis), the estate sought to value the rights in *Devil's Disciple* at $153,400 and the rights in *Pygmalion* at $1,140,000. The IRS contended that the fair market value of the rights was $30,000 for *Devil's Disciple* and $200,000 for *Pygmalion*. The tax court pointed out that, upon Pascal's death, no start had been made toward exploiting these rights. The experts who based their opinion on the success of *My Fair Lady* had not fairly valued the work based on reasonable expectations as of the date of death. Accordingly, the court concluded the correct fair market value was that contended for by the IRS.

More commonly, especially after the Tax Reform Act of 1976, the estate will seek a lower valuation to save estate taxes. The sculptor, David Smith, left four hundred and twenty-five works of substantial size and weight. His executors estimated the retail price of each piece if sold individually at the date of death. This totaled $4,284,000, which the executors discounted by 75 percent because any sale made immediately would have to be at a substantial discount. The IRS stayed with the original figure of $4,284,000, since the higher amount would yield the most in estate taxes. The court, in a "Solomon-like" decision, concluded the fair market value of the works to be $2,700,000.[8] Even so, Smith's estate lacked the cash to make an immediate payment of the taxes.

Fair market value is not only important for determining the value of an estate, but also for determining the value of gifts and contributions. Prior to the Tax Reform Act of 1969, writers could donate copyrights or manuscripts to universities or museums and take a charitable deduction for income tax purposes based on fair market value. Since 1969, such a donation by the writer creating the work (or a donee of the writer) would create a charitable deduction based only on the cost of the materials in the work—a negligible amount. In 1967 and 1968, when fair market value was still the relevant test, the well-known composer Maurice Jarre was requested to and did donate music manuscripts and related materials to the University of Southern California.[9] Jarre had won Academy Awards for his musical scores for the films *Lawrence of Arabia* and *Dr. Zhivago*. His donated manuscripts comprised over four thousand pages, including the scores for such films as *Dr. Zhivago, Grand Prix, Night of the Generals, Behold a Pale Horse, Is Paris Burning?*, and *Gambit*. Jarre retained the copyrights on the donated manuscripts.

One appraiser for Jarre found the fair market value of the donated materials to be $54,200 in 1967 and $61,900 in 1968, and this income tax deduction was claimed. At the trial another appraiser testified for him that the fair market value for the donations was $61,996 in 1967 and $35,918 in 1968. But the appraiser for the IRS believed the materials donated in 1967 had a value of $7,615, while the materials donated in 1968 had a value of $4,915. The tax court gave an excellent summary of the factors to be considered in determining the fair market value of manuscripts:

> the composer's standing in his field and popularity of his works in general; the critical acclaim and popular appeal of the particular works contributed; the relative place and importance of the contributed works in the composer's career; the condition and content of the contributed works; whether the contributed works are originals, fair copies, or photo copies, are written in the composer's own hand, are signed, or are in ink, pencil, or typed; the length of the individual contributed works and the sizes of the pages containing them; whether the mental processes of the composer are shown (i.e., working versus souvenir or finished manuscripts), including annotations; the demand in the market-place for the type of works contributed and for the particular works contributed; the associative character of the contributed works (such as the film, its actors and actresses, its director, or its subject); the quantity, or conversely the rarity, of the contributed material (including whether the composer is dead or alive); and the length of time necessary to sell the contributed works.[10]

The court concluded that the fair market value of the donations was $45,000 for 1967 and $31,000 for 1968—another compromise between conflicting appraisals. It is favorable to Jarre, because the court appeared impressed with the expertise of his appraisers.

These cases dealing with fair market value illustrate how extreme the variations in appraisals can be. Especially where estate taxes are concerned, the writer must prepare for variations in the valuation of the gross estate when attempting to gauge and prepare for the payment of estate taxes.

Taxable Estate

The gross estate is reduced by a number of important deductions to reach the taxable estate. The deductions include funeral expenses, certain administration expenses, casualty or theft losses during administration, debts and enforceable claims against the estate, mortgages and liens, the value of property passing to a surviving spouse subject to certain limitations, the value of property passing to an orphan under twenty-one subject to certain limitations, and the value of property qualifying for a charitable deduction because of the nature of the institution to which the property is given.[11]

The marital deduction provides an important tax saving. The deduction equals the greater of $250,000 or one-half of the value of the adjusted gross estate—which is the gross estate less all but the charitable and, of course, marital deductions—assuming property of that value is left to the surviving spouse. A spouse, especially a wife, is entitled in any case to a share of the deceased spouse's estate by law in most states. In New York, for example, a surviving spouse has a right to one-half of the deceased spouse's estate, but the right is reduced to one-third if there are also surviving children.[12] The value of property used for the marital deduction can satisfy these state requirements as well. But the property which goes to the surviving spouse for the marital deduction must basically pass in such a way that it will eventually be taxable in the estate of the surviving spouse. The marital deduction thus postpones estate taxes, but does not completely avoid them.

The Tax Reform Act of 1976 excludes from the gross estate the value of transfers to an orphaned minor child of the deceased. This applies if the decedent is not survived by a spouse and the child has no known surviving parent. The maximum amount of the exclusion for each such child is $5,000 multiplied by the number of years until the child reaches twenty-one.

The charitable deduction is of particular interest to the writer, since this provides the opportunity to give copyrights and manuscripts to institutions such as universities or museums which the writer may wish to benefit. As explained earlier, the income tax benefit from donating copyrights and manuscripts created by the writer is negligible. But the estate tax benefit can be very substantial, because the fair market value of such donated works is deducted from the writer's gross estate. A will clause is used stating that if the institution is not of the type to which a bequest qualifying for a charitable deduction can be made, the bequest will be made to a suitable institution at the choice of the executor.

If a copyright or manuscript is willed to charity, its fair market value is included in the gross estate, but the same fair market value is then subtracted as a charitable deduction in determining the taxable estate. But even if the estate tax rate were as high as 70 percent, keeping the copyright or manuscript would still pass 30 percent of the value on to the recipients under the will. However, if the estate does not have cash available to pay the estate taxes, charitable bequests may be an excellent way to reduce the amount of the estate taxes. Also, the intangible benefits, including perpetuating the writer's reputation, may well outweigh considerations of the precise saving or loss resulting from such bequests.

Once the gross estate has been reduced by the deductions discussed above, what is left is the taxable estate.

Unified Estate and Gift Tax

The Tax Reform Act of 1976 worked a major overhaul in the system of estate and gift taxation. It made the progressive tax, which had previously been separately applied to the fair market value of taxable gifts and the value of the taxable estate, apply to the cumulated total of taxable gifts and the taxable estate (and ended lower gift tax rates).[13] The progressive rates rise from 18 percent if the cumulated total of taxable gifts and the taxable estate is under $10,000, to 70 percent if the cumulated total is over $5,000,000. The amount of the tax on the cumulated total of the taxable gifts and taxable estate is reduced by a tax credit. The credit increases from 1977 to 1981, the applicable amount of the credit depending on the year in which the writer dies:

Year	Credit
1977	$30,000
1978	$34,000
1979	$38,000
1980	$42,000
1981	$47,000

A single writer who made taxable gifts of $70,000 and left an estate of $80,000 would owe, according to the rate schedule, a unified gift and estate tax of $38,800. If the writer died in 1978, the $34,000 credit would reduce this tax owed to $4,800. If the writer should die in 1981, the $47,000 credit would make no tax payable. A writer who dies in 1981 will only pay a tax if the cumulated total of taxable gifts and the taxable estate is greater than $175,625. If the writer who dies in 1981 is married and leaves sufficient property to a spouse to take advantage of the minimum marital deduction, no tax will be payable until the cumulated total of taxable gifts and the taxable estate exceeds $425,625 (because the minimum marital deduction is $250,000). It should be noted that the federal estate tax is reduced by either a state death tax credit or the actual state death tax, whichever is lesser.[14]

Liquidity

Estate taxes owed must normally be paid within nine months of death at the time the estate tax return is filed.[15] For the estate unable to make full payment immediately, it may be possible to spread payment out over a number of years.[16] One of the best ways to have the cash available to pay estate taxes is insurance policies on the life of the writer. The proceeds of life insurance payable to the estate are included in the gross estate. So are the proceeds of policies payable, for example, to a spouse or children if the insured writer keeps any ownership or control over the policy.[17] But policies payable to a spouse or children and not owned or controlled by the writer will not be included in the writer's gross estate. If a spouse or children are the beneficiaries under both insurance policies and the will, they will naturally want to provide funds to the estate to pay estate taxes so that the assets of the estate do not have to be sold immediately at lower prices. Such policies should probably be whole life insurance, rather than the less expensive term insurance which may be nonrenewable after a certain age or under certain health conditions. Also, such life insurance may sometimes best be maintained in a life insurance trust, especially where a trustee may have greater ability than the beneficiaries to manage the proceeds. This

stage of estate planning requires consultation with the writer's insurance agent to determine the most advisable course with regard
to maintaining such life insurance.

Gifts

If the writer makes gifts while alive, the value of the gross estate
at death could be reduced. The incentive for making gifts is a
yearly exclusion of $3,000 applicable to each gift recipient. If an
unmarried writer in one year gave copyrights with a fair market
value of $10,000 each to three children and two friends, there
would be total gifts of $50,000. The gift to each person, however,
would be subject to a $3,000 exclusion. This $3,000 exclusion applies each year to each person to whom a gift is given—one person
or a hundred. Thus, the $10,000 gifts to each child would be tax-
able only to the extent of $7,000. The total taxable amount would,
therefore, be $35,000. The writer who can afford gifts should
usually take advantage of the yearly exclusions.

If the writer were married rather than single, the writer and
spouse could elect to treat all gifts as being made one-half by each.
This has the effect of increasing to $6,000 the yearly exclusion for
each gift recipient. The Tax Reform Act of 1976 also allows a
writer to deduct 50 percent of the value of gifts made to a spouse
from the value of gifts subject to tax (by law, up to the first
$100,000 of gifts to a spouse is completely deductible, the second
$100,000 is not deductible at all, and the value of any gifts in ex-
cess of $200,000 is deductible at the 50 percent rate).[18]

Gifts must be complete and irrevocable transfers, including
transfers in trust, for the benefit of another person or group. The
entire copyright need not be transferred—for example, a valid gift
can be made of the right of exploitation in one medium—but a
mere gift of income must be avoided since such income will still be
taxable to the writer.[19] Every effort must be made to show a gift
has truly been given. There should be delivery of the gift, execution of a deed of gift, notification of the publisher, and, if
necessary, filing of a gift tax return. After the gift, the writer must
completely cease to exercise control over it. If the writer retains
powers, there will not be a valid gift for tax purposes. In that case

the income generated by the gift can be taxed to the writer instead of the donee, and the value of the gift will be included in the writer's gross estate.[20] The writer also should not serve as custodian of gifts given to minor children, since such custodianship will again cause the value of the gift property to be included in the writer's gross estate.[21] The complexity of this area makes legal advice necessary if the writer is to ensure that gifts will be effective.

A gift tax return must be filed in the first quarter of a calendar year in which taxable gifts exceed $25,000. If the total of taxable gifts during the year do not exceed $25,000, only one gift tax return need be filed at the end of the year. The failure to file a gift tax return can result in assessments of interest, penalties, and, in some cases, even criminal charges.

The writer can also make gifts to charities without having to pay a gift tax.[22] But charitable gifts have no advantage over charitable bequests under the will in terms of saving estate taxes. After the gift of a work, the writer of course would not own the work at death and its value could not be included in the gross estate. While the value of the same work would be part of the gross estate if owned at death, a charitable bequest would reduce the gross estate by the value of the work. The taxable estate is the same in either case. The estate of a wealthy, married individual might benefit more from charitable bequests than charitable gifts, since the larger adjusted gross estate may make possible a larger marital deduction.

Carry-Over Basis

Prior to the Tax Reform Act of 1976, the recipient of a copyright as a gift held the copyright as ordinary income property and took the basis of the writer who gave the gift. But a beneficiary who received a copyright under a will held the copyright as a capital asset with a stepped-up basis of the copyright's fair market value as included in the gross estate. For example, a writer in 1970 created a copyright with a zero basis. If the copyright were given to a daughter, the daughter would have a zero basis and receive ordinary income when she sold it. If the sale price were $5,000, she would receive $5,000 of ordinary income.

On the other hand, if the artist died in 1972 and the copyright were valued in the estate at $5,000, the daughter who received the copyright under the will would have a basis of $5,000. So if she sold it for $5,000, she would not have to pay any tax at all. If she sold it for $7,500, the tax would be on $2,500 at the favorable capital gains rates.

The Tax Reform Act of 1976 eliminates this discrepancy in treatment by providing for the carry-over of a decedent's basis in appreciated property to the beneficiaries who receive such property. For example, a writer creates a copyright in 1980 with a zero basis, leaves it to a daughter, and dies in 1982 when it has a fair market value of $5,000. If the daughter sells the copyright for $7,500, she will have to pay tax at ordinary income rates on the whole $7,500 because the writer's basis, which was transferred to the daughter, was zero. Also, the gain is an ordinary gain, rather than a capital gain, because of the provision of the tax laws denying treatment as a capital asset to copyrights where the basis of the owner is determined by reference to the basis of the writer who created the copyright.[23]

The effect of this provision on the beneficiaries of writers is most unfair, particularly since many believe that capital gains treatment should not automatically be denied to writers. Small estates will benefit from a provision increasing basis to a minimum of $60,000 (allocated to the assets in proportion to their net appreciation in relation to the overall appreciation in the estate). Also, works created before December 31, 1976, will be stepped up to their fair market value as of that date. To find the fair market value as of December 31, 1976, the number of days the work was in existence prior to December 31, 1976, is divided by the total number of days from the work's creation until the death of the writer. This fraction is then multiplied by the fair market value of the work as of the date of death. For example, a writer owns a work for two thousand days prior to death, and five hundred of the days are before December 31, 1976. Upon the writer's death, assume that the work, which had a zero basis for the writer, has a fair market value of $6,000. The basis to the beneficiary who receives the work will be $6,000 multiplied by 500/2000. This basis to the beneficiary, in other words, will be $1,500. But if the work had been created after December 31, 1976, the general rule would apply giving the beneficiary only the basis of the decedent, which, in this case, would be zero.

The Estate Plan

The planning of a writer's estate is a complex task often requiring the expertise of accountants, insurance agents, and bank officers, as well as that of a lawyer. But an informed writer can be a valuable initiator and contributor in creating a plan which meets both artistic and financial estate-planning needs.

13
Public Support
for Writers

The important role of the writer in society raises the issue of what assistance society should appropriately offer to the writer, especially to the creative writer. Earning a living has often been difficult for the novelist, the playwright, and the poet. Second careers are frequently a necessity. T.S. Eliot, for example, took employment in the foreign department of Lloyds Bank in London from 1917 through 1925, after which he worked for the rest of his life with the publishing house of Faber and Gwyer (later Faber and Faber). The horror with which some of Eliot's contemporaries viewed the full devotion of Eliot's working days to the bank was reflected in Ezra Pound's Bel Esprit scheme. Pound proposed to raise enough funds from those interested in the arts to permit Eliot to devote all his time to writing, but the plan never reached fruition. Thousands of writers less famous than Eliot struggle to create while maintaining other sources of livelihood such as teaching careers. A recent article estimates that only one hundred or so creative writers in the United States can live from the income generated by their books. And, as corporate conglomerates control more and more publishing houses, profit margins take precedence over any obligation to publish quality literature. This has led to fears that the younger, serious writers will find publication ever more difficult.[1]

Yet the 1975 National Report on the Arts, authored by the National Committee for Cultural Resources (the "committee") on the basis of extensive data, concluded that "interest in the arts has risen steadily over the past decade, and continues to rise. The work of the committee provides fresh evidence that both audiences and the number of arts organizations are continuing to grow in communities in every part of the nation. The American people themselves are making the strongest case for the arts."[2] A 1975 poll commissioned by the committee showed that 93 percent of the public believed the arts are important to the quality of life in the community; 85 percent believed arts activities are important to the business and economies of communities; and 41 percent would be willing to pay $25 or more in additional taxes to support the arts (51 percent would be willing to pay an additional $10 in taxes for the arts).

In the meantime the arts, as a growth industry, experienced an increased demand which could not be met by available revenues. This shortfall caused the committee to recommend increased support for the arts from individuals, corporations, foundations, counties, and cities. This local support, along with revenues raised from the arts, could meet 80 percent of needed budgeting. The committee proposed the other 20 percent come 10 percent from the states and 10 percent from the federal government. Since the federal government in fact only contributed 3.5 percent of gross arts expenditures in 1974–1975, the committee would have increased the year's federal support for the National Endowment for the Arts ("NEA") nearly threefold from about $74,700,000 to $209,000,000. For 1976–1977, when the NEA budget will be $82,000,000, the committee would recommend a budget of $225,000,000. These differences in magnitude would seem to be a severe criticism of government support for the arts, yet since the early 1960s the growth of state and federal support of the arts has been extraordinary. But the failure of the NEA to approach the support levels which the federal government provided in the 1930s—mainly under the Works Progress Administration's Federal Writers' Project—has caused those concerned for the arts to look both home and abroad for innovative models of government support.

The National Endowment for the Arts

The legislation creating the NEA in 1965 stated "that the encouragement and support of national progress and scholarship in the humanities and the arts, while primarily a matter for private and local initiative, is also an appropriate matter of concern for the Federal Government . . . [and] that the practice of art and the study of the humanities requires constant dedication and devotion and that, while no government can call a great artist or scholar into existence, it is necessary and appropriate for the Federal Government to help create and sustain not only a climate encouraging freedom of thought, imagination, and inquiry, but also the material conditions facilitating the release of this creative talent."[3] Whether the NEA has created such material conditions remains a matter of debate, since most supporters of the arts contend that far more must be done to aid writers and other artists than the NEA has achieved.

The budget for the NEA in 1966, the first year of operation, was $2,500,000. Over the next decade the budget continually increased to reach the level of $82,000,000 for the fiscal year beginning in October 1976. These budgets, however, had to be allocated among all the arts. Also, although grants are available to individuals (further information and application forms can be obtained from the Program Information Office, National Endowment for the Arts, Washington, D.C. 20506), grants are also given to the official arts agencies of the states and territories as well as to tax-exempt, nonprofit organizations.[4] In the 1975 fiscal year, for example, $1,746,778 was allocated to the Literature Program. Of this amount, $305,000 was spent on fellowships for creative writers, $300,000 on grants to literary magazines through the Coordinating Council of Literary Magazines, $64,080 to assist developing colleges in funding writers in residence, $266,095 on grants for small presses, $382,767 for general programs, and $428,801 for services to the field.[5] The service organizations include the P.E.N. American Center, Associated Writing Programs, Academy of American Poets, National Book Committee, Teachers and Writers Collaborative, and Poets and Writers, Inc., which provide a broad spectrum of assistance for writers. Funds from the NEA also aid writers in programs such as Artists-in-Schools and Developmental Theatre—New Plays, New Playwrights, New Forms. Funding for research and writing projects in the area of the humanities, as distinguished from the arts, may be available to writers through the National Endowment for Humanities, 806 15th Street, N.W., Washington, D.C. 20506.

Another source of support for writers could be the Comprehensive Employment and Training Act, which is providing federal funds to innovative state and local programs designed to create employment for the unemployed.[6] Early indications, however, show that few of these programs have been designed for writers. This situation could be improved upon if writers' groups would contact their local departments of employment, labor, or human resources to investigate the possibility of using available funds in programs for writers.

State Support

The first state arts council was created in 1902, but by 1960 only six such councils were in being. However, the period since 1960, when the New York State Council on the Arts was created, has seen the creation of an arts council in every state and territory, as the list of such councils in the appendix on pp. 228–232 indicates. During the ten years from 1965 to 1975, the appropriations of states in support of the arts increased from $1,700,000 to $55,000,000.[7] The impetus behind this increase in councils and funding is indicated, for example, in the California Arts Act of 1975, which states, "The Legislature perceives that life in California is enriched by art. The source of art is in the natural flow of the human mind. Realizing craft and beauty is demanding, however, the people of the state desire to encourage and nourish these skills wherever they occur, to the benefit of all."[8] In order to effectuate these legislative perceptions, the duties of the California Arts Council are described as follows:

> The council shall:
> (a) Encourage artistic awareness, participation and expression.

(b) Help independent local groups develop their own art programs.

(c) Promote the employment of artists and those skilled in crafts in both the public and private sector.

(d) Provide for the exhibition of art works in public buildings throughout California.

(e) Enlist the aid of all state agencies in the task of ensuring the fullest expression of our artistic potential.

(f) Adopt regulations in accordance with the provisions of the Administrative Procedure Act necessary for proper execution of the powers and duties granted to the council by this chapter.

(g) Employ such administrative, technical, and other personnel as may be necessary.

(h) Fix the salaries of the personnel employed pursuant to this chapter which salaries will be fixed as nearly as possible to conform to the salaries established by the State Personnel Board for classes of positions in the state civil service involving comparable duties and responsibilities.

(i) Appoint advisory committees whenever necessary. Members of an advisory committee shall serve without compensation, but each may be reimbursed for necessary traveling and other expenses incurred in the performance of official duties.

(j) Request and obtain from any department, division, board, bureau, commission, or other agency of the state such assistance and data as will enable it properly to carry on its power and duties.

(k) Hold hearings, execute agreements, and perform any acts necessary and proper to carry out the purposes of this chapter.

(l) Accept federal grants, for any of the purposes of this chapter.

(m) Accept only unrestricted gifts, donations, bequests, or grants of funds from private sources and public agencies, for any of the purposes of this chapter. However, the council shall give careful consideration to any donor requests concerning specific dispositions.

(n) Establish grant application criteria and procedure.

(o) Award prizes or direct grants to individuals or organizations in accordance with such regulations as the council may prescribe.[9]

The Writer in the Great Depression

One model for public support of writers was created in the 1930s, when the Great Depression made the precarious profession of the writer even more untenable. The federal government, as part of the overall effort to create work, developed the Works Progress Administration's Federal Writers' Project.[10] The project began in 1935 and lasted until 1943. To be employed by the project (at wages varying from $50.00 to $103.50 per month, the variance due to geographic adjustments), an individual had to meet a strict relief test. This made many talented writers ineligible, while the eligible people often had a very limited background in writing. The writer's specialty made no difference, so novelists, poets, advertising copywriters, newspaper reporters, and all other conceivable types of writers (including occasional and would-be writers) were joined together in the project. With rare exceptions, the projects did not permit creative writing, but instead employed the writers on such efforts as state guidebooks; research on the arts, history, and localities; preparation of special studies on topics in economics, sociology, the arts, and similar areas; preparation of a guide to governmental functions and publications; and information on the project itself. Also, the geographic distribution of jobs under the project had little bearing on where writers lived, causing unfortunate misallocations.

By 1942 the project had created over one thousand books, pamphlets, and leaflets which covered a vast range of subject matter drawn from the American experience. The employment peak came in April 1936 when the project had a work force of 6,686 men and women (women comprised about 40 percent of the employees). Included among those employed were many who later gained prominence, such as Nelson Algren, Saul Bellow, John Cheever, Loren Eiseley, Ralph Ellison, and Richard Wright. By 1939 the number of employees had been cut to 3,500 and by 1943 the project had been terminated. The total cost of the project was

$27,000,000, a different magnitude of support for writers than the NEA can generate today. But the project suffered from political turmoil, mainly accusations of Communist influence, which caused some to doubt its accomplishments and significance.

The need for a model—whether it be the NEA with the threefold budgetary increase proposed by the National Committee for Cultural Resources or a modified version of the Federal Writers' Project as it existed in the 1930s—suggests the value of looking abroad to where other countries have created their own systems to support and encourage writers and the arts. Some of these countries—the Netherlands, Ireland, Japan, and France—are presented as examples. Comparisons of the actual costs of supporting the arts between the countries would have little value, but the nature and variety of the programs as possible models are certainly of interest.

The Netherlands

The Netherlands supports a literature program under the aegis of its Ministry of Culture, Recreation and Social Work.[11] A Literary Fund, created in 1965, gives Dutch writers economic aid by paying grants to writers to supplement fees received from book and magazine publications, as well as by providing grants to enable writers to devote themselves solely to creative work for periods of varying duration. The government also supports various service organizations which offer aid to Dutch writers and, more generally, Dutch literature. For example, the Foundation for the Promotion of the Translation of Dutch Literature employs writers who translate the first chapter of works by Dutch writers. Such a chapter, along with a synopsis of the balance of the work, is offered to publishers abroad in order to propagate Dutch literature. The government regularly commissions writers for projects relating to the history of Dutch literature. Prizes are awarded to Dutch writers and special honoraria go to writers considered outstanding. Writers are paid for lecturing about their work in the schools by the Agency for Writers in the Schools. And writers may join the Writers Association, which is a professional association. Also, publishers can be subsidized in order to publish work which might otherwise never appear in published form or which, if published, would be at an unacceptably high price.

Ireland

In 1969 the government of Ireland enacted an unprecedented law designed to give tax relief to writers, artists, and composers within the boundaries of Ireland. The minister of finance, in presenting the legislation to the Dail Eireann, stated, "The purpose of this relief is . . . to help create a sympathetic environment here in which the arts can flourish by encouraging artists and writers to live and work in this country. This is something completely new in this country and, indeed, so far as I am aware, in the world . . . I am convinced that we are right in making this attempt to improve our cultural and artistic environment and I am encouraged by the welcome given from all sides both at home and abroad to the principle of the scheme. I am hopeful that it will achieve its purpose."

The legislation completely frees the writer, regardless of nationality, from any tax obligation to Ireland with respect to income derived from writing.[12] The main requirement for application is that the writer be resident in Ireland for tax purposes. Simply explained, this requires the writer to rent or purchase a home in Ireland and work at that home during a substantial part of the year. However, while the residence must be uninterrupted, a writer does not necessarily have to be in Ireland for the entire year. Brief trips back to the United States, for example, would not affect a writer's tax status as a resident of Ireland. Every United States writer should remember, however, that the United States reserves the right to tax its citizens anywhere in the world, so consult pp. 179–182 for the United States tax effect of living abroad.

Once a writer is resident in Ireland, there are two methods to qualify for tax relief. An established writer, who has produced "a work or works generally recognized as having cultural or artistic merit," would use Artists Application Form 1. A less established artist would use Artists Application Form 2 for the exemption of a particular work "having cultural or artistic merit." In both cases the determination of "cultural or artistic merit" is made by the

Irish revenue commissioners after consultation, if necessary, with experts in the field. Once a writer qualifies under either Artists Application Form 1 or Form 2, all future works by the writer in the same category will be exempt from Irish tax. The offices of the revenue commissioners are in Room 5, Cross Block, Dublin Castle, Dublin 2, Ireland. For the writer exempt from Irish tax, the sole Irish tax requirement is that a tax return showing no tax due be prepared and filed with the revenue commissioners in Dublin.

By early 1976, however, only about 500 persons had qualified to live tax free in Ireland. This was true despite the ease of application, absence of excessive tax paper work, and high percentage of applicants approved by the revenue commissioners. Of those who qualified, about 69 percent were writers and 3 percent composers, while 22 percent were painters and 6 percent sculptors. The assistance to the individual writer who comes to Ireland is certainly valuable, but Ireland's hope to create a new Byzantium has yet to be realized.

Japan

Japan has a unique approach whereby an organization or an individual can be registered as a "Living National Treasure."[13] Legislation in 1955 created the National Commission for Protection of Cultural Properties which, by 1967, had designated fifty-seven persons and seven organizations as living national treasures for their role in aiding and continuing the culture and arts of Japan. Fields where living national treasures have been designated include ceramic art, dyeing and weaving, lacquered ware, metalwork, special dolls, Noh and Kabuki acting, Banraku puppets, music, dance, singing and so on. The living national treasures receive a stipend in order to be able to improve their special artistic talent while training students to perpetuate their art form. If the United States were to adopt analogous legislation, poets, novelists, and playwrights might well be designated living national treasures for our country.

France

France has an innovative system for the support of publishers as well as writers.[14] The *Centre National des Lettres* provides grants for writers, but also offers interest-free loans to French publishers for works of cultural significance. This concept of interest-free loans is a valuable one, since it draws upon the existing strengths of the publishing industry to permit financially marginal books to reach the public. In a modified form, a system of interest-free loans for publishers in the United States could prove a valuable initiative.

Victor Hugo advocated a national literary fund financed by a tax on the sale of books in the public domain. Thus, the writers of the past might give a bequest to the writers of the present. *The Caisse Nationale des Lettres* was created after the Second World War, but the sources of funding could not be agreed upon. Faced with imposing a tax of 5 percent on publishing companies, the law simply was not implemented. In 1948 an amendment proposed funding the law by a 6 percent tax on the sale price of books in the public domain, with only school books, scholarly books, and devotional books exempted from the tax. The defeat of this proposal came from the belief that the financing would not only be inadequate, but would also impose an unfair surcharge on the best literary works. For eight years the law remained dormant due to the impasse over funding.

Finally, in 1956, agreement was reached on a mixed system of funding. A direct subsidy, which has increased year after year, is provided by the government. A tax of .2 percent is imposed on French publishers, except for books for exportation and scientific or school books. Writers contribute to the fund through a .2 percent tax on royalties and a levy under their social security system. An ever more important funding source is the extension of the copyright term for fifteen years. This extension has kept the works of such writers as Emile Zola, Guy de Maupassant, Mallarme, and Jules Verne from going into the public domain. The royalties realized on their works during the period of the extension belong to the national literary fund. In addition, the repayment of loans and project funds on hand but not yet due to be paid provide sources of support.

In 1973 this structure of taxation, support for writers, and interest-free loans was taken over by the *Centre Nationale des Lettres*, superseding the *Caisse Nationale des Lettres*. The interest-free loans continue to be focused on works of cultural value which need aid in order to be published. This problem is more acute in

France than in the United States with respect to the classics and specialized books, since the French-language reading public is much smaller in size. To obtain a loan, a publisher applies to the *Centre Nationale des Lettres* and gives an estimate of projected costs. A committee makes the decision whether to accept or reject the loan application, basing its decision on the cultural merit of the work. The result has been the publication of highly diverse works, including the complete works of Diderot, the correspondence of George Sand, translations of Lewis Carroll, reference works, critical essays, historical works, dictionaries of languages and of culture, new editions of works not available in libraries, and poetry magazines and books.

The loans must be repaid by the publisher within ten years. However, payments are coordinated with sales of the book. The risk of poor sales is mainly borne by the literary fund, since the publisher which has not earned back the initial investment within ten years will have had its loss cushioned by the use of the interest-free funds.

Interest-free loans funded by an extension of the copyright term (or a tax on public domain works) offer a model which could be highly effective if used in the United States. While our publishing industry and reading public are far larger than those in France, many obstacles render difficult the publication of certain types of culturally valuable works. For example, of the limited number of first novels published each year, many disappear into obscurity because budgeting for promotion has been reserved for more marketable books. Interest-free loans could be used for promotion as well as publication of novels and other works of cultural merit which would otherwise not reach the public. By drawing upon the strengths of the publishing industry, writers, publishers, and the reading public would all benefit. Interest-free loans might also provide a valuable funding source for the national nonprofit presses proposed in the article, "A Publishing Alternative," on pp. 222–224.

United States Proposals

Many proposals to aid writers have been introduced as bills in Congress. One of the most intriguing would have created a poet laureate for the United States under the NEA.

There is hereby established the office of Poet Laureate of the United States. The Poet Laureate of the United States shall perform such duties as the President shall prescribe, but they shall not be such as to prevent him from continuing his creative work.

The Poet Laureate of the United States, who shall be appointed by the President after consideration of the recommendations of the National Council on the Arts, shall be a poet whose works reflect those qualities and attributes that are associated with the historical heritage, present achievement, and future potential of these United States. He shall be appointed for a term of office of five years, and shall receive compensation at such rate as shall be set by the President.[15]

Another bill proposed that $20,000,000 be allocated to the NEA to employ unemployed writers, painters, musicians, actors, and other artists during any fiscal year in which the national rate of unemployment exceeded 6.5 percent.[16] This concept focuses attention on the lack of unemployment insurance for the self-employed, a more general problem which might well be the subject of future reforms, as well as the possibility of developing special employment programs for the arts in which unemployment and underemployment are chronic. One issue which any such arts employment program must resolve will be whether the program's purpose is solely economic relief, solely the creation of a national artistic legacy, or a balancing of each of these goals.

Numerous bills have sought a charitable deduction of fair market value instead of just the cost of creating the work (which is usually zero) for writers who donate their literary property to charities and other suitable organizations.[17] It has also been proposed that the proceeds from sales of literary property be taxed as capital gains income in appropriate circumstances, instead of being taxed at the less favorable rates applicable to ordinary income.[18] This idea has become especially important in view of the carryover basis provisions of the Tax Reform Act of 1976, discussed on pp. 207–209.

One proposal which has attracted great interest would permit each taxpayer to make a donation to the NEA by either designating a portion of a tax overpayment for such use or including a contribution with the tax return.[19] The advantage of such a proposal would be the ease with which the contributions could be made.

Other proposals have been discussed but not introduced as bills. For example, the Irish model might be considered for those writers who must struggle to maintain a precarious financial equilibrium. Michael Pantaleoni, former Executive Director of the Volunteer Lawyers for the Arts in New York City, has suggested that writers and other artists who earn less than $10,000 per year be entitled to a reduced rate of tax as long as their income is from their art-related work.[20] The cost of such a program to aid writers and other artists might be surprisingly little, since the arts provide a substantial stimulus to the economies of communities.[21]

A different approach would seek to aid writers by substantially increasing the opportunities for publishing creative writing of high quality. The following article is republished by permission of *The Nation* where it originally appeared.

A Publishing Alternative
by Tad Crawford

American theater survived the 1960s, and American fiction can survive the 1970s. This is so despite the fact that strains in the publishing industry have become increasingly visible over the last decade, strains due to inefficient business practices and the conglomerate structures into which most major publishing companies have been integrated. As a result, extensive reductions in the number of works of fiction and nonfiction of good quality are reflected in the 1975 lists of the commercial publishers; and recently came the disturbing news that half as many first novels were published in 1975 as were published in 1974. Clearly, if the survival of American fiction is to have the fullest cultural significance, a process similar to that which saved theater must soon be initiated in book publishing.

At present, there is no adequate alternative to commercial publishing. The small presses and the university presses—which are, in the main, nonprofit entities—lack capital or endowments of the magnitude necessary to permit publishing and promoting books on a national scale. Foundation, state and federal grants to writers are likewise limited in terms of the funds available. Groups of writers who pay for the publication of their own work, such as the much publicized Fiction Collective, can contribute only marginally to filling the vacuum created by the activities of the immensely larger commercial publishers. Vanity presses, which also publish at the writer's expense, are generally unsatisfactory because they have little interest in the quality of the books they issue. They derive their profits from the author's subsidy rather than from sales, and that factor further complicates the ordinary vagaries of distribution.

These shortcomings, however, at least point to the requisites for a viable alternative to commercial publishing. Briefly, there must be publishing houses that can: (1) be concerned primarily with quality, not revenues; (2) publish large selections of fiction and nonfiction; (3) promote and distribute on a national scale; (4) maintain book prices at attractive levels—perhaps 50 percent of the comparable book prices charged by commercial presses; (5) give consideration to all manuscripts submitted to them; (6) remunerate writers adequately for work published.

Nonprofit publishing houses of national scope could best satisfy all the listed requisites. Such a nonprofit cultural initiative would follow a model already proved successful in American theatre. Only a decade ago concern was frequently voiced for the survival of our serious theatre, but today nonprofit theatre has enabled men like Joseph Papp to introduce exciting talents and productions. Nonprofit presses, raising their funds in large part from grants and contributions, would be concerned only with quality. National scope—in quantity of books issued, in promotion and in distribution—would require that the capital of such presses be of a new magnitude, much as vastly increased support was necessary to advance nonprofit theatre. Promotion is crucial, since the public sensibility has to a substantial extent been conditioned to lesser quality by the advertising campaigns of the commercial publishers. The size of the endowment of these presses should be large enough to permit book prices to be subsidized in order to increase readership. Nonprofit presses would have no impediments to reading the manuscripts of unpublished and unrepresented writers, and could help create an atmosphere in which diversity is encouraged. Finally, some remuneration could be offered to writers of disparate cultural orientations, who, under the present commercial system, can expect little in material rewards.

Leadership and funding are the critical needs which must be met if such national nonprofit presses are to be established. As the plight of American theater inspired personal sacrifice on the part of persons who loved the theater and labored to insure its cultural survival, so the plight of American writing must arouse writers, editors, literary agents and readers to action. Funding will prove a difficult task, but it should not be impossible. Grants and support from individuals will have to be raised. Some income may come from the nonprofit presses themselves, once these are in full operation. Successful novelists might be persuaded to contribute new literary works to the presses as a new and useful form of patronage. Lobbying efforts could seek favorable changes in the tax laws to benefit such presses. There could be a far wider use of community fund-raising drives for the arts. These and other possibilities will be limited only by the desire and ingenuity of those who come forward to organize such national nonprofit publishing houses.

The challenge of creating a national literary endowment is much the same as the challenge already overcome by American theater. If the model of the theater is a true guide, we are now waiting for the men and women of good will and imagination who can create an environment in which our literary heritage will not only survive but thrive as well.

The Democratic Platform

These proposals offer evidence of the concern felt for the status of the writer. The intangible contribution of the writer, especially the creative writer, to society is seldom matched by comparable tangible benefits given in return. While society rewards its favorites well, those who struggle are often forgotten. In this context the perceptions and pledges contained in the 1976 Democratic platform are especially significant:

> We recognize the essential role played by the arts and humanities in the development of America. Our nation cannot afford to be materially rich and spiritually poor. We en-

dorse a strong role for the federal government in reinforcing the vitality and improving the economic strength of the nation's artists and arts institutions, while recognizing that artists must be absolutely free of any government control. We would support the growth and development of the National Endowments for the Arts and Humanities through adequate funding, the development of special anti-recession employment programs for artists, copyright reforms to protect the rights of authors, artists and performers, and revision of the tax laws that unfairly penalize artists.

Appendixes

Volunteer Lawyers

Increasing numbers of lawyers across the country are volunteering to assist qualifying writers, other artists, and arts organizations. Up-to-date information on the volunteer lawyers closest to a specific location can be obtained from one of the following established groups:

CALIFORNIA
Hamish Sandison, Executive Director
Bay Area Lawyers for the Arts
25 Taylor Street
San Francisco, California 94102
(415) 775-7200

ILLINOIS
Tom Leavens, Executive Director
Lawyers for the Creative Arts
111 North Wabash Avenue
Chicago, Illinois 60602
(312) 263-6989

NEW YORK
James Fishman, Executive Director
Volunteer Lawyers for the Arts
36 West 44th Street
New York, New York 10036
(212) 575-1150

State Arts Agencies

**Alabama State Council on the Arts
and Humanities**
M. J. Zakrzewski, Exec. Director
449 S. McDonough Street
Montgomery, Alabama 36130
(205) 832–6758

Alaska State Council on the Arts
Roy H. Helms, Exec. Director
360 K Street, Suite 240
Anchorage, Alaska 99501
(907) 279–3824 or 272–5342

American Samoa Arts Council
Palauni M. Tuiasosopo, Chairman
Office of the Governor
Pago Pago
American Samoa 96799

**Arizona Commission on the Arts
and Humanities**
Mrs. Louise Tester, Exec. Director
6330 North Seventh Street
Phoenix, Arizona 85014
(602) 271–5884

**The Office of Arkansas State Arts
and Humanities**
Dr. R. Sandra Perry,
Exec. Director
Old State Capitol
300 West Markham
Little Rock, Arkansas 72201
(501) 371–2539 or 2530

California Arts Council
Clark Mitze, Exec. Director
808 "O" Street
Sacramento, California 95814
(916) 445–1530

**The Colorado Council on the Arts
and Humanities**
Robert N. Sheets, Exec. Director
1550 Lincoln Street, Room 205
Denver, Colorado 80203
(303) 892–2617 or 2618

**Connecticut Commission
on the Arts**
Anthony S. Keller, Exec. Director
340 Capitol Avenue
Hartford, Connecticut 06106
(203) 566–4770

Delaware State Arts Council
Mrs. Sophie Consagra,
Exec. Director
Wilmington Tower, Room 803
1105 Market Street
Wilmington, Delaware 19801
(302) 571–3540

**D.C. Commission on the Arts
and Humanities**
Executive Director
1023 Munsey Building
1329 E Street, N.W.
Washington, D.C. 20004
(202) 347–5905 or 5906

Fine Arts Council of Florida
Mrs. Anna Price, Exec. Director
Division of Cultural Affairs
Department of State
The Capitol Building
Tallahassee, Florida 32304
(904) 487–2980

**Georgia Council for the Arts
and Humanities**
John Bitterman, Exec. Dir.
Suite 1610
225 Peachtree Street, NE
Atlanta, Georgia 30303
(404) 656-3990

Insular Arts Council of Guam
Mrs. Louis Hotaling, Director
P.O. Box EK (Univ. of Guam)
Agana, Guam 96910
729-2466

**Hawaii State Foundation
on Culture and the Arts**
Alfred Preis, Exec. Director
250 South King Street, Room 310
Honolulu, Hawaii 96813
(808) 548-4145

**Idaho State Commission on Arts
and Humanities**
Miss Suzanne Taylor,
Exec. Director
c/o State House
Boise, Idaho 83720
(208) 384-2119

Illinois Arts Council
Michele Brustin, Director
111 North Wabash Avenue
Room 1610
Chicago, Illinois 60602
(312) 793-3520

Indiana Arts Commission
Janet I. Harris, Exec. Director
Union Title Building, Suite 614
155 East Market
Indianapolis, Indiana 46204
(317) 633-5649

Iowa State Arts Council
Jack E. Olds, Exec. Director
State Capitol Building
Des Moines, Iowa 50319
(515) 247-4451

Kansas Arts Commission
Jonathan Katz, Exec. Director
117 West Tenth Street, Suite 100
Topeka, Kansas 66612
(913) 296-3335

Kentucky Arts Commission
Miss Nash Cox, Exec. Director
100 W. Main Street
Frankfort, Kentucky 40601
(502) 564-3757

Louisiana State Arts Council
Mrs. E. H. (Lucile) Blum, President
c/o Department of Education
State of Louisiana
P.O. Box 44064
Baton Rouge, Louisiana 70804
(504) 389-6991

**Maine State Commission on the
Arts and the Humanities**
Alden C. Wilson, Director
State House
Augusta, Maine 04330
(207) 289-2724

Maryland Arts Council
Kenneth Kahn, Exec. Director
15 West Mulberry
Baltimore, Maryland 21201
(301) 685-7470

Massachusetts Council on the Arts and Humanities
Miss Louise G. Tate,
Exec. Director
1 Ashburton Place
Boston, Massachusetts 02108
(617) 727-3668

Michigan Council for the Arts
E. Ray Scott, Exec. Director
Executive Plaza
1200 Sixth Avenue
Detroit, Michigan 48226
(313) 256-3735

Minnesota State Arts Board
Stephen Sell, Exec. Director
314 Clifton Street, South
Minneapolis, Minnesota 55403
(612) 874-1335

Mississippi Arts Commission
Lida Rogers, Exec. Director
301 North Lamar Street
P.O. Box 1341
Jackson, Mississippi 39205
(601) 354-7336

Missouri State Council on the Arts
Mrs. Emily Rice, Exec. Director
111 South Bemiston, Suite 410
St. Louis, Missouri 63105
(314) 721-1672

Montana Arts Council
David E. Nelson, Exec. Director
235 East Pine
Missoula, Montana 59801
(406) 543-8286

Nebraska Arts Council
Gerald Ness, Exec. Director
8448 West Center Road
Omaha, Nebraska 68124
(402) 554-2122

Nevada State Council on the Arts
James Deere, Exec. Director
560 Mill Street
Reno, Nevada 89502
(702) 784-6231 or 6232

New Hampshire Commission on the Arts
John G. Coe, Exec. Director
Phenix Hall, 40 North Main Street
Concord, New Hampshire 03301
(603) 271-2789

New Jersey State Council on the Arts
Brann J. Wry, Exec. Director
27 West State Street
Trenton, New Jersey 08625
(609) 292-6130

The New Mexico Arts Commission
Bernard Blas Lopez, Exec. Director
Lew Wallace Building
State Capitol
Santa Fe, New Mexico 87503
(505) 827-2061

New York State Council on the Arts
Robert A. Mayer, Exec. Director
80 Centre Street
New York, New York 10013
(212) 488-5222

North Carolina Arts Council
Halsey North, Exec. Director
N.C. Dept. of Cultural Resources
Raleigh, North Carolina 27611
(919) 829-7897

**North Dakota Council on the
Arts and Humanities**
Glenn Scott, Exec. Director
Department of English
North Dakota State University
Fargo, North Dakota 58102
(701) 237-7143

Ohio Arts Council
L. James Edgy, Exec. Director
50 West Broad Street, Suite 2840
Columbus, Ohio 43215
(614) 466-2613

**Oklahoma Arts and Humanities
Council**
William Jamison, Exec. Director
2101 North Lincoln Boulevard
Oklahoma City, Oklahoma 73105
(405) 521-2931

Oregon Arts Commission
Peter deC. Hero, Exec. Director
328 Oregon Building
494 State Street
Salem, Oregon 97301
(503) 378-3625

**Commonwealth of Pennsylvania
Council on the Arts**
Otis B. Morse, Exec. Director
2001 North Front Street
Harrisburg, Pennsylvania 17102
(717) 787-6883

Institute of Puerto Rican Culture
Luis M. Rodriguez Morales,
Exec. Director
Apartado Postal 4184
San Juan, Puerto Rico 00905
(809) 723-2115

**Rhode Island State Council on
the Arts**
Mrs. Anne Vermel, Exec. Director
4365 Post Road
East Greenwich,
Rhode Island 02818
(401) 884-6410

South Carolina Arts Commission
Rick George, Exec. Director
829 Richland Street
Columbia, South Carolina 29201
(803) 758-3442

**South Dakota State Fine Arts
Council**
Mrs. Charlotte Carver,
Exec. Director
108 West 11th Street
Sioux Falls, South Dakota 57102
(605) 339-6646

Tennessee Arts Commission
Norman Worrell, Exec. Director
222 Capitol Hill Building
Nashville, Tennessee 37219
(615) 741-1701

**Texas Commission on the Arts
and Humanities**
Maurice D. Coats, Exec. Director
P.O. Box 13406, Capitol Station
Austin, Texas 78711
(512) 475-6593

Utah State Division of Fine Arts
Ruth Draper, Director
609 East South Temple Street
Salt Lake City, Utah 84102
(801) 533-5895

Vermont Council on the Arts
Ellen McCulloch-Lovell,
Exec. Director
136 State Street
Montpelier, Vermont 05602
(802) 828-3291

**Virginia Commission of the Arts
and Humanities**
Frank R. Dunham, Exec. Director
400 East Grace Street
Richmond, Virginia 23219
(804) 786-4492

**Virgin Islands Council
on the Arts**
Stephen J. Bostic, Exec. Director
Caravelle Arcade
Christiansted, St. Croix
U.S. Virgin Islands 00820
(809) 773-3075, x3

**Washington State
Arts Commission**
James L. Haseltine, Exec. Director
1151 Black Lake Boulevard
Olympia, Washington 98504
(206) 753-3860

**West Virginia Arts and
Humanities Council**
Norman Fagan, Exec. Director
Science and Cultural Center
State Capitol Complex
Charleston, West Virginia 25305
(304) 348-3711

Wisconsin Arts Board
Jerrold Rouby, Exec. Director
123 W. Washington Avenue
Madison, Wisconsin 53702
(608) 266-0190

Wyoming Council on the Arts
Michael Haug, Exec. Director
200 West 25th Street
Cheyenne, Wyoming 82002
(307) 777-7742

Selected
Bibliography

Law Books

Baumgarten, Paul A., ed. *Legal and Business Problems of Motion Picture Industry*. New York: Practicing Law Institute, 1973.

Baumgarten, Paul A., and Farber, Donald C. *Producing, Financing and Distributing Film*. New York: Drama Book Specialists, 1973.

Cartoonists Guild. *Syndicate Survival Kit*. New York: Cartoonists Guild, 1975

Farber, Donald C. *From Option to Opening*. New York: Drama Book Specialists, 1970.

Farber, Donald C. *Producing on Broadway*. New York: Drama Book Specialists, 1969.

Goldberg, Morton David, ed. *Current Developments in Copyright Law*. 2 vols. New York: Practicing Law Institute, 1977.

Goodale, James C., ed. *Communications Law 1976*. New York: Practicing Law Institute, 1976.

Gross, Stephen H., and Perle, E. Gabriel, eds. *Magazine Publishing Industry*. New York: Practicing Law Institute, 1973.

Lindey, Alexander. *Entertainment, Publishing and the Arts*. 2 vols. New York: Clark Boardman Co., Ltd., 1963. Supp. 1975.

Nimmer, Melville. *Nimmer on Copyright*. 2 vols. New York: Matthew Bender, 1963, Supp. 1976.

Olsson, Harry R., Jr., ed. *Legal and Business Problems of Television and Radio 1976*. New York: Practicing Law Institute, 1976.

Perle, E. Gabriel, ed. *Book Publishing and Distribution: Legal and Business Aspects*. New York: Practicing Law Institute, 1974.

Pilpel, Harriet F., and Zavin, Theodora S. *Rights and Writers—A Handbook of Literary and Entertainment Law.* New York: Dutton, 1960.

Rothenberg, Stanley. *Legal Protection of Literature, Art, and Music.* New York: Clark Boardman Co. Ltd., 1960.

Wincor, Richard. *Literary Property.* New York: Clarkson N. Potter, Inc., 1967.

Wittenberg, Phillip, *The Protection of Literary Property.* Boston: The Writer, Inc., 1968.

Other Reference Books

Balkin, Richard. *A Writer's Guide to Book Publishing.* New York: Hawthorn Books, 1977.

Henderson, Bill, ed. *The Publish-It-Yourself Handbook: Literary Tradition & How-To.* Yonkers, New York: The Pushcart Book Press, 1973.

LMP (Literary Market Place). New York: R.R. Bowker, Co., revised annually.

Mangione, Jerre. *The Dream and the Deal: The Federal Writers Project, 1935-1943.* New York: Avon Books, 1972.

Writer's Handbook. Boston: The Writer, Inc., revised annually.

Writer's Market. Cincinnati: Writers *Digest, Inc.,* revised annually.

LMP, Writer's Handbook, and *Writer's Market* contain lists of great interest to writers, such as national, regional, and local writers' organizations. Conferences, contests, agents, and, most importantly, markets are thoroughly listed and kept up to date.

Notes

Books listed in the Selected Bibliography are cited by title only in the notes. The form for the notes is modified from that provided in *A Uniform System of Citation* (11th ed., Cambridge: Harvard Law Review Association, 1967) in order to be accessible to the writer as well as to the lawyer. After a full citation to a source is given in the notes for a chapter, additional references to the same source in that chapter are in shortened form.

Chapter 1. Copyright

1. p. 4. *See*, as to **Eugene O'Neill**, *The Protection of Literary Property*, p. 51, and as to **J. D. Salinger**, *New York Times*, November 3, 1974, p. 1, and *New York Times*, November 10, 1974, p. 75.

2. p. 5. Sheldon v. Metro-Goldwyn Pictures Corporation, 81 F.2d 49, 55 (2d Cir. 1936).

3. p.5. For a case where two writers created highly similar but noninfringing articles based on interviews with the same individual, *see* Morse v. Fields, 127 F. Supp. 63 (S.D.N.Y. 1954).

4. p. 6. *Nimmer on Copyright*, Sec. 41, pp. 169–72; Reyher v. Children's Television Workshop, 387 F. Supp. 869 (1975); *contra*, to the effect that to avoid infringement public domain materials must be copied from the public domain and not a copyrighted derivative work, Leon v. Pacific Telephone and Telegraph Co., 91 F.2d 484 (9th Cir. 1937).

5. p. 6. 17 United States Code Sec. 7.

6. p. 6. *See Nimmer on Copyright*, Sec. 30, pp. 134–37.

7. p. 6. *Id.*, Sec. 95, pp. 357–60.

8. p. 7. Chamberlain v. Feldman, 300 N.Y. 135, 89 N.E.2d 863 (1949); *but see,* for a case where a right of reproduction passed upon the sale of a physical art work, Pushman v. New York Graphic Society, 287 N.Y. 302, 39 N.E. 2d 249 (1942).

9. p. 7. United States v. First Trust Company of St. Paul, 251 F.2d 686 (8th Cir. 1958).

10. p. 7. Baker v. Libbie, 210 Mass. 599, 97 N.E. 109 (1912); Eyre v. Higbee, 22 How. Prac. 198 (N.Y. Sup. Ct. 1861); *Nimmer on Copyright,* Sec. 64, pp. 247–49.

11. p. 8. Estate of Hemingway v. Random House, 23 N.Y.2d 341, 347, 296 N.Y.S.2d 771, 777 (1969); *see,* as to public performance of plays, Ferris v. Frohman, 223 U.S.424, 434 (1912), Palmer v. DeWitt, 47 N.Y. 532 (1872); as to public reading of speeches and songs, King v. Mister Maestro, Inc., 224 F. Supp. 101 (S.D.N.Y. 1963), Heim v. Universal Pictures Co., 154 F.2d 480 (2d Cir. 1946); as to public broadcast of a radio script, Uproar Co. v. National Broadcasting Co., 8 F. Supp. 358, 362 (D. Mass. 1934).

12. p. 9. For a case where fraud was raised, *see* Twentieth Century-Fox Film Corp. v. Dieckhaus, 153 F.2d 893 (8th Cir.) *rev'g* 54 F. Supp. 425 (D.C. Mo. 1944), *cert. denied,* 329 U.S. 716 (1946).

13. p. 10. 17 United States Code Sec. 1.

14. p. 10. *Id.* Sec. 2.

15. p. 11. *Id.* Sec. 9.

16. p. 11. *Id.,* Sec. 24.

17. p. 11. *Nimmer on Copyright,* Sec. 49, pp. 193–96.

18. p. 12. White v. Kimmell, 193 F.2d 744, 746–47 (9th Cir. 1952); *see,* as to circulation for criticism, Dieckhaus v. Twentieth Century-Fox Film Corporation, 54 F. Supp. 425 (D.C. Mo. 1944), *rev'd on other grounds,* 153 F.2d 893 (8th Cir.), *cert. denied,* 329 U.S. 716 (1946).

19. p. 12. Dieckhaus v. Twentieth Century-Fox Film Corp., 54 F. Supp. 425, 426 (D.C. Mo. 1944), *rev'd on other grounds,* 153 F.2d 893 (8th Cir.), *cert. denied,* 329 U.S. 716 (1946); Fader v. Twentieth Century-Fox Film Corp., 169 F. Supp. 880 (S.D.N.Y. 1959).

20. p. 12. American Visuals Corp. v. Holland, 239 F.2d 740 (2d Cir. 1956); Hirshon v. United Artists Corp., 243 F.2d 640 (Ct. of Ap. D.C. 1957).

21. p. 12. Code of Federal Regulations, Title 37, Chap. II, Sec. 202.4(a), 202.5.

22. p. 13. 17 United States Code Sec. 19.

23. p. 13. *See,* as to more complicated issue of the name to be used in a notice where an assignment of a statutory copyright has been made but not recorded in the Copyright Office, *Nimmer on Copyright,* Sec. 123.4, pp. 536–38.

24. p. 13. 17 United States Code Sec. 20.

25. p. 13. Siewek Tool Company v. Morton, 128 F. Supp. 71 (E.D. Mich. 1954).

26. p. 13. Kraft v. Cohen, 32 F. Supp. 821, 823 (E.D. Pa. 1940), *rev'd on other grounds*, 117 F.2d 579 (3d Cir. 1941).

27. p. 13. Siewek Tool Company v. Morton, 128 F. Supp. 71 (E.D. Mich. 1954); Deward & Rich v. Bristol Savings and Loan Corporation, 34 F. Supp. 345, 349 (W.D. Vir. 1940).

28. p. 13. *See Nimmer on Copyright*, Sec. 119.1, 119.2, pp. 510–16.

29. p. 14. Goodis v. United Artist Television, Inc., 425 F.2d 397, 403 (2d Cir. 1970).

30. p. 14. 17 United States Code Secs. 10, 19, 24.

31. p. 14. B & B Auto Supply, Inc. v. Plesser, 204 F. Supp. 36, 40 (S.D.N.Y. 1962); Wrench v. Universal Pictures, 104 F. Supp. 374, 378–79 (S.D.N.Y. 1952).

32. p. 15. *Nimmer on Copyright*, Sec. 85.4, p. 313.

33. p. 15. *Id.*, Sec. 85.3, pp. 311–12.

34. p. 15. 17 United States Code Sec. 21; *see Nimmer on Copyright*, Secs. 90.1, 90.11, 90.12, 90.13, 90.14, pp. 338–41.

35. p. 15. *Nimmer on Copyright*, Sec. 85.2, p. 309.2–310.

36. p. 16. Code of Federal Regulations, Title 37, Chap. II, Secs. 202.6, 202.7, 202.8.

37. p. 16. *Nimmer on Copyright*, Sec. 92.1, pp. 345–48; *cf.* 17 United States Code Sec. 24.

38. p. 16. 17 United States Code Sec. 209; Scherr v. Universal Match Corp., 297 F. Supp. 107 (S.D.N.Y. 1967), *aff'd* 417 F.2d 497 (2d Cir. 1969), *cert. denied*, 397 U.S. 936 (1970).

39. p. 17. 17 United States Code Sec. 5; *Nimmer on Copyright*, Secs. 12.23, 94, pp. 50–51.1; 355–57.

40. p. 17. 17 United States Code Sec. 16; *see Nimmer on Copyright*, Secs. 96–98, pp. 360–69.

41. p. 18. 17 United States Code Sec. 22.

42. p. 18. *Id.* Sec. 23.

43. p. 18. *Id.* Sec. 9 (c).

44. p. 19. The Berne Convention For the Protection of Literary and Artistic Works (Paris Text, July 24, 1971) in *Nimmer on Copyright*, Appendix P, pp. 1033–71; *see*, as to moral rights, Article 6 *bis*.

45. p. 19. *See*, for an interpretation that the common law provides sufficient recognition of moral rights without federal legislation and, moreover, that Article 6 *bis* does not require moral rights to be inalienable, Melville Nimmer, "Implications of the Prospective Revisions of the Berne Convention and the United States Copyright Law," *Stanford Law Review*, Vol. 19, pp. 518–24 (1967).

46. p. 19. 17 United States Code Sec. 26.

47. p. 19. Brattleboro Publishing Co. v. Winmill Publishing Corp., 369 F.2d 565 (2d Cir. 1966); *Nimmer on Copyright*, Secs. 6.3, 62, pp. 11–14, 238.1–244.

48. p. 20. 17 United States Code Sec. 28.

49. p. 20. *Id.* Section 30; *see*, for a case where delayed recordation resulted in a loss of rights, Vidor v. Serlin, 119 U.S.P.Q. 104 (N.Y Sup. Ct. 1958).

50. p. 20. 17 United States Code Sec. 24; *see generally, Nimmer on Copyright*, Secs. 113–18, p. 460.2–508.

51. p. 21. Shapiro, Bernstein & Co., Inc. v. P. F. Collier & Son Company, 26 U.S.P.Q. 40, 43 (S.D.N.Y. 1934); *see generally, Nimmer on Copyright*, Sec. 145, pp. 643–56.6.

52. p. 24. *See generally, Nimmer on Copyright*, Secs. 131–65, pp. 567–713.

53. p. 24. 17 United States Code Sec. 101(b).

54. p. 24. *Id.; see Nimmer on Copyright*, Sec. 154, pp. 677–95.

55. p. 24. 17 United States Code, Secs. 101(a), 101(c), 101(d), 104, 105, 116.

Chapter 2. The Copyright Revision Act of 1976

1. p. 26. 17 United States Code Sec. 201(e). All references in the notes for Chapter 2 to 17 United States Code refer to the Copyright Revision Act of 1976, 90 Stat. 2541 (October 19, 1976), which will take effect on January 1, 1978. The legislative history of the act is contained in S. Rep. No. 94–473, (94th Cong., 1st Sess.), H.R. Rep. No. 94–1476 (94th Cong, 2nd Sess.), and H.R. Rep. No. 94–1733 (94th Cong., 2nd Sess.). H.R. Rep. No. 94–473 and H.R. Rep. No. 94–1733 are contained in 1976 U.S. Code Cong. and Adm. News, p. 6089 *et. seq.*

2. p. 27. 17 United States Code Sec. 102.

3. p. 27. 17 United States Code Sec. 101.

4. p. 27. *Id.*

5. p. 27. *Id.*, Section 103(a); *see* H.R. Rep. No. 94–1476, pp. 57–58.

6. p. 28. 17 United States Code Sec. 103(b).

7. p. 28. *Id.*, Sec. 105; S. Rep. No. 94–473, pp. 56–57, H.R. Rep. No. 94–1733, p. 69–70.

8. p. 28. 17 United States Code Sec. 301(a).

9. p. 29. *Id.*, Sec. 106.

10. p. 29. *Id.*, Sec. 109.

11. p. 29. *Id.*, Sec. 104(a).

12. p. 29. *Id.*, Sec. 104(b).

13. p. 30. *Id.*, Sec. 302(a).
14. p. 30. *Id.*, Sec. 302(b).
15. p. 30. *Id.*, Sec. 302 (c).
16. p. 30. *Id.*, Sec. 302(d).
17. p. 30. *Id.*, Sec. 302(e).
18. p. 30. *Id.*, Sec. 303.
19. p. 30. *Id.*, Sec. 304(a).
20. p. 31. *Id.*, Sec. 304(b).
21. p. 31. *Id.*, Sec. 101.
22. p. 31. *Id.*
23. p. 31. *Id.*
24. p. 32. *Id.*, Sec. 408(a).
25. p. 32. *Id.*, Sec. 408(e).
26. p. 32. *Id.*, Sec. 410(c).
27. p. 32. *Id.*, Sec. 411.
28. p. 32. *Id.*, Sec. 408(b)(1), (2).
29. p. 32. *Id.*, Sec. 408(b)(4).
30. p. 32. *Id.*, Sec. 408(c)(1).
31. p. 33. *Id.*, Sec. 408(c)(2).
32. p. 33. *Id.*, Sec. 408(c)(3).
33. p. 33. *Id.*, Sec. 708(a)(1), (2).
34. p. 33. *Id.*, Sec. 401(a).
35. p. 33. *Id.*, Sec. 401(b).
36. p. 33. *Id.*, Sec. 401(c).
37. p. 34. *Id.*, Sec. 405(a).
38. p. 34. *Id.*, Sec. 406(b).
39. p. 34. *Id.*, Sec. 101.
40. p. 34. *Id.*, Sec. 201(c).
41. p. 34. *Id.*, Sec. 404(b).
42. p. 34. *Id.*, Sec. 406(a).
43. p. 35. *Id.*, Sec. 201(c).
44. p. 35. By letter dated December 20, 1976, an attorney-adviser in the office of the register indicated this to be a "gray area" probably governed by the case law developed prior to the act.
45. p. 35. 17 United States Code Sec. 601, H.R. Rep. No. 94–1476, pp. 164–169; H.R. Rep. No. 94–1733, pp. 80–81.
46. p. 37. 17 United States Code Sec. 201(b).
47. p. 37. *Id.*, Sec. 101.
48. p. 38. *Id.*
49. p. 38. H.R. Rep. No. 94–1476, p. 121.
50. p. 38. 17 United States Code Sec. 101.
51. p. 38. *Id.*, Sec. 202.
52. p. 38. *Id.*, Sec. 101.

53. p. 38. *Id.*, Sec. 204.
54. p. 39. *Id.*, Sec. 205(e).
55. p. 39. *Id.*, Sec. 203.
56. p. 39. *Id.*, Sec. 201(d)(1).
57. p. 39. *Id.*, Sec. 107.
58. p. 40. *Id.*
59. p. 40. *Id.*, Sec. 108.
60. p. 41. *Id.*, Sec. 101.
61. p. 41. *Id.*, Sec. 110(1;).
62. p. 41. *Id.*, Sec. 110(1), (8).
63. p. 41. *Id.*, Sec. 110(3;).
64. p. 41. *Id.*, Sec. 110(4).
65. p. 41. *Id.*, Sec. 110(9).
66. p. 42. *Id.*, Sec. 504(b).
67. p. 42. *Id.*, Secs. 502, 503, 504(c), 505, 506.
68. p. 42. *Id.*, Sec. 412.
69. p. 42. *Id.*, Sec. 507(b).
70. p. 42. *Id.*, Sec. 405(b).
71. p. 42. *Id.*, Sec. 406(a).

Chapter 3. Rights of the Writer

1. p. 44. Lord Byron v. Johnston, 2 Mer. 29, 35 Eng. Rep. 851 (1816).

2. p. 45. Berne Convention for the Protection of Literary and Artistic Works, June 26, 1948 (Brussels), Art. 6 *bis.* (1), in, *Nimmer on Copyright*, Appendix O, p. 1020) *compare* the more recently adopted text of the Berne Convention, July 10, 1974 (Paris), Art. 6 *bis.* (1), in, *Nimmer on Copyright*, Appendix P, pp. 1037-38.

3. p. 45. Law of March 11, 1957 on Literary and Artistic Property. *See generally*, as to moral rights under French law, Jean-Loup Tournier, "The French Law of March 11, 1957 on Literary and Artistic Property," *Bulletin of the Copyright Society of the U.S.A.*, Vol. 1, No. 6 (1958), pp. 1-26; Raymond Sarraute, "Current Theory of the Moral Rights of Authors and Artists Under French Law," *American Journal of Comparative Law*, Vol. 16 (1968), pp. 465-86.

4. p. 45. *Compare* William Strauss, "The Moral Right of the Author," *Copyright Law Revision*, Study No. 4 (1959), pp. 109-42, with Melville B. Nimmer, "Implications of the Prospective Revisions of the Berne Convention and the United States Copyright Law," *Stanford Law Review*, Vol. 19 (1967), pp. 518-25; "Copyright: Moral Right—A Proposal," *Fordham Law Review*, Vol. 43 (1975), pp. 793-819; "Toward Artistic In-

tegrity: Implementing Moral Right Through Extension of Existing American Legal Doctrines," *Georgetown Law Journal*, Vol. 60 (1972), pp. 1539–62; and James M. Treece, "American Law Analogues of the Author's 'Moral Rights'," American Journal of Comparative Law, Vol. 16 (1968), pp. 487–506.

5. p. 46. Shaw v. Time-Life Records, 38 N.Y.2d 201 (1975). *See generally* J. Thomas McCarthy, *Trademarks and Unfair Competition* (Rochester, New York: Lawyers Cooperative Publishing Co., 1973), pp. 265–318.

6. p. 47. Patten v. Superior Talking Pictures, Inc., 8 F. Supp. 197, 198 (S.D.N.Y. 1934); *see* Fisher v. Star Co., 231 N.Y. 414, 433, 132 N.E. 133, 139, *cert. denied* 257 U.S. 654 (1921).

7. p. 47. Hemingway v. Film Alliance of the U.S., 174 Misc. 725, 21 N.Y.S.2d 827 (Sup. Ct. 1940).

8. p. 47. Children's Television Workshop v. Sesame Nursery, 171 U.S.P.Q. 105 (Sup. Ct., N.Y., 1970).

9. p. 47. International Film Service Co., Inc. v. Associated Producers, Inc., 273 F.585 (S.D.N.Y. 1921).

10. p. 47. Fishler v. Twentieth Century-Fox Film Corporation, 159 F. Supp. 215 (S.D. Cal. 1958).

11. p. 48. Granz v. Harris, 198 F.2d 585, 588 (2d Cir. 1952). *See,* with respect to the distortion of films by television commercials, Stevens v. National Broadcasting Co., 148 U.S. P.Q. 755 (Cal. Super. Ct. 1966), in which it was stated that the network could "insert commercials; however, the commercials must not be inserted so as to alter or adversely affect or emasculate the artistic or pictorial quality of the film, or destroy or distort materially or substantially the mood, the effect or the continuity of the film. In other words, the defendants in inserting commercials must give primary consideration as to whether the insertion of the commercials will substantially or materially distort the mood, effect or continuity of the film." *But see,* for the unhappy end result of this dispute, Stevens v. National Broadcasting Co., 150 U.S.P.Q. 572 (Cal. Super. Ct. 1966). *See,* for a case favorable to writers involving mutilation by editing, *Gilliam* v. *American Broadcasting Companies, Inc.*, 538 F.2d 14 (2d Cir. 1976).

12. p. 48. Granz v. Harris, 198 F.2d 585, 589 (2d Cir. 1952).

13. p. 48. Vargas v. Esquire, Inc., 164 F.2d 522 (7th Cir. 1947).

14. p. 48. *Nimmer on Copyright*, Sec. 110.5, pp. 449–52; *see* Poe v. Michael Todd Company, 151 F. Supp. 801 (S.D.N.Y. 1957).

15. p. 49. Clemens v. Belford, Clark & Co., 14 F. 728 (C.C.N.D. Ill. 1883).

16. p. 49. *Black's Law Dictionary* (4th ed. St. Paul, Minn.: West Publishing Company, 1952), pp. 505, 1060, 1559.

17. p. 50. D'Altomonte v. New York Herald Co., 154 App. Div. 453, 139 N.Y.S. 200, *mod.* 208 N.Y. 596, 102 N.E. 1101 (1913).

18. p. 50. Clevenger v. Baker Voorhis & Co., 8 N.Y.2d 187, 168 N.E.2d 643 (1960).

19. p. 50. Geisel v. Poynter Products, Inc., 295 F. Supp. 331, 353 (S.D.N.Y. 1968); *see* Carte v. Ford, 15 Fed. 439, 447 (C.C.D. Md. 1883).

20. p. 50. *See Corpus Juris Secundum,* Vol. 53, *Libel and Slander,* Sec. 134(c), pp. 221–22; Fisher v. The Washington Post Co., 212 A.2d 335 (D.C. App. 1965); Fitzgerald v. Hopkins, 70 Wash.2d 924, 425 P.2d 920 (1967).

21. p. 51. Buckley v. Vidal, 327 F. Supp. 1051 (S.D.N.Y. 1971).

22. p. 51. Montandon v. Triangle Publications, Inc., 120 Cal. Rptr. 186, 191, 45 Cal. App.3d 938, 946 (Ct. App. 1975), quoting Cepeda v. Cowles Magazine and Broadcasting, Inc., 392 F.2d 417, 419 (9th Cir.), *cert. denied* 393 U.S. 840 (1968).

23. p. 52. Shostakovich v. Twentieth Century-Fox Film Corp., 196 Misc. 67, 80 N.Y.S.2d 575 (1948), *aff'd* 275 App. Div. 692, 87 N.Y.S.2d 430 (1949).

24. p. 52. *See* Soc. Le Chant du Mond v. Soc., Fox Europe et Fox Americaine Twentieth Century, (1954) D. Jur. 16, 80 (Cour d'appel, Paris).

25. p. 52. Seroff v. Simon & Schuster, Inc., 6 Misc.2d 383, 162 N.Y.S.2d 770 (1957).

26. p. 53. Williams v. Weisser, 78 Cal. Rptr. 542 (1969).

27. p. 53. *Compare* Eliot v. Jones, 66 Misc. 95, 120 N.Y.S. 989 (1910), *aff'd* 140 App. Div. 911, 125 N.Y.S. 1119 (1910); Kerby v. Hall Roach Studios, 53 Cal. App.2d 207, 127 P.2d 577 (1942); *with* D'Altomonte v. New York Herald Co., 154 App. Div. 453, 139 N.Y.S. 200, *mod* 208 N.Y. 596, 102 N.E. 1101 (1913).

28. p. 53. Ellis v. Hurst, 70 Misc. 122, 128 N.Y.S. 144 (1910); *compare* Ellis v. Hurst, 66 Misc. 235, 121 N.Y.S. 438 (1910).

29. p. 53. Geisel v. Poynter Products, Inc., 295 F. Supp. 331, 355 (S.D.N.Y. 1968).

30. p. 53. Rand v. Hearst Corp., 31 App. Div.2d 406, 298 N.Y.S.2d 405, *aff'd* 26 N.Y.2d 806, 309 N.Y.S.2d 348, 257 N.E.2d 895 (1969).

31. p. 53. *See* Haelan Laboratories v. Topps Chewing Gum, 202 F.2d 866 (2d Cir.), *cert. denied* 346 U.S. 816 (1953); Uhlaender v. Henricksen, 316 F. Supp. 1277, 1278–79 (D. Minn. 1970); "Transfer of the Right of Publicity," *U.C.L.A. Law Review,* Vol. 22 (1975), pp. 1103–28.

32. p. 54. Namath v. Sports Illustrated, 48 App. Div.2d 487, 371 N.Y.S.2d 10 (1975), *aff'd* 39 N.Y.2d 897, 386 N.Y.S. 2d 397, 352 N.E.2d 579 (1976).

33. p. 54. Price v. Hal Roach Studios, 400 F. Supp. 836 (S.D.N.Y. 1975).

34. p. 54. *See generally* J. Thomas McCarthy, *Trademarks and Unfair Competition* (Rochester, New York: Lawyers Cooperative Publishing Co., 1973), pp. 318–44.

35. p. 55. Gilroy v. American Broadcasting Company, Inc., 47 App. Div.2d 728, 365 N.Y.S.2d 193 (1975).

36. pp. 56. Gilroy v. American Broadcasting Company, Inc., ____ App. Div.2d ____, ____ N.Y.S.2d ____ (1977), *appeal pending*.

Chapter 4. The Content of Written Works

1. p. 57. It is beyond the scope of this work to deal with the tension between the First Amendment's guarantee of free speech and the Sixth Amendment provision that "In all criminal prosecutions, the accused shall enjoy the right to a speedy and public trial, by an impartial jury of the state and district wherein the crime shall have been committed . . ." At issue are gag orders handed down by courts in order to prevent the publication of information which would prejudice a criminal defendant's opportunity for a fair trial. This form of prior restraint on publication has been extensively curtailed by the guidelines delineated in Nebraska Press Association v. Stuart, 96 S. Ct. 2791 (1976).

2. p. 58. William L. Prosser, *The Law of Torts* (4th ed. St. Paul, Minn.: West Publishing Company, 1971), Sec. 112, pp. 753–54. Much of the material on defamation and invasion of privacy is drawn from *The Law of Torts*.

3. p. 58. *Corpus Juris Secundum*, Vol. 53, *Libel and Slander*, Sec. 148, pp. 231–32. This liability is stated to be, "in full, without apportionment." *See The Law of Torts*, Sec. 113, pp. 775–76.

4. p. 58. *Corpus Juris Secundum*, Vol. 53, *Libel and Slander*, Sec. 137, pp. 223–27. The defense of truth need not be literal as to every detail, but the gist of the defamation must be substantially true. Partial truth or a showing of general bad character will not be sufficient to invoke the defense of justification due to truthfulness. (*The Law of Torts*, Sec. 116, pp. 796–99).

5. p. 58. Kimmerle v. New York Evening Journal, 262 N.Y. 99, 102, 186 N.E. 216, 218 (1933).

6. p. 58. *The Law of Torts*, Sec. 111, p. 740–41.

7. p. 58. *Id.*, p. 743; *see* Ben-Oliel v. Press Publishing Co., 251 N.Y. 250, 167 N.E. 432 (1929).

8. p. 59. *The Law of Torts*, Sec. 111, pp. 741–42.

9. p. 59. *Id.*, Sec. 113, p. 768.

10. p. 59. *See,* for an entertaining survey which conveys a writer's outrage at this state of affairs, Tom Wallace Lyons, "Libel: Names Will Always Hurt Me," *the new renaissance,* Vol. II, No. 3 (1973), pp. 8–30.

11. p. 59. Youssoupoff v. Metro-Goldwyn-Mayer, (1934), 50 T.L.R. 581, 584, 99 A.L.R. 864, 870.

12. p. 59. "Libel: Names Will Always Hurt Me," p. 21.

13. p. 60. *Restatement of the Law, Torts,* Ch. 24, Sec. 564, Comment.

14. p. 60. *See,* for a sample libel release form, *Entertainment, Publishing and the Arts,* Vol. 1, Part 5, Sec. I, pp. 542–43.

15. p. 61. Hulton and Co., Ltd. v. Jones, (1910), 26 T.L.R. 128, 129.

16. p. 61. Clare v. Farrell, 70 F. Supp. 276, 279–80 (D. Minn. 1947).

17. p. 62. *The Law of Torts,* Sec. 112, pp. 749–51.

18. p. 62. *New York Times* v. Sullivan, 376 U.S. 254 (1964).

19. p. 62. Time, Inc. v. Firestone, 96 S. Ct. 958 (1976).

20. p. 62. Gertz v. Robert Welch, Inc., 418 U.S. 323 (1974).

21. p. 62. *Corpus Juris Secundum,* Vol. 53, *Libel and Slander,* Secs. 74–76, 260, pp. 124–27, 372–75.

22. p. 63. *The Law of Torts,* Sec. 116, pp. 799–801.

23. p. 63. *See The Law of Torts,* Sec. 111, p. 745; Walter P. Armstrong, "Nothing But Good of the Dead?", Vol. 18, *American Bar Association Journal* (1932), pp. 229–32.

24. p. 63. *The Law of Torts,* Sec. 117, pp. 802–18.

25. p. 64. Friedan v. Friedan, 414 F. Supp. 77, 79 (S.D.N.Y. 1976).

26. p. 65. Sidis v. F-R Pub. Corporation, 113 F.2d 806, 809 (2d Cir.), *cert. denied* 311 U.S. 711 (1940).

27. p. 65. *Id.*

28. p. 65. Virgil v. Time, Inc., 527 F.2d 1122 (9th Cir. 1975), *cert. denied,* 96 S. Ct. 2215 (1976). The quotation is from the decision on remand, 424 F. Supp. 1286, 1289(S.D. Cal. 1976).

29. p. 65. 424 F. Supp. on p. 1289. It could be argued, however, that the question of unconscionability is not for the jury to determine. *Cf.* Monitor Patriot Co. v. Roy, 401 U.S. 265, 276–77 (1971).

30. p. 66. Briscoe v. Reader's Digest Association, 4 Cal. 3d 529, 537, 483 P.2d 34, 40 (1971).

31. p. 66. Time, Inc. v. Hill, 385 U.S. 374, 387–88 (1967).

32. p. 67. Spahn v. Julian Messer, Inc., 18 N.Y.2d 324, 221 N.E.2d 543 (1966), *vacated and remanded,* 387 U.S. 239 (1967), *aff'd,* 21 N.Y.2d 124, 233 N.E.2d 840 (1967), *appeal dismissed,* 393 U.S. 1046 (1968).

33. p. 67. Rosemont Enterprises, Inc. v. Random House, Inc., 58 Misc.2d 1, 294 N.Y.S.2d 122, *aff'd* 32 A.D.2d 892, 301 N.Y.S.2d 948 (1968).

34. p. 68. Pearson v. Dodd, 410 F.2d 701, 705 (D.C. Cir.), *cert. denied*, 395 U.S. 947 (1969).

35. p. 68. Dietemann v. Time, Inc., 449 F.2d 245, 249 (9th Cir. 1971).

36. p. 68. *See* Note 14 of this chapter for reference to a release form covering invasion of privacy as well as libel.

37. p. 68. *The Protection of Literary Property*, pp. 199–203; *see*, for an excellent introduction to the law of obscenity as well as a compendium of cases which provide a sense of the history of censorship, Edward De Grazia, *Censorship Landmarks* (New York: R.R. Bowker Company, 1969).

38. p. 70. Miller v. California, 413 U.S. 15, 24 (1973).

39. p. 70. Memoirs v. Massachusetts, 383 U.S. 413, 418 (1966).

40. p. 70. Miller v. California, 413 U.S. 15, 30–34 (1973). The clarification of the phrase "contemporary community standards" may come on the appeal from the conviction of the publisher of *Hustler* magazine for "pandering obscenity" and "engaging in organized crime" under the relevant Ohio statutes.

41. p. 70. Marks v. United States, 45 U.S.L.W. 4233 (U.S. March 1, 1977).

42. p. 70. Ginsberg v. New York, 390 U.S. 629, 637–43 (1968).

43. p. 70. Roaden v. Kentucky, 413 U.S. 496 (1973).

44. p. 71. President's Council, District 25 v. Community School Board No.25, 457 F.2d 289, 293 (2d Cir.), *cert. denied*, 409 U.S. 998 (1972).

45. p. 71. Minarcini v. Strongsville City School District, 541 F.2d 577, 582 (6th Cir. 1976).

46. p. 71. One case now in litigation involves the actions of the Island Trees School Board in Nassau County, New York. The board removed nine contemporary works of fiction from the school library and banned their classroom use. The books included Bernard Malamud's *The Fixer*, Kurt Vonnegut's *Slaughterhouse Five*, and Piri Thomas's *Down These Mean Streets*.

Chapter 5. Contracts: An Introduction

1. p. 72. General principles of contract law are drawn from sources such as the *Restatement of Contracts* (1932) and the multivolume treatises *Corbin on Contracts* (1963) and *Williston on Contracts* (1957, 1975 Supp.). A good single volume text is John Calamari and Joseph Perillo, *The Law of Contracts* (St. Paul, Minn.: West Publishing Company, 1970).

2. p. 73. Crawford v. Mail and Express Publishing Co., 163 N.Y. 404, 57 N.E.616 (1900), contract for newspaper articles; Haven v. Russell, 34 N.Y.S. 292 (Sup. Ct. 1895), contract for a play. *See* Calamari and Perillo, *The Law of Contracts*, Sec. 153, pp. 240–42; *Williston on Contracts*, Vol. 5, Sec. 675A, pp. 189–209.

3. p. 73. *American Jurisprudence 2d*, Vol. 17, *Contracts*, Sec. 272–74, pp. 680–88.

4. p. 73. *Id.*, Secs. 82, 344, pp. 422–24. *See*, for a contract which had not been fully performed and was held unenforceable for a failure to specify royalty rates, Hindes v. Wilmington Poetry Society, 138 A.2d 501, 116 U.S.P.Q. 301 (1958).

5. p. 74. N.Y. General Obligations Law Sec. 1-202; Cal. Civil Code Sec. 25.

6. p. 75. Roddy-Eden v. Berle, 108 N.Y.S.2d 597, 600, 202 Misc. 261, 264 (Sup. Ct. 1951).

7. p. 75. *Williston on Contracts*, Vol. 4, Sec. 568, p. 30; *see*, for a case in which a check was returned despite the absence of a truly restrictive covenant, Cooke v. Manhattan Galleries, 48 App. Div.2d 793, 369 N.Y.S.2d 165 (1975).

8. p. 76. 17 United States Code Sec. 204 (eff. Jan. 1, 1978).

9. p. 76. *Id.*, Sec. 101.

10. p. 76. Uniform Commercial Code Sec. 1-206(1); *see Nimmer on Copyright*, Sec. 169.21, pp. 731–33.

11. p. 76. *See, e.g.*, N.Y. General Obligations Law Sec. 5-701(1); Cal. Civil Code Sec. 1624(1).

12. p. 76. *Compare Corpus Juris Secundum*, Vol. 77, *Sales*, Secs. 306, 309 with Uniform Commercial Code Sec. 2-313, Official Comment 7.

13. p. 76. *Corpus Juris Secundum*, Vol. 77, *Sales*, Sec. 301, pp. 1115–16.

14. p. 77. *Id.*

15. p. 77 Loew's Inc. v. Wolff, 101 F. Supp. 981 (D.C. Cal. 1951).

16. p. 77. *American Jurisprudence 2d*, Vol. 6, *Assignments*, Sec. 13, p. 198; Foster v. Callaghan & Co., 248 F.944 (D.C. N.Y. 1918); Wooster v. Crane & Co., 73 N.J. Eq. 22, 66 A. 1093 (1907).

17. p. 77. *American Jurisprudence 2d*, Vol. 6, *Assignments*, Sec. 19, pp. 200–201.

18. p. 78. *See* Brockhurst v. Ryan, 2 Misc.2d 747, 146 N.Y.S.2d 386 (Sup. Ct. 1955).

19. p. 78. *Id.*, 2 Misc.2d at p. 753, 146 N.Y.S.2d at p. 392.

20. p. 79. Wagner-Larscheid Co. v. Fairview Mausoleum Co., 190 Wis.357, 362, 208 N.W.241, 242 (1926).

21. p. 79. *See generally Williston on Contracts*, Sec. 805, pp. 838–57.

22. p. 79. *See Corpus Juris Secundum,* Vol. 17A, *Contracts,* Secs. 334, 511, pp. 311, 831.

23. p. 79. Annotation, "Specific Performance of Contracts for Services," *American Law Reports,* Vol. 135, pp. 289–90 (1941).

24. p. 79. *Corbin on Contracts,* Vol. 5A, Sec. 1146, p. 154; Benziger v. Steinhauser, 154 F. 151 (C.C. N.Y. 1907).

25. p. 80. *Compare* N.Y. Civil Practice Law and Rules Sec. 213(2) with Cal. Code of Civil Procedure, Secs. 337, 339.

26. p. 80. *Corpus Juris Secundum,* Vol. 53, *Limitations of Actions,* Secs. 67–69, pp. 1028–36.

27. p. 80. *See,* for a case reviewing the relevant issues when a unique manuscript is lost by a printer, Gerschel v. St. Crispin Bindery, *New York Law Journal,* March 2, 1970, p. 23 (Sup. Ct. 1970). Another issue which might arise is whether all of the writer's bailments are for mutual benefit, or whether certain bailments would either be for the sole benefit of the bailor or the sole benefit of the bailee. If the bailment is for the sole benefit of the bailor, the bailee will only be liable for gross negligence. If the bailment is for the sole benefit of the bailee, the bailee can be liable even through reasonable care is taken with the goods. A bailment for mutual benefit will usually be found where the bailee takes possession of the goods as an incident to the bailee's business, even if no consideration is received. *American Jurisprudence 2d,* Vol. 8, *Bailments,* Sec. 10, pp. 914–15.

28. p. 80. *See,* for a thorough discussion of the law pertaining to the protection of ideas, *Nimmer on Copyright.* Secs. 166–73, pp. 714–60; "Beyond the Realm of Copyright: Is There Legal Sanctuary for the Merchant of Ideas?", *Brooklyn Law Review,* Vol. 41 (1974), pp. 284–324; and Louis Bernard Jack, "The Legal Protection of Abstract Ideas: A Remedies Approach," *IDEA,* Vol. 18, No. 2 (1976), pp. 7–24.

29. p. 82. *Id.*

Chapter 6. Agency Contracts

1. p. 86. Dramtists Guild, Inc., Minimum Basic Production Contract for Off-Broadway Dramatic Productions, Schedule of Additional Producduction Terms, Sec. 30.

2. p. 86. *New York Jurisprudence,* Vol. 2, *Agency,* Secs. 203, 206, pp. 338–39, 341–42; *California Jurisprudence 3d,* Vol. 3, *Agency,* Secs. 96–97, pp. 133–36.

3. p. 87. Conde Nast Press v. Cornhill Pub. Co., 255 Mass. 480, 152 N.E. 240 (1926).

4. p. 87. *Corpus Juris Secundum,* Vol. 2A, *Agency,* Secs. 86–87, pp. 682–92.

5. p. 89. Wilck v. Herbert, 178 P.2d 25, 28, 78 Cal. App.2d 392, 395 (Cal. D. Ct. App. 3d Div. 1947).

6. p. 89. *Id.*

7. p. 89. *Corpus Juris Secundum,* Vol. 3, *Agency,* Sec. 343, pp. 152–55.

8. p. 89. 178 P.2d at pp. 37–38, 78 Cal. App.2d at pp. 412–13, quoting from *Restatement of the Law, Agency,* p. 1058, Sec. 449, Comment 6.

9. p. 90. *Corpus Juris Secundum,* Vol. 2A, *Agency,* Sec. 112(a), pp. 729–30.

10. p. 90. *But see Id.,* Sec. 118, pp. 740–41, which states, "To constitute an agency coupled with an interest, the agent must have a present interest in the property upon which the power is to operate . . . where an agent receives a commission for making a sale . . . he does not have a power coupled with an interest such as to make it irrevocable." *Compare New York Jurisprudence,* Vol. 2, *Agency,* Secs. 58–59, pp. 229–32.

11. p. 92. Dramatists Guild, Inc., Minimum Basic Production Contract for Off-Broadway Dramatic Productions, Schedule of Additional Production Terms for Off-Broadway Productions, Section 29(a).

12. p. 92. *New York Jurisprudence,* Vol. 2, *Agency,* Secs. 208–09, pp. 343–44.

13. p. 92. Dramtists Guild, Inc., Minimum Basic Production Contract for Off-Broadway Dramatic Productions, Schedule of Additional Production Terms for Off-Broadway Productions, Section 31.

14. p. 92. Dramatists Guild, Inc., Minimum Basic Production Contract for Off-Broadway Dramatic Productions, Paragraph Fifth (a).

Chapter 7. Marketing Literary Property

1. p. 97. The provisions of the standard book contract are also examined in *Literary Property,* pp. 91–106; *The Protection of Literary Property,* pp. 221–49; Irwin Karp, "What the Writer Should Look for in His First Book Contract," *Writer's Yearbook* (1967), p. 27; Richard Dannay, "A Guide to the Drafting and Negotiating of Book Publication Contracts," *Bulletin of the Copyright Society of the U.S.A.,* Vol. 15 (1967–68), pp. 295–322; and Andrew O. Shapiro, "The Standard Author Contract: A Survey of Current Draftsmanship," *ASCAP Copyright Law Symposium,* No. 18 (1970), pp. 135–73.

2. p. 106. The Authors Guild, "Children's Book Royalties," (no date). The survey of children's book royalties had extensive coverage in the January, April, and June, 1971, issues of the *Authors Guild Bulletin.*

3. p. 106. The royalty rates for professional, scientific and technical books, as well as textbooks, are discussed in *A Writer's Guide to Book Publishing*, pp. 75–76.

4. p. 110. Fugate v. Greenberg, 16 Misc.2d 942, 945, 189 N.Y.S.2d 948, 952 (Sup. Ct. 1959).

5. p. 112. *See*, for a case in which the writer could only recover nominal damages for the failure of the publisher to proceed with publication (due to the difficulty of proving what royalties would have been earned), Freund v. Washington Square Press, 34 N.Y.S.2d 379, 314 N.E.2d 419 (1974), *modifying* 41 App. Div.2d 371, 343 N.Y.S.2d 401 (1973). When the publisher's default leaves the writer with a salable literary property which can be placed elsewhere, damages will be difficult to establish. However, if the nature of the property is such that the delay decreases its value—for example, a book about a current news event—the writer should be able to recover damages based upon expert testimony as to the royalties which would have been earned had the publisher fulfilled its obligations. *See* the discussion on pp. 54–56.

6. p. 112. *See*, for a case in which the writer received damages for the publisher's sale of rights after the book had gone out of print, Fugate v. Greenberg, 16 Misc.2d 942, 947–48, 189 N.Y.S.2d 948, 954 (Sup. Ct. 1959).

7. p. 114. Such warranty provisions have been held not to violate public policy in D. Appleton & Co. v. Warbasse, 92 Misc. 42, 155 N.Y.S. 987 (Sup. Ct. 1915). *See*, for a case involving a warranty against obscenity, Fugate v. Greenberg, 16 Misc.2d 942, 946, 189 N.Y.S.2d 948, 953 (Sup. Ct. 1959) in which the court stated that a writer's warranty against obscenity would be against public policy if the writer were required to hold the publisher harmless from the publisher's own illegal acts.

8. p. 120. *But see*, for a holding that an arbitrator can award only compensatory damages, not punitive damages, Garrity v. Lyle Stuart, Inc., 40 N.Y.2d 354, 353 N.E.2d 793 (1976).

9. p. 121. *See*, for several forms of collaboration contracts, *Entertainment, Publishing and the Arts*, Vol. I, Sec. H, pp. 98–107.

10. p. 121. *See*, for a thorough analysis of joint authorship, *Nimmer on Copyright*, Secs. 67–80, pp. 270–98. A writer and illustrator were held joint authors in Donna v. Dodd, Mead & Co., Inc., 374 F. Supp. 429 (S.D.N.Y. 1974).

11. p. 122. *See*, for an unusual case in which a publisher was found to have breached its contractual obligation to use "best efforts" in promotion, Van Valkenburg v. Hayden Pub. Co., 33 App. Div.2d 766, 306 N.Y.S.2d 599 (1969), *aff'd* 30 N.Y.2d 34, 281 N.E.2d 142 (1972), *cert. denied* 409 U.S. 875 (1972).

12. p. 125. A number of syndication agreements for comic strips ap-

pear in Cartoonists Guild, *Syndicate Survival Kit* (New York: Cartoonists Guild, 1975).

13. p. 128. *See, From Option to Opening*, pp. 6–34, and *Producing on Broadway*, pp. 3–79.

14. p. 129. Warner Brothers Pictures, Inc. v. CBS, 216 F.2d 945 (9th Cir. 1954), *cert. denied* 348 U.S. 971 (1955).

15. p. 130. *See generally Producing, Financing and Distributing Film*, pp. 1–26.

Chapter 9. Income Taxation

1. p. 157. *Compare* Sec. S46-2.0, N.Y.C. Adm. Code (as amended by L.L. 1971, No. 36, June 30) with N.Y. Tax Law Sec. 703 (McKinney 1975). New York City no longer permits a professional exemption from the unincorporated business tax. New York State will allow an exemption for self-employed authors, poets, and dramatists, but not for self-employed advertising copywriters or other creators of material having a business purpose. Opinion of Counsel, Department of Taxation and Finance, October 28, 1966; Opinion of Counsel, Department of Taxation and Finance, March 21, 1968, NYTB–V.1, p. 56 (issued 1/69); Gordon Auchincloss, Decision of State Tax Commission, August 12, 1966; Alfred Stern, Decision of State Tax Commission, December 28, 1971. *See*, for a case in which a writer challenged New York City's gross receipts tax and lost, Steinbeck v. Gerosa, 4 N.Y.2d 302, 151 N.E.2d 170, *cert. denied*, 358 U.S. 39 (1958). This gross receipts tax was repealed by Chapter 772, Laws 1966 (effective July 1, 1965).

2. p. 159. Jacob Mertens, Jr., *Law of Federal Income Taxation*, Vol. 2 (1974, 1976 Supp.), Sec. 10.07, pp. 31–33; James Gould Cozzens, 19 T.C. 663 (1953).

3. p. 160. The exact calculation, of course, involves the subtraction of net short-term capital loss from net long-term capital gain prior to application of one of the alternative methods for computing the tax provided by Internal Revenue Code of 1954, Secs. 1201, 1201; Treas. Reg. Sec. 1.1202-1.

4. p. 160. Internal Revenue Code of 1954, Sec. 1221(3). *See*, for cases involving "similar property," Cranford v. United States, 338 F.2d 379 (Ct. Cl. 1964); Stern v. United States, 164 F. Supp. 847 (E.D. La. 1958), *aff'd per curiam*, 262 F.2d 957 (5th Cir. 1959). Sec. 1221(3)(c) also excludes a holder "in whose hands the basis of such property is determined, for purposes of determining gain from a sale or exchange, in whole or part by reference to the basis of such property" in the hands of the cre-

ator, so as to deny copyrights being capital assets in the hands of a donee.

5. p. 160. Internal Revenue Code of 1954, Sec. 1348, *as amended* 90 Stat. 1554 (October 4, 1976).

6. p. 161. Internal Revenue Code of 1954, Sec. 117.

7. p. 162. Internal Revenue Code of 1954, Sec. 74; Treas. Reg. Sec. 1.74-1.

8. p. 163. Internal Revenue Code of 1954, Sec. 280A, added, 90 Stat. 1569 (October 4, 1976).

9. p. 166. Internal Revenue Code of 1954, Sec. 162; Stern v. United States, 71-1 USTC Par. 9375 (D.C. Cal. 1971); *but see* Rev. Rul. 73-395, 1973-2 Cum. Bull. 87, which raises the threat of capitalizing research costs. That ruling has been at least temporarily suspended by IR-1575 (News Release, March 17, 1976). in, *Federal Taxes*, Vol. 6 (Prentice-Hall, 1976), p. 54, 927. For the effect of the Tax Reform Act of 1976 on this issue, *see* note 15 for Chapter Eleven. The requirement that "away from home" expenses be for overnight travel is not supported by the language of Sec. 162, but the Supreme Court approved a "sleep or rest" test in United States v. Correll, 389 U.S. 299 (1967).

Chapter 10. Income Taxation: II

1. p. 172. 42 United States Code Sec. 403(f)(5). The Authors Guild has published a question and answer sheet explaining the interplay of benefits and earnings.

2. p. 174. *See* Rev. Rul. 60-31, 1960-1 Cum. Bull. 174 example (3); E.K. Gann, 31 T.C. 211 (1958), *acquiesced* to by the Internal Revenue Service; William R. Hoffman, Jr., "Tax Planning for Authors," *Taxes* (July, 1968), pp. 434-35.

3. p. 175. *See* Rev. Rul. 234, 1953-2 Cum. Bull. 29; Hoffman, "Tax Planning for Authors," pp. 435-36.

4. p. 179. Internal Revenue Code of 1954, Sec. 911.

5. p. 180. 60 T.C. 277 (1973); *see* Renato Beghe, "The Artist, the Art Market and the Income Tax," *Tax Law Review*, Vol. 29 (1974), pp. 491-524.

6. p. 181. "League Wins Tax Decision for Nonresident Author," *Authors Guild Bulletin* (March-May, 1976), p. 4.

7. p. 182. Internal Revenue Code of 1954, Sec. 911(a) *as amended* 90 Stat. 1610 (October 4, 1976).

8. p. 182. Internal Revenue Code of 1954, Sec. 871; *see* Steven Duke, "Foreign Authors, Inventors, and the Income Tax," *Yale Law Review*, Vol. 72 (1963), pp. 1093-169.

9. p. 182. *See* Richard S. Brawerman and Robert C. Kopple, "Income Tax Planning for Composers, Entertainers and Others Performing Personnel Services," *Taxes*, Vol. 49 (1971), pp. 211–25. This article discusses the problem fo royalties being passive income with respect to a Subchapter S corporation on pp. 217–18.

10. p. 184. Internal Revenue Code of 1954, Sec. 501(c)(3).

11. p. 184. *See* Fides Publishers Association, (DC) 67-1 USTC Par.9251, 263 F.Supp. 924; Rev. Rul. 66-104, 1966-1 Cum. Bull. 135; Rev. Rul. 60-351, 1960-2 Cum. Bull. 169. *Compare* Elisian Guild, Inc., (CA-1) 69-2 USTC Par. 9483, *rev'g* (DC), 68-2 USTC Par. 9659, 293 F.Supp. 219.

12. p. 184. *See generally* Herrick K. Lidstone and R.J. Ruble, *Exempt Organizations and the Arts* (New York: Volunteer Lawyers for the Arts, 1976).

Chapter 11. The Hobby Loss Challenge

1. p. 185. This chapter is based on an unpublished article by the author. Tad Crawford and Herrick Lidstone, "Hobbies, Horses and the Struggling Artist," *Art and the Law* (Summer 1975), pp. 3–4, should be consulted for detailed citations on hobby losses. *See generally* Internal Revenue Code of 1954, Sec. 183.

2. p. 185. Internal Revenue Code of 1954, Sec. 183(d).

3. p. 186. Internal Revenue Code of 1954, Sec. 183(e)(4), added 90 Stat. 1954 (October 4, 1976).

4. p. 186. Treas. Reg. Sec. 1.183-2(b).

5. p. 188. Nemish v. Semmir, 452 F.2d 611 (9th Cir. 1972), *aff'g per curium* 29 T.C.M. 1249 (1970).

6. p. 189. *Id.*, p. 1251.

7. p. 189. *Id.*

8. p. 189. *Id.*

9. p. 189. John R. Baltis, 31 T.C.M. 213 (1972).

10. p. 190. *Id.*, p. 214.

11. p. 190. *Id.*

12. p. 190. Chaloner v. Helvering, 69 F.2d 571 (D.C. Cir. 1934).

13. p. 190. Lamont v. Commissioner, 339 F.2d 377 (2d Cir. 1964); *see*, to the same effect, G. Szmak, 376 F.2d 154 (2d Cir. 1967).

14. p. 190. 339 F.2d at p. 381.

15. p. 191. Stern v. United States, 71-1 USTC Par. 9375 (D.C. Cal. 1971). The IRS indicated that it would not follow this case in Rev. Rul. 73-395, 1973-2 Cum. Bull. 87, but that has been at least temporarily suspended by IR-1575 (News Release, March 17, 1976), in *Federal Taxes,*

Vol. 6 (Prentice-Hall, 1976), p. 54,927. Suspension of Rev. Rul. 73-395 has been continued with respect to publishers by the Tax Reform Act of 1976, Sec. 2119, 90 Stat. 1912 (October 4, 1976). Any regulations issued by the IRS will be applicable to the future only. Nothing in Sec. 2119 indicates an intention on the part of Congress to change the result of the Stern decision. The capitalization of the costs of producing books and similar property is required for taxpayers (other than regular corporations) by the Tax Reform Act of 1976, Sec. 210, 90 Stat. 1544 (October 4, 1976), but this provision appears relevant only to investors—not writers who develop material for their own work. The Senate Finance Committee stated, "This rule is to apply to persons . . . engaged in the service of producing, displaying, or distributing a film, . . . book, or similar property (such as a play, etc.). . . . Thus, the production costs will be written off by the taxpayer over the useful life of the asset which he has acquired as a result of his investment." (S. Rep. No. 94-938, 94th Cong., 2d Sess., pp. 77–78).

16. p. 191. Stern v. United States, 71-1 USTC Par. 9375 (D.C. Cal. 1971), at p. 86, 420.

17. p. 191. Cornelius Vanderbilt, Jr., 16 T.C.M. 1081 (1959).

18. p. 192. *Id.*, p. 1085.

19. p. 193. *d.*

20. p. 193. Crymes v. Commissioner, 31 T.C.M. 4 (1972). *But see* note 15 for this chapter.

21. p. 193. *Id.*, p. 5.

22. p. 193. Sebastian de Grazia, 21 T.C.M. 1572 (1962). *See*, for a recent case very favorable to writers, C. West & Gloria Churchman v. Commissioner, 68 T.C. No. 59 (1977).

Chapter 12. The Writer's Estate

1. p. 196. Israel Shenker, "Donor's Anger at N.Y.U.'s Handling of Her Literary Collection Leads to Switch of Letters to Public Library," *New York Times*, October 11, 1976, p. 15.

2. p. 197. Arthur and Barbara Gelb, *O'Neill* (New York: Harper & Row, rev. ed., 1973), pp. 861–62, 938, 951–53.

3. p. 198. 17 United States Code Sec. 24.

4. p. 199. *See generally*, Internal Revenue Code of 1954, Secs. 2031–44.

5. p. 200. *Id.*, Sec. 2032.

6. p. 200. Treas. Reg. Sec. 20.2031-1(b).

7. p. 200. Estate of Gabriel Pascal, 22 T.C.M. 1766 (1963). "7. Patents and Copyrights. There is no definite rule for valuing these intangibles,

but the burden is on the executor to prove their value based on the probable earning power, previous earnings, remaining life, and other factors." J. G. Denhardt, Jr. *Complete Guide to Estate Accounting and Taxes,* (Englewood Cliffs, N.J.: Prentice-Hall, Inc., 1964), p. 72.

8. p. 201. Estate of David Smith, 57 T.C. 650 (1972), *aff'd.* 510 F.2d 479 (2d Cir. 1975), *acquiesced in,* I.R.B. 1974-27, 8.

9. p. 201. Jarre v. Commissioner, 64 T.C. 183 (1975).

10. p. 202. *Id.,* p. 188.

11. p. 203. Internal Revenue Code of 1954, Secs. 2051–57.

12. p. 203. N.Y. Estates, Powers and Trusts Law Sec. 5-1.1.

13. p. 204. Internal Revenue Code of 1954, Sec. 2001, *as amended* 90 Stat. 1846 (October 4, 1976).

14. p. 205. *Id.,* Sec. 2011.

15. p. 205. Treas. Reg. Secs. 20.6151-1, 20.6075-1.

16. p. 205. Another method for easing estate liquidity problems may be available to a writer's estate. The Tax Reform Act of 1976 provides that upon a showing of reasonable cause (as opposed to the prior undue hardship standard), the district director may extend the time for payment up to ten years (Internal Revenue Code of 1954, Sec. 6161, *as amended* 90 Stat. 1867, October 4, 1976). However, the interest on such unpaid taxes, which has been 4 percent, now reflects the current prime interest rate (Internal Revenue Code of 1954, Sec. 6621). The Tax Reform Act of 1976 adds a new provision which can prove helpful to the estates of writers. If more than 65 percent of the adjusted gross estate consists of an interest in a closely held business (such as being the sole proprietor engaged in the business of being a writer), the tax can be paid in ten equal yearly installments. And, if the executor so elects, the first installment need not be paid for five years. Interest payable on the estate tax attributable to the value of the business property (up to $1,000,000) receives a special rate of 4 percent (Internal Revenue Code of 1954, Sec. 6166, *added by* 90 Stat. 1862, October 4, 1976).

17. p. 205. Internal Revenue Code of 1954, Sec. 2042; Treas. Reg. Sec. 20.2042-1.

18. p. 206. Internal Revenue Code of 1954, Sec. 2056(c)(1), *as amended* 90 Stat. 1854 (October 4, 1976).

19. p. 206. *See* William R. Hoffman, Jr., "Tax Planning for Authors," *Taxes* (July 1968), pp. 436–39; Rev. Rul. 54-599, 1954-2 Cum. Bull. 52.

20. p. 207. *Compare* Wodehouse v. Commissioner, 177 F.2d 881 (2d Cir. 1949) with Wodehouse v. Commissioner, 178 F.2d 987 (4th Cir. 1949). *See* Warren S. Shine, "Some Tax Problems of Authors and Artists," *Tax Law Review,* Vol. 13 (1958), pp. 451–57.

21. p. 207. Internal Revenue Code of 1954, Sec. 2038; Rev. Rul. 57-366, 1957-2 Cum. Bull. 618; Rev. Rul. 59-357, 1959-2 Cum. Bull. 212.

22. p. 207. Internal Revenue Code of 1954, Sec. 2522(a); Treas. Reg. Sec. 25.2522(a)-1(a).

23. p. 208. Internal Revenue Code of 1954, Secs. 1014, 1221(c). This opinion was contained in a memorandum dated November 29, 1976, from a staff member of the Joint Committee on Internal Revenue Taxation to a congressman. The memorandum, which follows, refers to art works but applies with equal force to copyrights.

> SUBJECT: Character of income from sale of art objects inherited from artist who created the objects.
>
> Code section 1221(3) provides that the term "capital asset" does not include an artistic composition held by a taxpayer whose personal efforts created the property or by a taxpayer whose basis in the property is determined in reference to the basis of the taxpayer who created the property. Prior to enactment of the Tax Reform Act of 1976, this provision did not preclude capital gains treatment of sales of art work by a deceased artist's executor, heirs, or legatees.
>
> The Tax Reform Act of 1976 provides a carryover basis rule for property acquired or passing from a decedent. Under this rule, the decedent's executor, heir, or legatee will take the same basis in property for determining gain or loss as the decedent had immediately before death, subject to certain adjustments for death taxes imposed on the unrealized appreciation. As a result of the interplay of this carryover basis rule and the definition of a capital asset, a gain realized with respect to art work by the executor, heir, or legatee of an artist will always be treated as ordinary income.
>
> I do not recall that anyone focused on this aspect of the application of the carryover basis rule to art work in the hands of an artist's executor, heir, or legatee.

The prior rule with respect to beneficiaries is reflected in Gershwin v. United States, 153 F. Supp. 477 (Ct. Cl. 1957). *See*, as to purchasers, Holt v. Commissioner, 35 T.C. 588, 600–01 (1961), *aff'd. on other grounds*, 303 F.2d 687 (9th Cir. 1962). The IRS has acquiesced in this decision. *See*, as to whether a transaction will qualify as a sale instead of a mere license, Rev. Rul. 60–226, 1960-1 Cum. Bull. 26-27.

The Authors League will seek changes in the law to allow capital gains treatment for sales by a writer's estate or heirs (letter to the author, dated March 1, 1977, from Peter Heggie, Executive Director of the Authors Guild).

Chapter 13. Public Support for Writers

1. p. 210. *See* John Leonard, "Critic's Notebook: For Many Writing Is a Hungry Trade," *New York Times*, February 10, 1976, p. 39; Marylin Bender, "Macmillan Under the Gun," *New York Times*, Section 3 (Financial), December 1, 1974, p. 1; Tom Buckley, "Michener Fears Publishing Take-Over May Ground Fledgling Novelists," *New York Times*, October 27, 1975, p. 31; Ronald Sukenick, "Author as Editor and Publisher," *New York Times*, (Book Review Section), September 15, 1974, p. 55.

2. p. 211. The National Committee for Cultural Resources, *National Report on the Arts* (New York: The National Committee for Cultural Resources; 1975), p. 1.

3. p. 212. 20 United States Code Sec. 951(5), in National Foundation on the Arts and Humanities Act of 1965, 20 United States Code Sec. 951 *et. seq.*

4. p. 212. *See generally* The National Endowment for the Arts, *Guide to Programs* (1976–77 ed.; Washington, D.C.: Superintendent of Documents; August, 1976).

5. p. 212. The National Endowment for the Arts and the National Council on the Arts, Annual Report, 1975 (Washington, D.C.: Superintendent of Documents: March, 1976), pp. 48–52.

6. p. 213. Comprehensive Employment and Training Act, 29 United States Code Sec. 801 *et. seq., as amended,* Emergency Jobs and Unemployment Assistance Act of 1974, 29 United States Code Sec. 961 *et. seq.* (also codified in sections of 20, 29, 42 United States Code), and the Emergency Jobs Program Extension Act of 1976, Public Law No. 94-444 (October 1, 1976).

7. p. 213. *National Report on the Arts,* p. 11.

8. p. 213. Cal. Government Code Sec. 8750 (West's, 1976 Supp.).

9. p. 215. *Id.* Sec. 8753 (West's 1976 Supp.); *see,* for some interesting speculations with respect to appropriate roles for state arts councils, Monroe E. Price, "State Arts Councils: Some Items for a New Agenda," *Hastings Law Journal,* Vol. 27, No. 5 (May 1976), pp. 1183–1205.

10. p. 215. *See The Dream and the Deal: The Federal Writers Project, 1935-43,* pp. 8, 45, 88, 97–98, 100, 156–57, 352, 369.

11. p. 216. *See generally* Kingdom of the Netherlands, *Facts and Figures,* Vol. 16, *The Arts* (The Hague, Netherlands: Government Printing Office, 1970–71), pp. 57–61.

12. p. 217. Irish Finance Act of 1969, Part I, Sec. 2.

13. p. 218. *See generally* National Commission for Protection of Cultural Properties, *Living National Treasures of Japan* (Tokyo, Japan: Minichi Newspapers, 1967), pp. 2–3.

14. p. 218. The section on the French literary fund is drawn from Jules Marc Baudel, *"La Caisse Nationale des Lettres," Bulletin of the Copyright Society of the U.S.A*, Vol. 16 (1968–69), pp. 1–15, as well as more recent materials supplied by the *Centre Nationale des Lettres*, 6 rue Dufrenoy, Paris 75016, France.

15. p. 221. H.R. 1885, 94th Cong., 1st Sess. (1975).

16. p. 221. H.R. 8563, 94th Cong., 1st Sess. (1975).

17. p. 221. H.R. 1739 and H.R. 2046, 95th Cong., 1st Sess. (1977).

18. p. 221. H.R. 696, 93rd Cong., 1st Sess. (1973).

19. p. 221. S.1080 and H.R. 3018, 95th Cong., 1st Sess. (1977).

20. p. 220. Michael Pantaleoni, "Comment: Priorities for Tax Reform," *Art and the Law* (December 1974), p. 2; Tad Crawford, "A Proposal for the Arts," *New York Law Journal* (May 19, 1976), p. 1.

21. p. 220. National Report on the Arts, p. 17.

Index

ABOUT THE AUTHOR

A member of the New York Bar, Tad Crawford served as a judge's clerk on the New York Court of Appeals after his graduation from Columbia Law School. He is the author of *Legal Guide for the Visual Artist* and has published numerous articles and short stories. Mr. Crawford teaches writing at the School of Visual Arts in New York City, is on the board of the Foundation for the Community of Artists, and has a novel in progress. He lives in New York City with his wife Phyllis.